Embracing Sisterhood

Embracing Sisterhood

Class, Identity, and Contemporary Black Women

Katrina Bell McDonald

ROWMAN & LITTLEFIELD PUBLISHERS, INC.
Lanham • Boulder • New York • Toronto • Oxford

ROWMAN & LITTLEFIELD PUBLISHERS, INC.

Published in the United States of America
by Rowman & Littlefield Publishers, Inc.
A wholly owned subsidiary of The Rowman & Littlefield Publishing Group, Inc.
4501 Forbes Boulevard, Suite 200, Lanham, Maryland 20706
www.rowmanlittlefield.com

PO Box 317
Oxford
OX2 9RU, UK

British Library Cataloguing in Publication Information Available

Library of Congress Cataloging-in-Publication Data

McDonald, Katrina Bell, 1961–
    Embracing sisterhood : class, identity, and contemporary Black Women / Katrina
Bell McDonald.
        p.   cm.
    Includes bibliographical references and index.
    ISBN-13: 978-0-7425-4574-8 (cloth : alk. paper)
    ISBN-10: 0-7425-4574-1 (cloth : alk. paper)
    ISBN-13: 978-0-7425-4575-5 (pbk. : alk. paper)
    ISBN-10: 0-7425-4575-X (pbk. : alk. paper)
    1. African American women—Social conditions.   2. African American women—
Attitudes.   3. African American women—Race identity.   4. Winfrey, Oprah—Public
opinion.   5. Winfrey, Oprah—Influence.   6. Group identity—United States.   7.
Public opinion—United States.   I. Title.
E185.86.M395   2006
305.48′896073—dc22   2006006467

Printed in the United States of America

∞ ™ The paper used in this publication meets the minimum requirements of American
National Standard for Information Sciences—Permanence of Paper for Printed Library
Materials, ANSI/NISO Z39.48-1992.

This book is dedicated to my mother,
Gladys Murrel Bell,
a lioness of a mother
and a treasure of the sisterhood.

Contents

Tables

Acknowledgments

Embracing Sisterhood was finally completed after many months of global, national, and personal turmoil, much of which is simply now a blur. My sweetest sister-friend and maternal grandmother, Florastein Bell, passed away in February of 2004 while I was sharing Mardi Gras in New Orleans with my oldest and dearest friend, Myrna Dean. (Just a few months later, Myrna lost her father and then faced the threat of breast cancer.) My grandmother's death was closely followed by the death of my Aunt Grace, with whom I share a middle name (Margaret), and who helped othermother my baby boy, Jordan, when I was in graduate school. Then an intruder decided to steal my laptop (and numerous other valuables), which contained a number of critical documents related to this project, from my home. Just as I had resettled to continue my work, my dear mother and close friend, Gladys Bell, suffered a terrible stroke, which left her sorely limited on her right side. Since then, I have proudly served as her sole caregiver; she would do no less for me. My Aunt Precious Craft, who lives up to her name in so many ways, came to my rescue in January 2005, only to fall and break her hip on the stairs in my home. Soon after, I learned that my Uncle Babe was being treated for prostate cancer and that the firstborn child of my cousin, Monica, came into the world four months premature, weighing just over a pound. The stress of all this, and the struggle to rescue my marriage from strife, made having the surgery that I had put off so long absolutely necessary in July of 2005.

What is more, these family trials were wedged between the September 11 attacks, the second war in Iraq, the sniper shootings in the D.C. area (where I happened to be commuting for work during my research sabbatical), the tsunami and earthquake in the East, and hurricanes Katrina and Rita in the South. It was the strangest of times.

The good news is, however, that through it all, the sisterhood of black women in my little corner of the world held fast: Carla Henry Hopkins and the entire Henry clan stuck close by and prayed me through, Judy Ford bent over drafts of book chapters with me in the wee hours, Marsha Davenport and April Garrett gave valuable feedback, my mother cheered me on even from her nursing-home bed (she's now in her own place just a block from me!), and my sister-cousins Pamela Parker and Paula Birdsong were as supportive as they have always been. And it certainly helped that Ms. Oprah Winfrey launched the twentieth season of her talk show in 2005; thanks, Oprah, for reminding us of what we black women owe.

Most of all, my colleagues in the Sociology Department at Hopkins; my deans Daniel Weiss and Adam Falk; and my editor, Alan McClare at Rowman & Littlefield Publishers, were phenomenally fair and compassionate. My dear husband Ray (I love you immensely, Bubba) and my son Jordan Ray (now age sixteen and college bound) took the brunt of this drama; they were far more understanding than I could have ever hoped.

This study would also not have been possible without the generous participation of the eighty-eight black women who permitted me into their homes, cell blocks, and workplaces or agreed to hang out with me at their favorite restaurants and hair salons. I would like to give special thanks to study women "Erin" and "Laura" for facilitating my data collection at the department of corrections and at one hair salon, and especially my dear friend Wanda Randall for directing me to study women of various kinds, sorority women in particular. (Keep building bridges, girlfriend!) Thanks also go to Alpha Kappa Alpha Sorority, Inc., ("skee-wee") and Sigma Gamma Rho Sorority, Inc., for their vital support.

Several of my colleagues were particularly helpful to me in conceptualizing and theoretically framing my analysis, and these are Andrew Cherlin, Giovanni Arrighi, Beverly Silver, and Sara Berry. Comments from other faculty members were also extremely helpful. In addition, I am grateful for the long-time support from my mentors at the University of California, Davis, Carole Joffe and James Cramer, and from Frank Furstenberg Jr. at the University of Pennsylvania.

I began this research on a shoestring, literally the small bit I had in my personal checking and faculty expense accounts. I felt that I had to strike while the iron was hot, so I set out to recruit my study women with what I had on hand. In time, substantial financial support was provided by the American Association of University Women in the form of a 2002–2003 postdoctoral research leave fellowship and research grant. Funds for this project were also awarded as a sabbatical research grant and a summer research grant from the Zanvyl Krieger School of Arts and Sciences at Johns Hopkins University, and a new program development grant jointly by the National Institutes of Health and the Hopkins Population Center (with my friend and colleague Thomas A. LaVeist).

Invaluable research assistance was provided by a number of individuals at different stages of the research process. My heartfelt thanks to Antonia Bad-way, Mindelyn Buford, Lauren Charles, Senchal Dashiell, Megan Kashdin, Seo Hee Koh, Leslie Strothers, and Suzumi Yasatuke. Thanks also to those graduate students who provided me with a crucial "safe place" with which to argue out loud about the substance of this work: Mark King, Adia Harvey, Bedelia Richards, Travis Gosa, and Christian Villenas.

Finally, there are the names of those too numerous to list who prayed, cried, laughed, and fed me through to the end. Among them are my department administrators, Binnie Bailey and Mary Ann Zeller; my in-laws—the Seviers, McDonalds, and Kellys; my stepchildren, Sharon and David; the Voices of Faith (the spiritual body that has nurtured me since childhood); my dear cousin Reverend Curtis Parker, and heaps of other cousins; the Reverend Sharon Smith; friends and colleagues Siba Grovogui and Floyd Hayes; and close sister-friends Myrna Dean, Leah Hall, Carla Hopkins, Sandi Jackson, and Rachel Jackson. With the support of all of these people, I now resume cooking homemade meals.

Chapter One

Introduction: Metaphorically Speaking

Given the ideological differences within the black community, we must heed [Toni] Morrison's call and not empirically or theoretically assume we can take for granted an undifferentiated, ungendered black community or that, for black women at least, there is a contradiction between their intersecting identities with both women and blacks.

—Michael C. Dawson, political scientist and
African-American studies scholar[1]

The new public safe space provided by black women's success allowed long-standing differences among black women structured along axes of sexuality, social class, nationality, religion, and region to emerge. At this point, whether African American women can fashion a singular "voice" about the black woman's position remains less an issue than how black women's voices collectively construct, affirm, and maintain a dynamic black women's self-defined standpoint. Given the increasingly troublesome political context affecting black women as a group, such solidarity is essential. Thus, ensuring group unity while recognizing the tremendous heterogeneity that operates within the boundaries of the term "black women" comprises one fundamental challenge now confronting African American women.

—Patricia Hill Collins, sociologist and black feminist scholar[2]

Though the subject of this text has been of great interest to me for more than ten years, it was a chance encounter with a young black woman a few years back that provided me with the impetus to develop its particular line of inquiry. I was waiting in the lobby of an oil-and-lube shop for my car to be returned when suddenly I heard music from the lobby television announcing a promotion of a popular national talk show. Curious about what the topic of that day's show would be, I looked up to watch the brief overview. A twenty-something-year-old black woman standing near the television set, also waiting for her car, did the same. Just as the promo ended, the young woman looked back over her shoulder at me and said, "She ain't even black anymore. I don't even bother to watch her silly little show." I answered, "Really? What makes you say that?" She replied, "Nothing about her is real anymore. Look at what she says and who she says it to." The talk show in question was *The Oprah Winfrey Show.*

It was hardly the first time I had heard such sentiments expressed about Oprah. Black folk have had extremely high expectations for what this cele-brated, extraordinary, insanely wealthy African-American woman could do for the progress of our people. Some have been dismayed by her actions, oth-ers continue to hold out hope, and still others feel that tending to "us" is not what she's about and that that's just good business. But I was taken aback by the conviction of this particular young woman's words and, more impor-tantly, by the obvious assumption on her part of "sisterhood" between her and me on the issue. The tone with which she spoke was one of "girlfriend, you know what I'm talkin' about," and indeed I did. I understood, but I did not concur. All manner of explanations raced through my mind in an attempt to characterize the moment of estrangement I then felt from my "sister." What might best explain why she had such difficulty embracing Oprah and I had so little? If I had said more in response to her comments, would she have dismissed me as a "fake sister" and built up a wall of distrust? Of course I knew virtually nothing about this young black woman, only her strong opin-ion about the likes of Oprah, and that only superficially. But I imagined sociologically so much more. As is often the case among my sister-friends and sister-scholars, my sociological imagination turned toward differences in social class status as the explanation for the estrangement I experienced, par-ticularly given the frequently cited increase in socioeconomic diversity within black America. Since that day, "embracing Oprah" has served as my primary metaphor for the challenge that twenty-first-century black women face in negotiating gender-ethnic bonds[3] across class lines.

More recently, a second metaphor has helped in guiding my thinking about my experience of estrangement. Imagining the "black stepsister" came as I sought to capture the complexity of the gender-ethnic dynamics revealed in that exchange at the oil-and-lube shop as well as that reported across a vast interdisciplinary literature. Stepsisters are generally characterized in one of two ways—one from the sociology of the family and the other from fairy tales, most notably the tale of Cinderella. In the real world, a stepsister (or stepbrother) is said to be more likely to bond with her siblings under certain conditions,[4] the following of which are also relevant for a healthy black woman collective: social similarity and shared experiences, frequent contact, and perceived mutual benefit of association. Conversely, tension among sib-lings is likely under conditions of dissimilarity, disparate life experiences, infrequent contact, and where the perception of mutual benefit of association is low. The stepsister relationship, therefore, is clearly the product of environment.

The "evil" commonly associated with fairy-tale versions of the stepsister, on the other hand, is rarely presented as a reflection of the woman's environment but rather of the woman herself. In an extremely intriguing passage from a commencement speech that Nobel Prize winner Toni Morrison gave back in the 1980s, it is this image—though not exclusively, knowing Morrison—that is projected on certain black women:

> I want not to ask you but to tell you not to participate in the oppression of your sisters. . . .
>
> I am alarmed by the violence that women do to each other; professional violence, competitive violence, emotional violence. I am alarmed by the willingness to enslave other women. I am alarmed by a growing absence of decency on the killing floor of professional women's worlds. . . . I am suggesting that we pay as much attention to our nurturing sensibilities as to our ambition. We are moving in the direction of freedom and the function of freedom is to free somebody else. You are moving toward self-fulfillment, and the consequences of that fulfillment should be to discover that there is something just as important as you are and that just-as-important thing may be Cinderella—or your stepsister. . . . In your rainbow journey toward the realization of personal goals, don't make choices based only on your security and your safety. Nothing is safe. . . . But in pursuing your highest ambitions, don't let your personal safety diminish the safety of your stepsister. In wielding the power that is deservedly yours, don't permit it to enslave your stepsisters. Let your might and your power emanate from that place in you that is nurturing and caring.[5]

In her own analysis of this black stepsister phenomenon, Clenora Hudson-Weems offers the following summation:

> Here Morrison comments on her amazement at the cruel manner in which women treat each other every day, particularly in the workplace. Her statement offers profound insights into the nature and source of the absence of sisterhood on the part of many women toward each other, an unfortunate phenomenon which violates the very foundation of female relationships.[6]

Thus, taken together, sociological and fictional literature suggest that certain socioenvironmental conditions, such as increased socioeconomic diversity, may serve to unearth tensions within the contemporary "family" of black women, tensions likened to poor bonding among stepsisters, even erupting in oppressive language and behavior by those of higher social standing.

Over the past several years, I have partaken in, eavesdropped on, and refereed a good deal of folk talk on the challenge of "embracing Oprah" (literally and figuratively) and of embracing the "black stepsister." It frequently emerges as the high point of dinner parties, sorority luncheons, Sunday school classes, and professional and academic activities where African-

American women gather. I have imagined, and anecdotally I have evidenced, hundreds of such conversations taking place across the country each day. Scholars generally know or care very little about the significance of these conversations. They miss the opportunity to understand more deeply the potential psychosocial and sociopolitical effects of growing socioeconomic diversity on what many assume—both within and outside the academy—to be a virtually indestructible web of cultural solidarity and trust among black women.

In an effort to enlighten these scholars and other persons less engaged with this subject, *Embracing Sisterhood* describes the contemporary state of the black woman collective and how the legacy of black sisterhood plays out in these times. Its primary agenda is to determine the relative degree of black sisterhood (unity) and black stepsisterhood (class discord) that exists through an examination of how both of these ideas are articulated and experienced among today's African-American women. The concept "discord" is significant here, as it conveys not only a lack of agreement or harmony within a group but also disharmony among those expected to be unified. In this instance, such an expectation stems from the cultural-historical notion that black women's gender-ethnic identity and consciousness are highly uniform even across class lines.

With this purported new "era of high-profile, megasuccessful black women who are changing the face of every major field worldwide"[7] and of growing socioeconomic diversity among black women as the backdrop, this book seeks to determine where contemporary black women's ideas of black womanhood and sisterhood merge with social class status to shape certain attachments and detachments among them. Similarities as well as variations in how black women of different social backgrounds perceive and live black womanhood are interpreted from a range of social contexts—from small, intimate, and very tangible social contexts as well as in broader, more abstract, more ideological terms. *Embracing Sisterhood* draws its analysis from in-depth interviews with eighty-eight contemporary black women age eighteen to eighty-nine, covering a variety of issues prompted by a survey questionnaire that captured various dimensions of gender-ethnic identity and consciousness.[8]

This book confirms what many of today's African-American women and most other interested observers have known for some time: conceptions and the experience of black womanhood are quite diverse and at least appear to have grown more diverse over time. And while there is concern about the discord that exists among black women, this discord is generally accepted as a natural outgrowth of that diversity. Discordant sentiment and experience are revealed in two basic forms: as collective ambivalence, where as a whole the women are largely unsettled on certain issues, and as significantly divided tendencies among subgroups of women in supporting or rejecting certain ideas.

Discordant sentiment and experience among these women largely reflects the varying ways in which they work to fully immunize themselves against the public's general negative regard for them, a public sentiment that stems from a complex and denigrating mythology about black women. Internalizing this oppression frequently produces intragroup tension and at times evokes conscious and unconscious discriminative behavior toward those whose skin tone, body type, wardrobe, hairstyle, and so on African-American women have been programmed to reject. It also rears it ugly head in the competitiveness that black women sometimes feel and show toward one another in the labor market and in the dating and marriage market.

But chances are that those who have anticipated class "polarization" or "schism" from my analysis—including my oil-and-lube-shop sister, the study women, and especially me—will be surprised to find how relatively little there is around issues of gender-ethnic identity and consciousness. Class discord is no doubt the predominant discord of all that are observed in this study, and one of my objectives is to etch out as much as possible these classed patterns of sentiment and experience. But this discord is primarily revealed in differences of small or moderate degree rather than by polar opposition. Areas where class differences are evident are much more subtle than generally anticipated: the proportions of middle-class black women supporting or rejecting certain ideas are for the most part virtually the same as or are only moderately different from those for the lower classes. This is true even when the women specify the sort of black woman who who they say would qualify as their "black stepsister."

There are clearly instances, however, where class discord runs deeper. These are where the middle classes are contrasted with the most marginalized of the lower classes: the incarcerated. Black incarcerated women—whose circumstances have led most scholars to cast them as members of the urban "underclass"—show that for the most part they want not to stand out so much as black women (positively or negatively) but to live relatively undetected in the mainstream of American society. Women of the middle classes, on the other hand, view their gender-ethnicity as worthy of special recognition and act accordingly. These differences notwithstanding, I contend that on the whole, the class discord observed among contemporary black women falls far short of that typically projected by the scholarly and public rhetoric of "class warfare."

The potential for a pervasive and polarizing black stepsisterhood is considerably undermined by the passion with which these women cling to the promises of cross-class gender-ethnic "community" and group determination. Expressions of strong sisterly attachments to other black women in families, neighborhoods, churches, workplaces, and other social spaces are prominent and compelling. As was true for their foremothers, what unifies black women today is their strong self-esteem and sense of pride manifested by, among other things, their strong feelings of identification and their virtual personification with the notion of "struggle." Contemporary African-American women are generally well versed in the oppression they have suffered personally and as a group historically. Knowledge and experience of this oppression helps fuel the great pride these women take in their collective accomplishments and advancements and in being black women with proven resiliency. A large proportion share black feminist and humanist ideas about the interracial and interethnic world in which they live, and there is strong agreement about the importance of regularly immersing themselves and their families in things historically, aesthetically, and culturally "black." In sum, the analyses conducted for *Embracing Sisterhood* reveal that notions of class polarization, schism, and cleavage in scholarly and public rhetoric overdramatize the condition of today's black woman collective and unduly overshadow the gender-ethnic unity that contemporary black women exemplify.

Before venturing further, readers should note that "black" and "African American" are used interchangeably in this text and refer to a specific subset of people of African descent living in the United States. They refer to those whose "identity is based on putative common descent, claims of shared history, and symbols of peoplehood."[9] Their "common descent" from free and enslaved Africans in the United States during the sixteenth through the nineteenth centuries and their "shared history" in the United States from that time forward qualifies them as a black ethnic group. Though they clearly share a forced "racial" category with other groups of African descent, the nature and timing of their involuntary immigration to the United States distinguishes them in important ways from other blacks. In addition, the "ethnic" portion of the "gender-ethnic" designation is used to convey a shared ethnicity (African American) and racial status (black) among the women I study.

MEGASUCCESS AND IMPRESSIONS
OF BLACK STEPSISTERHOOD

America has always had a certain, though often warped, fascination with the black woman. Of late there has even been a growing appetite, dare I say genuine appreciation, for her in a variety of areas. In a recently published work entitled *The Black Female Body: A Photographic History*,[10] we are reminded, for example, just how deeply curious nonblack artists and scientists were about what they saw as the most foreign and "exotic" of the human form as much as three hundred years ago, as well as how more modern artists have captured representations of black women who are determined to reclaim their own bodies. And there have been newly cast spotlights on the significant literary and political contributions of a host of black women both past and present, an illumination reminiscent of the 1970s and 1980s when celebrations of black women abounded in reaction to "unrelenting misogynistic attacks."[11] This, as Patricia Hill Collins attests, is part of the "new public safe space" enjoyed by contemporary African-American women as the result of their having a "new-found," "self-defined," "collective standpoint."[12]

What I have found most intriguing, however, is the steady stream of both solicited and unsolicited books, commentaries, and news articles circulating in recent years on the socioeconomic success of black women, something some believe is a direct consequence of their having forged this new public regard—at least in the fields of academia and literature—and "achieved a visibility unthinkable in the past."[13] Unlike the typical reports of the 1970s, 1980s, and early 1990s that condemned "underclass" black women for many of society's ills, the vast majority of these reports center on the gains that African-American women have made occupationally, educationally, and materially over the past thirty years. Writing several years after the academic world had well documented such trends, they give resounding praise to the thousands of black women who remain steadfast in their pursuit of higher degrees and in their dogged attempts to secure highly influential jobs in government and in corporate America. As one *Newsweek* article stated, the fruits of their labor are borne out by their ascension to the professional-managerial class. Today, about 24 percent of black women occupy such positions.[14]

We know that such reports must be somewhat tempered, however. The class designations used in reporting these and other related statistics (i.e., the U.S. census) do not capture the full reality of black college-degreed, professional-managerial status. As sociologist Elizabeth Higginbotham has stated,

> Empirical research indicates that the occupational positions of educated Black women are still problematic. . . . Black employees in professional and managerial positions are concentrated in the public sector. When they are in the private sector, Black middle-class employees are in the marginal areas of production (such as personnel, public relations, and the like).[15]

Further, black women's representation in many top positions remains significantly less than that for women overall. Yet, despite seriously ingrained race and gender barriers, many believe that black women's presence "atop the nation's foreign-policy pyramid" and in "'white men's jobs" generally will continue to rise.[16]

Paradoxically, as a consequence of their recent and rapid social ascension, middle-class black women may be experiencing increased frustration with finding suitable husbands and partners, as well as greater loneliness and isolation. Indeed, many of the women contributing their personal stories to these published accounts—sources which also include *USA Today*, *Honey* magazine, and Veronica Chambers's *Having It All?* to name a few—do find that the black male/black female achievement gap severely limits the pool of compatibly successful men with which to form committed unions. The "black marriage problem" is apparently just as severe (if not more so) for black women at the other end of the spectrum, where a much larger proportion of the black female population remains trapped in the poor, working poor, and working classes and where joblessness and forms of social dislocation plague their black male counterparts. Without diminishing the seriousness of these dilemmas for black women, *Embracing Sisterhood* is primarily concerned with what impact upward mobility for some and social stagnation for others may have on relations among contemporary black women, that is, other than creating potential interpersonal conflicts that might erupt in an effort to secure black husbands.

Locating Black Stepsisterhood in Social Class

In order to statistically verify a pattern of sharpening socioeconomic divisions among African-American women, I compiled 1970 and 2000 census data for women age twenty-five or older.[17] Using typical categories of educational attainment as proxies for social class status, these data suggest that the most dramatic changes over the past thirty years have been in wages, income, employment, homeownership, and marriage. Women of the middle classes (i.e., with four or more years of college) have enjoyed increases in both wages and total personal income and in their rates of homeownership, and women of the lower classes (i.e., who have not completed high school) have experienced a large drop in employment rates. Middle-class black women, like their lower-class counterparts, however, have experienced a decrease in marriage rates. Therefore, on the whole, there is no clear indication that there has been a "pulling away" of the class structure "at both ends"[18] among black women; by most measures, gains and losses are roughly the same across class categories.

A number of scholars have argued that class divisions among African Americans are best understood through examining the total amount of income earned by this population and how that income is distributed among it members. Studies using this method have demonstrated a consistent pattern where the income shares for the lowest two-fifths of black families and black adult men have decreased over time, and the income shares for the upper two-fifths of these populations have increased.[19] The most recent of these studies tracks these changes over a thirty-year period:[20] between 1970 and 2000, the income share for black families of the lowest strata decreased from 15.2 percent to 12.8 percent, while the share for the upper strata increased from 68.2 percent to 72 percent—hence the pulling away at both ends. But does this pattern hold for African-American women as well? No, just the opposite: the aggregate income shares for the lowest two-fifths of adult black women (age twenty-five and older) have increased over time, and shares for the upper two-fifths have decreased (see table 1). It is not simply that evidence of growing class polarization in the black community tends to be much more evident from individual-level analyses of men than of women, as Michael C. Dawson contends,[21] but rather that the trends may flow in the opposite direction. Nonetheless, because family-level data (said to be more revealing than individual-level data) have consistently shown economic polarization, and because women play such an integral economic role in black families, poor and well-to-do alike, class schism for African-American women is indirect yet inevitable.

Equally important as these facts of changing social class structure is the commonly held belief that these changes have caused a waning of collective gender-ethnic identity and consciousness. This belief extends largely from recent observations of the black community at large, such as that reported by sociologist Lois Benjamin. Using in-depth interviews with three generations of black professionals, Benjamin illustrates what she calls "the changing cultural tradition of sharing and caring in the Black community," "frayed connections," and "broken bonds."[22] Reinforcing this belief is a handful of empirical research studies focused specifically on women, such as that showing that time-honored black maternal kin networks appear to be less likely to meet their objectives. These networks are the epitomized and most frequently cited expression of black women's solidarity. Elaine Bell Kaplan's ethnographic study,[23] for example, revealed that black teenage mothers often feel emotionally abandoned, even by their own mothers, and that emotional support to these young mothers is sometimes even withheld. A recent collection of statistically rigorous studies finds that extended-kin support for young black mothers is often ineffective or nonexistent.[24] Fully one-third of black single mothers in one study were without an extended-kin network from which to draw support of any kind. Anne Roschelle's study of family networks concludes that black families are less likely than white families to be involved in giving intergenerational assistance to young and/or needy mothers.[25]

Further, another study of black maternal caregiving to disadvantaged women found social class to play a significant role in estranging caregivers from those they sought to assist. The primarily middle-class Birthing Project, an informal collective of black women based in Sacramento, California, struggled to maintain cross-class fictive-kin relations in an urban area that had suffered—like so many others—the erosion of traditional community infrastructures. Many of the middle-class "sister-friends" I interviewed there expressed disillusionment about their work to provide maternal support to young, disadvantaged mothers. They often found their efforts undermined by an increasing divergence of experiences, resources, and interests among black women, both real and perceived. There I argued that this divergence is realized for today's black women activists in the "burnout" they suffer in trying to meet the demands of upwardly mobile work, family, and community life; in the differentiated "street wisdom" exhibited by lower-class (versus middle-class) black women that fosters resentment between them around issues of materialism, opportunism, and trust; and, most importantly, in their fear of, and frustration with, drugs and drug-related crime that is too often associated with urban black existence.[26] Given that we have come to understand the motivation for black women to sustain kin support networks as derived from a conjunction of empathy for other black women who suffer similar social advantages and of African-American norms of solidarity, responsibility, and accountability (what I call "normative empathy"[27]), news that this cultural system may be in jeopardy is certainly disturbing.

In *Further to Fly: Black Women and the Politics of Empowerment,*[28] I find a kindred spirit deeply concerned about the state of black sisterhood and about whether changing socioeconomic and sociopolitical conditions have undermined the power of the black woman collective. For nearly twenty years, author and black activist Sheila Radford-Hill has warned that an era of "crisis" has come for black sisterhood:[29]

> What caused black women to become immobilized? Why are black women resisting the "necessary moves to correct what's not [working] in their lives"? What, in short, is the cause of the present crisis of black sisterhood? . . . I raise the question, who was asleep at the switch when the crisis of black womanhood first started?[30]

Sociologist Patricia Hill Collins rightly notes that unity among black women has long been threatened by differences among them, including differences in social class status. This moment in history is really not so different:[31] Collins argues that the purported "crisis" is better described as the observation of "emerging" disunity from beneath the surface and brought about by significant current events. In our time, such events would include the occupation of high-level white-collar positions by a significant number of black women and the gracing of *Fortune* magazine's list of billionaires by the first black woman to do so.[32] Hence, "emergence" in Collins's statement does not signify that the challenge of black sisterhood is unusual, only that it confronts us at unique historical moments.

Nonetheless, it is difficult to shake the impression that black sisterhood is declining contemporarily under changing socioeconomic conditions. Such impressions are evident in Radford-Hill's powerful, succinct analysis of the confluence of factors that purportedly gave rise to the heyday of black sisterhood and how ultimately the demise of black women's solidarity was realized in class polarization. She describes how black women came together in unprecedented numbers against racist violence and injustice in the 1950s and early 1960s. Spirited themes of black woman's pride and beauty rang out from political rallies and from popular culture, and expectations ran high for what future rewards black women would reap from their sacrifices. Then, she argues, significant changes and events helped to unravel that optimism. Black men "adopted the patriarchal traditions of their white counterparts as the standard for black male-female relationships,"[33] effectively casting black women's traditional gender roles in the community as deviant. Aiding in this were the release of the infamous Moynihan Report and the death of Malcolm X in 1965. In placing the onus of the responsibility for the ills of the black community on black mothers, the Moynihan Report undermined the credibility of black women as social change agents. Had Malcolm X not been assassinated, Radford-Hill believes he may have "challenged the notion that the black matriarch was responsible for deviant black families."[34] He might have provided a "serious challenge" to the ideologies of race and gender that helped deflate black women's community power. In the aftermath of these occurrences and the less sensationalized enactments of Great Society policies that actually helped to increase social inequalities both interracially and intraracially (in the late 1960s and 1970s), the "crisis" of black womanhood began to unfold, manifest in conflicts over what the proper community roles of black women should be (even, and particularly, among black feminists); a "rupture" in black women's gender identity; and therefore a diminished activist sisterhood. Little progress in black women's solidarity, she says, has been made since this time, due in part to what may be sharply held differences among black women. In sum,

> It is commonly believed that the loss of social cohesion among African Americans is a consequence of ending legal discrimination in America and of expanding the black middle class, whose obligation to the race declined with its increased access to the social and economic mainstream. An equally crucial but rarely discussed cause for the decline in ethnic solidarity is the deterioration of black women's political culture. This loss of political infrastructure and organizing is connected to the inability of black women to define and promote social roles that incorporate traditional standards of black womanhood.[35]

Though my own theorizing on this makes less distinction between the problems of the expanding black social class structure and the "social disintegration and cultural malaise"[36] of black women's community, I share Radford-Hills's concern for the potential for crisis. My past work employs the term "schism" (rather than "crisis") to connote that estrangement among African-American women may be growing, a term common among my social science colleagues who work in this general area. I, along with others, have bemoaned the class polarization of the black community and its potential to dismantle gender-ethnic solidarity. We have had to face the fact that the strong traditions of black sisterhood are not immune to such problems as urbanization and its dislocation of women from the "once familial" character of cross-class social relationships.[37] Portions of Patricia Hill Collins's highly acclaimed *Black Feminist Thought: Knowledge, Consciousness, and the Politics of Empowerment* follow suit:

> The entire community structure of bloodmothers and othermothers is under assault in many inner-city neighborhoods, where the very fabric of African-American community life is being eroded.[38]

Further, Radford-Hill proclaims,

> Ultimately, the crisis reflects black women's ambivalence toward the value of maintaining ethnic community. This ambivalence reflects the constraints that family and career place on political action, as well as the frustrations of reconciling the social, economic, and political differences of divergent class interests and needs. When black women equivocate about the value of their communities and about their roles in maintaining them, they erode the development of their political culture.[39]

Over the past century, numerous scholars have predicted that divergent class experiences or interests would eventually undermine significantly the "racial" bonds of African Americans, though relatively little attention has been given to how race and class might intersect with gender. Their debate is with other scholars equally committed to theorizing about whether collective "race consciousness" will prevail over or ultimately give way to a stronger "class consciousness" as significant social progress for blacks is realized. The concerns addressed in Michael Dawson's *Behind the Mule: Race and Class in African-American Politics* and, more recently, in his *Black Visions: The Roots of Contemporary African-American Political Ideologies* are indicative of those addressed by various intellectual pundits: of central interest is how class polarization affects the degree to which blacks are homogeneous in their racial identity and in their social and political interests and actions.

The "Race School"

The "race school" of black intellectuals has tended to emphasize the fact that the passage of the civil rights bills, the widespread societal changes of the 1960s, and the economic booms of the 1980s and 1990s did not guarantee blacks freedom from racist oppression, and that therefore the extent of class polarization is tempered by racism's lingering effects.[40] Their philosophy condemns the social injustice of racism and highlights the linked fate of all blacks to racist practices, leading them to predict that race will remain the predominant shaper of all African-American life and will continue to bind blacks to a common identity and to common interests and ways of the race, regardless of class differences. The success or failure of any one African American is seen as necessarily linked to the fate of the entire race.

Though they differed in how racial progress should best be achieved—either through assimilation and accommodation or through resistance and preservation of culture—Booker T. Washington and W. E. B. DuBois have been credited with having conceived and advanced decades ago the idea that middle-class blacks are the group best equipped to tend to the social advancement of the mass of African Americans. Better educated and socioeconomically situated, and somewhat less vulnerable to adverse social and economic trends, middle-class blacks (or the "talented tenth" of black America, as DuBois called them) were bestowed the duty of race leadership for the elevation of black people and the obligation to serve as role models, educators, supporters, and advocates.[41] Every middle-class success story must also be a tale of how one fulfilled his or her moral obligation to "uplift" others.[42]

E. Franklin Frazier[43] did not have the confidence of his two predecessors in the black middle-class's ability or desire to fulfill their obligation to uplift the race. Characterizing blacks that had achieved a relatively high economic, educational, and occupational status as an isolated "black bourgeoisie," Frazier concluded that the black middle class lacked a cultural tradition, rejected identification with the black masses, conformed to white bourgeoisie values, and suffered an "inferiority complex." Combined, Frazier stated, these factors rendered the group useless to the cause of black uplift. Thirty years later, Harold Cruse[44] would find the "new" black middle class to be as "empty" in their social mission as those Franklin had encountered.

Despite Frazier's pessimism, or perhaps because of it, race school intellectuals have continually addressed this issue of middle-class black obligation and racial solidarity. Joe Feagin and Melvin Sikes's investigation[45] of how the contemporary middle class was holding up under the "frustration and rage over persisting discrimination" revealed that a large proportion of the African-American middle class continues to feel conscious of and willing to pursue their obligations and duties to the larger black community. Cornell West and Charles Banner-Haley,[46] on the other hand, were concerned about how this "new" black middle class, those who emerged as a legacy of civil rights victories in the 1960s and 1970s, would organize itself in order to meet the challenges of 1990s-style racism and fulfill its crucial role in leading the black community to political resistance and cultural consciousness. West remained optimistic: "The relation of [the middle class's] unprecedented opportunities and privileges to the revolt of the black masses is quite obvious to them. . . . [They] possess the requisite skills and legitimacy in the eyes of the majority of African Americans for the articulation of the needs and interests of African America."[47] Speaking to the fact that many members of the middle class are "morally torn" between their racial obligations and their class interests in modern times, Bill E. Lawson asked to what extent they were obligated to uplift the disadvantaged.[48]

Because historically the mechanism for racial uplift has been the practice of formal political action and power, the voices of black intellectual women on the subject generally are absent from the mainstream of "race school" thought. Women's discussions of race consciousness are most likely to be found in a separate literature analyzing the work of black club women, suffragists, feminists, and other black women activists. It is understandable, however, that an intellectual tradition promoting racial solidarity might not welcome an interest in issues exposing gender differences within the African-American community or class differences among black women.

The "Class School"

One important intellectual counter to the race school is the "class school," whose advocates argue that in the last twenty years, sweeping social and economic changes have created a situation where race has ceased to be the major determinant of the fate of African Americans. They believe that class consciousness now supercedes race consciousness, that the persistence of racism in modern times does not sufficiently explain the class polarization that has emerged and that continues to strengthen among African Americans.[49] Credited in large part to sociologist William Julius Wilson, this school of thought has tended to emphasize the role of past racism in creating the labor and socioeconomic separation of blacks and whites. Social dislocation among blacks contemporarily, however, is attributed to "impersonal shifts in the economy" (versus racism), black social "disabilities" (versus racial discrimination), and middle-class self-interest (versus racial solidarity); these are what have led to the socioeconomic and cultural isolation of a new, relatively privileged class and an underprivileged "underclass" of blacks.[50] *Contemporary Sociology*[51] ranked Wilson's *The Declining Significance of Race* among the "Ten Most Influential Books in the Past Twenty-Five Years."

Emphasis in these class studies is placed far more on the condition of black men than of black women. Typically, analyses focus on the lack of labor-market opportunities for lower-class black men and its negative consequences for black family formation and stability. The spatial concentration of disorganized, unskilled, and alienated underclass black male populations is said to be directly linked to declines in black marriage and positive family functioning. Nonetheless, this theme of alienation has been useful in theorizing about the constellation of interlocking sociohistorical factors that have crippled many black women. An extensive discussion of this theme is offered in the work of sociologist William Julius Wilson, where a framework is provided with which to interpret the plight of disadvantaged urban black women and the severing of ties between them and the culturally obligated black women of the middle class. It is argued that as a direct consequence of a self-interested black middle-class exodus from the inner city, blacks who remain do so without the so-called economic and social buffer provided by a more stable black middle class. It is argued that, lacking the interpersonal trust and moral cohesion provided through traditional cultural relationships, the lower class is increasingly isolated, and the opportunities for moving beyond the confines of lower-class existence are progressively closed. Further, relations antithetical to these traditions have emerged between the upper classes and the disadvantaged, the latter of whom opportunistically engage in distrustful, alienating, and sometimes criminal social and economic activities that further undermine cultural solidarity. Most recently, these images of bifurcation in the black community are described as a conflict between the "Afristocracy" ("upper-middle-class blacks and the black elite") and the "Ghettocracy" ("the desperately unemployed and underemployed . . . trapped in underground economies, and those working-poor folk who slave in menial jobs at the edge of the economy.")[52]

The theoretical debate on the black urban underclass continues to be misguided in its preoccupation with restoring black men to economic stability—that is, to their rightful place as family wage earners and productive male citizens—and in its lack of appreciation for what black women have accomplished across class.[53] Still, the class school's analysis of how the economic transformation of the inner city undermined the middle class's identification with and support of the black masses provides a basis from which to better understand the potential estrangement of black women from one another. It is insufficient, however, in that it downplays the continued significance of white racism and thus certain other realities. For example, critics from the race school characterize the new black middle class as highly vulnerable to future economic downturns—a vulnerability reflective of deep-seated racial discrimination.[54] Further, the peculiar nature of this racism is such that any negative social messages "sent" by the black underclass are generalized to affect the status of African Americans as a whole; this spillover effect could regularly remind members of the middle class of their race embeddedness and obligation.[55]

Two recent urban ethnographies help to remind us of the complex ways that race and class (and other axes of difference) intersect for African Americans today. In *Harlemworld*, John L. Jackson Jr. observes how black Harlemites "behave interpersonally" as an indicator of "their particular class placement," and he argues that "black people often theorize class as always already articulated with race."[56] He focuses on "the intraracial, class-stratified contexts wherein African Americans are forced to negotiate class differences in their everyday lives."[57] And similar to the picture of Chicago drawn by Mary Pattillo-McCoy in *Black Picket Fences*, Jackson draws the following conclusion:

> Harlem residents not only have life histories that transcend the discrete categories of "black underclass" and "black middle-class," they not only live in close proximity

to other residents with markedly different socioeconomic realities, they also have
social interactions that cut across many class lines.[58]

The trick, he says, is to unravel the mysteries of "folk theories of class" and
the "mutable and fluid property of class and class-consciousness that makes
discussions of socioeconomic differences within a racialized space like Harlemworld so rich an endeavor."[59] Pattillo-McCoy, in her analysis of the
"privileges and perils" of the black middle class, underscores one of the
"many manifestations of simultaneous racial and class stratification."[60] For
the middle class, this is in part shown in the way their lives regularly and
impressionably straddle that of their poorer counterparts. She argues that
popular ideas about the social isolation and out migration of middle-class
blacks from the inner city downplay or miss altogether the "long reach of the
ghetto outside of high-poverty neighborhoods."[61] Particularly for black
youth, this "in-between position" and "peculiar limbo" help to explain how
the life outcomes of similarly situated African Americans become so different and unequal.[62] In neither of these studies, however, are the social location
of women (or girls) and their ideas about and experiences with the race-class
intersection given adequate attention. There are admittedly "loud silences of
gender's present absences,"[63] though certainly neither scholar dismisses gender as deserving in these discussions.

Black Feminist Theory

Two decades ago, Cheryl Townsend Gilkes enthusiastically announced that
"a sociology which accounts for the integral and unique role of the Black
woman within Black society is being developed."[64] Since that time, black
feminist (and womanist) scholarship has significantly advanced the view that
the black woman's experience is a "central thread in the interpretation of
culture and society."[65] Black feminist intellectual thought is dedicated to
issues not only of black women's racial consciousness but also of their unique
gender consciousness—a dual consciousness formed from a history of racial
and sexist oppression and resistance.[66] The concepts of "double jeopardy"
and "double burden" have been frequently employed to describe this dual
consciousness.[67] In recent years, this framework has been expanded to reflect
black women's "multiple" consciousness stemming from their class, sexual,
and other social locations.
    Like the black male theorists most often credited with generating black
intellectual thought, black feminist theorists have also addressed the class
polarization of the black community and its potential undermining of the traditional philosophies of racial consciousness; for black feminists, however,
the concern is also for the undermining of gender-ethnic consciousness.
Implicitly, their critique of both the "race school" and the "class school" is

that these two traditions narrowly focus attention on the androcentric conceptualization and operationalization of racial uplift, obligation, and leadership.[68] Contrastingly, black women's visions of these activities have included mainstream, male-dominated political/intellectual channels as well as community- and women-centered ones.

Clues from black feminists about whether a tension between gender-ethnic consciousness and class consciousness among black women exists are scarce, though some acknowledge that the commonality black women have shared historically may be giving way to experiences of race, gender, and class oppression that are more variegated than they were in the past. In a thoughtful and frequently cited essay originally written for *Newsweek* in 1980 and later reproduced in an anthology on race, class, and gender, black woman journalist Leanita McClain revealed what many other black women like her have likely experienced—that her social mobility had increasingly distanced her from folks in the ghetto and made her fearful of ever returning there: "I am uncomfortably middle-class."[69] In *Yearning: Race, Gender, and Cultural Politics*, feminist scholar bell hooks warns of the tendency of "gifted brilliant black women" and "feminist divas" to "begin thinking of [themselves] as different from and superior to other black women."[70] Further, as sociologist Patricia Hill Collins puts it, there looms the "ominous" potential for "negative relationships" to "develop among Black women of different social classes" because of changing socioeconomic patterns.[71] (Recall that I suggested earlier the caution that should be taken in analyzing such statements. By Collins's own admission, negative relationships among black women are not new; therefore, the implication that the "development" of such relationships contemporarily is something new is misleading, even as the conditions under which these relationships take place is changing.) Despite their providing a rather limited understanding of intragroup class dynamics, transcending these differences has been a focused agenda of black women intellectuals: "The process of empowerment cannot be simplistically defined in accordance with our own particular class interests. We must learn to lift as we climb."[72]

My own work in this area only helps to further muddy these waters. The art of applying black feminist theory to sociological research was taught to me by an enlightened interdisciplinary faculty, and that experience strongly influenced (and continues to influence) my approach to the study of social problems confronting contemporary black women. In recognizing the value of "adding flesh" to what was then just a hint of what might be a waning of gender-ethnic solidarity among black women—that is, the value of convincingly and legitimately processing social data for academic consumption—I conducted the study of the Birthing Project sister-friends, described earlier, from which issues of social class and black stepsisterhood reared their ugly heads. But I also observed that despite a sense of growing estrangement among contemporary black women, there was much to honor and celebrate in sisterhood at the Birthing Project. (Now, more than a decade since I first met these extraordinary women, the sister-friends are still actively committed to expending personal and group resources across class to help preserve the lives of mothers and children.) Though these maternal activists were frequently disheartened by the interpersonal strife that would erupt between them and the disadvantaged women they served, the very fact that they committed themselves to the revitalization of the extended-kin community structure is itself testimony of an enduring solidarity. Further, their activities, and that of other black collectives like them, harkens back to the gender-ethnic solidarity of their activist foremothers—black club women of the late nineteenth and early twentieth centuries—who fought against the devastating poverty and pervasive health problems that plagued the black community after Reconstruction. In both eras, these women sought to fulfill their duty as "community othermothers"[73] and to meet their moral obligation to gender-ethnic survival. Their actions reflect empathy for other less fortunate black women with whom they felt inextricably tied; their actions also reflect African-American norms of community solidarity and individual responsibility and accountability.

As is often the case in comparing and contrasting various schools of thought on a subject, past theorizing on intraracial solidarity among African Americans—including black feminist theory which is committed to bringing women in from the margins of such discourse—leads us to anticipate contemporary outcomes reflecting a compromise of these ideas. Both theory and empirical evidence (including some of my own) suggest that there is a need to balance the idea of a thriving, cross-class black woman collective that has persisted despite an expanding class structure, with a sense of growing and debilitating estrangement among black women.

In applying this compromise of theory to the current study, I anticipated a good mix of sisterhood and stepsisterhood evidenced both through direct testimony and through my analysis of the whole of the data I gathered. Despite my strong predisposition to assume that gender-ethnic identity and consciousness would align themselves neatly along class lines, I worked to accommodate both the admission by some that black women's traditions cannot be expected to withstand the challenges presented by urbanization and growing class divergence, and what others cite as historical proof of how, when faced with great challenges, certain aspects of traditional black sisterhood have survived across class.

The ideas and sentiments shared by the women of this research offer us some experientially based insights into concerns that were revisited by my oil-and-lube-shop encounter (described at the start of this chapter), as well as into the contemporary social structure within which black women exist. From this investigation, I ultimately argue that the legacy of black women's collective strength will continue to be one that makes us proud and that the black sisterhood—restimulated by a new social project and by effective new leadership—is not likely to dissipate into a morass of community discord. It is my hope that this book is received as part of the womanist tradition of bringing African-American women in from the margins of social study through the exploration of this particular substantive and contemporary dilemma. Still, readers should know that this is undoubtedly a political hotbed upon which I, in the name of black sisterhood, am somewhat reluctant to tread. (There's that "airing of dirty laundry" thing to worry about.) But given that much of the research on African-American women either assumes a homogeneity of identity and experience (among them and as well as indistinguishable from black men), focuses on only one of many social categories of black women (e.g., women of the so-called underclass), or is preoccupied with interracial dynamics, *Embracing Sisterhood* makes an important contribution.

COMMUNING WITH BLACK SISTERS: THE RESEARCH METHODOLOGY

What is the relative degree of black sisterhood and black stepsisterhood that exists among contemporary African-American women? How are these two ideas articulated and experienced in black women's everyday lives within and across class lines? From March 2001 to April 2002, I held intimate conversations with eighty-eight African-American women, hoping to discover the answer to these questions. These women on the one hand were perfect strangers and on the other were just like me. As April L. Few and her colleagues explain,

> As Black women researchers, we share race and gender with our informants, but barriers are possible because of differences in class, sexual orientation, ethnicity, or nationality. . . . Sharing certain identities is not enough to presume an insider status. Idiosyncrasies are embedded in our identities that inevitably create moments of intimacy and distance between the informant and the researcher.[74]

While I felt warmly received almost immediately by each woman, I was never more grateful for my rigorous training in fieldwork and for my ability to establish a reasonable degree of trust between my informants and me. (This was the last place I wanted to stumble by inadvertently exuding an air of superiority or prejudgment.) For the most part, it appeared that I successfully negotiated the differences between us, at least while we were face to face. I judged this by the appreciation that many of the women showed me for providing them the rare opportunity to voice their concerns and share their experiences with "sister-friend" candor. I cannot be certain, however, that all of the women found me to be nonthreatening and adequately sensitive.

The women of this study were among the 126 African-American women who were invited from the Greater Baltimore Area to be interviewed for this research. One of the more interesting, unique facts about the study sample is that, as Baltimoreans, many of the women had witnessed, indirectly as media consumers and as distant social acquaintances, Oprah Winfrey make her initial mark in the television news and talk-show world. Many have distinct memories of her having visited their public schools or local performances, or of just seeing her on the street as she shopped or socialized. None knew her personally—though some did know folks who did—but a good number had had the opportunity to meet her. While black women's talk of praise or condemnation of Oprah is common across the nation, the study women have a unique purview on the subject, perhaps even more so than black women in Chicago, since her huge celebrity very likely limits her interaction with the masses there.

Limiting the pool of prospective study participants to this geographic space clearly limits theoretically the degree to which the findings discussed in this book can be generalized to the population of black women as a whole. Further, despite attempts to sample women from a wide range of socioeconomic backgrounds, the women of this study are disproportionately from the middle classes (about 60 percent) relative to the Greater Baltimore Area (about 21 percent). This figure is based on the women's occupational prestige—executive, managerial, and professional occupations.[75] Fifty-one percent of these women also hold postbaccalaureate degrees. The fact that 32 percent hold no college degree led me to examine each case more closely to determine if she should be reclassified as "lower class" (i.e., from the poor and working classes). Note that throughout this text I use the terms "lower classes" and "middle classes" to reflect my having collapsed several smaller groups, meaningful in their own right, into these simple dichotomous categories. Clues about the women's class status were ascertained from field notes and interview data, such as how they described their work setting and the nature of their leisure time, and family income was also considered. Incorporating additional information such as this resulted in seventeen of the women being reclassified as "lower class," and there was also some reclassification of those originally designated "lower class" based on such information (six in all). This process ultimately yielded a somewhat smaller proportion of middle-class study women (about 55 percent).[76]

The overrepresentation of middle-class black women in this sample provides a strong base for substantive discussion of the particular issues addressed in this research. The *African American Review* reports that "trends of thought" adopted by middle-class African Americans continue to "identify and to establish a collaborative perspective acceptable to and representative of African American people."[77] Similarly, Yanick St. Jean and Joe R. Feagin state, "Rare are contemporary studies of middle-class African American women, those whose persisting experiences with discrimination, despite their educational and occupational achievements, provide strong evidence of the central play of discrimination in the lives of contemporary African Americans."[78] On the other hand, the number of study women from the lower and middle classes is roughly the same (forty-one and forty-seven women, respectively), which provides a rare opportunity for women from each class group to contribute equally to the research discussion.

Invitations to participate were facilitated by a variety of individuals who, to my surprise and delight, were rather easily persuaded to let me venture into their institutions to "discuss relationships among today's black women." The sites from which prospective interviewees were identified were chosen on the basis that they employ, serve, and/or attract black women from diverse socio-economic backgrounds, making it likely that—at least in the time spent at these sites—these women interacted regularly face to face.[79] Further, since I anticipated that the context of the women's interaction would likely shape that interaction, the sites were intentionally chosen so as to be differentiated by how they are regulated—by culture, by the market, and by the state. No hypotheses were intended, however, as to how gender-ethnic identity and consciousness might vary by these contexts; the objective was primarily to derive a diverse research sample.

For the purposes of this study, I define culture-regulated sites as those established and managed for the express purpose of serving some cultural (i.e., gender-ethnic) imperative. The local chapters of two well-respected black sororities were chosen to represent such sites, given that their focus is on community outreach and racial uplift for African-American women. Women members of the black faculty and staff association at a local, predominantly white elite university were selected for similar reasons. Two local black hair salons were chosen to represent market-regulated sites; though they are also unique cultural spaces for black women (most outsiders have no clue just how much so!), their primary motive is clearly profit making. The two state-regulated research sites fall under the umbrella of public safety and corrections administration. I chose these latter two sites specifically for their large representation of black women from the lower class and for the opportunity to include in the study hard-to-reach women with substance abuse, domestic abuse, and criminal justice problems.

At each of these seven sites, I recruited women from all levels of the hierarchy: parole officers and ex-offenders, hair stylists and clients, legal counsel and clerical staff, organizational executives and general management. Additionally, I pursued other women that were referred to the study by interviewees, even if these women were not associated with any of the targeted research sites, provided that they were not close relatives or friends of other interviewees. About 80 percent of the research sample was recruited from three areas: local chapters of two national black sororities, local offices of state correctional agencies and institutions, and by respondent referrals. The women range in age from eighteen to eighty-nine years, with a median age of thirty-six years; their age distribution makes them a bit younger than black women in the Greater Baltimore Area generally. About 54 percent of the women had never married, though 18 percent of these never-married women were currently cohabitating; 28 percent were currently married. Sixty-one percent of the women were mothers; others closely mothered siblings and other kin. Sixteen of the eighty-eight women (18 percent) were being held at a local women's facility while they awaited criminal trial or reassignment to another, more long-term facility.

This project employed intensive interviews and a written survey. It was my original intent to use the survey as primarily a conversation piece (something for the women to tinker with in preparation for the in-depth conversation we were to hold together) and as a guide for me to use in conducting the interview. But at the analysis stage of the project, I recognized that the survey provided an important conceptual framework for interpreting the interview data, that the survey results were of equal importance to the interview data, and that these results made for a richer and more complete understanding of my material. Still, the intensive interview data is clearly the centerpiece and provides substantially more detail.

The intensive interview was the method best suited for eliciting detailed responses to questions about the sensitive and potentially explosive issue of gender-ethnic identity and consciousness among black women. April L. Few and her colleagues elucidate the "fit" of such a method to the black feminist/womanist agenda:

> The use of qualitative methods, particularly interviews or narrative documents, has been instrumental in informing researchers of the various dynamics that shape sexuality, race, and gender interactions. . . . The process of focusing primarily on Black women's experiences provides the researcher with knowledge and also affords the informant the opportunity to revisit the phenomena at her own pace and in her own words.[80]

I spent approximately one and a half hours with each woman, and, excepting those cases where the woman was incarcerated, virtually all of the interviews took place in the woman's home. I designed these interviews to probe as deeply as possible the women's gender-ethnic identities and consciousness, most importantly their feelings of attachment to (or detachment from) black women as a whole, as well as to specific groups of black women. The women were strongly encouraged to tie their feelings to specific individuals and events. While highly subjective data content can be problematic in some studies, here it plays a direct role in the research analysis and therefore constitutes valid data.

The written survey that was administered may best be described as an augmented and "feminized" version of the Multidimensional Model of Racial

Identity (MMRI) scale constructed by Robert Sellers and his colleagues in 1997.[81] It is mingled with language borrowed from the personal- and group-identity sections of the National Survey of Black Americans, the National Black Politics Study, and the Racial Identity Attitude Scale,[82] and it concludes with a short set of vignettes created specifically for this research. In feminizing the substantive portions of the survey instrument, I attempted to crudely capture the women's ideas about and experiences with solidarity, as well as baseline measures of their gender-ethnic identities across four dimensions—centrality, private regard, public regard, and sociopolitical ideology (see table 2).[83] Additionally, basic demographic data were also collected. Each of the women was asked to complete the survey prior to the interview, generally no more than a week to ten days prior. Only five of the eighty-eight women failed to do so for one reason or another.

My conversations with these women were launched by asking the respondent to elaborate on her reaction to the one survey item that seemed to epitomize the concerns of this project: "I have a strong attachment to other black women." I asked the women in various ways to state whether they are concerned about the current state of the black woman collective and what potential threats to the collective they believe exist. As our meeting progressed, special attention was also given to the set of questions asking how close the interviewee believes she is to various groups of women "in her feeling and ideas about things." Four of these groups represented different social classes.

In addition to the intensive interview and the survey, I engaged in participant observation as frequently as possible at four of the research sites—the two hair salons and two divisions of the public safety and corrections administration. There were also occasions to attend sorority meetings and other events. Permission was generally easy to obtain, sometimes in exchange for such favors as assisting with appointment scheduling in the hair salon or providing educational counseling to inmates. Extensive field notes were taken after each interview and after each visit to the research sites, and both interview data and field notes were tape-recorded and later transcribed verbatim.

Data analysis first involved identifying from the interviews recurring themes among the study women and matching these themes to the predetermined constructs reflected in the written survey—for instance, dimensions of gender-ethnic identity, feelings of closeness to women of various sociodemographic categories, and thoughts the women have most frequently when pondering the condition of the black woman collective today. Coupling this information with the women's survey responses,[84] I worked to distinguish the more unified sentiments from those that were more ambivalent, as well as those that tended to organize along class lines. The proportions of women tending in certain directions on a given survey item did not always jibe with the amount or intensity of that content offered in the interview; thus it took a

very intimate acquaintance with the whole of this research data to derive the
conclusions I do.

ORGANIZATION OF CHAPTERS

There would be little concern about stepsisterhood among contemporary
black women were it not for such a rich history of fostering black sisterhood.
Therefore, this book begins with a discussion of what I call the "master narrative" of some of that history. It is a narrative brought to light through an
interdisciplinary body of literature that elucidates the power of womanhood
and the primacy of sisterhood among African-American women. It is a literature composed of theory, social history, poetry, and essay, much of which
documents the history of African-American women and their efforts to build
and sustain a conscious gender-ethnic community across class. Chapter 2,
"The Legacy of Black Sisterhood: Deep Collective Roots," begins with an
examination of precolonial and colonial African influences on black sisterhood, as it is frequently noted that many aspects of both past and contemporary African-American culture are reflective of an African way of being.

The next two chapters demonstrate what I find to be the most compelling
evidence from this study: the continuity of that legacy in contemporary
America. In chapter 3, "The Contemporary Currency of Black Sisterhood,"
"currency" refers to the widespread acceptance of the idea and practice of
black sisterhood among today's African-American women. This currency, I
argue, is reflected in their fostering and maintaining shared gender-ethnic
identity and consciousness. Its specific reflections are shown in their endear-
ing use of the term black "sister," their formation and maintenance of sisterly
attachments, their strong gender-ethnic centrality and private regard, their
ability to maintain this centrality and private regard in the face of the public's
general disregard for them, and their shared sociopolitical ideology. Chapter
4, "'Struggle' as a Marker of Authentic Black Womanhood," discusses the
strong commitment black women have to the notion of "struggle" and how
they embrace it as uniquely relevant to their gender-ethnic identity and consciousness. In general, the women's ideas about their struggle are articulated
in four ways and are at times particularized by social class. Further, these
articulations lend some understanding of who black women consider to be a
"real sister"; relations are said to be shaped and unshaped in large part on the
basis of whether the women in question align in their ideas of authenticity.

Chapter 5, "Discord in the Sisterhood: Classed Patterns of Sentiment and
Experience," presents all the evidence from this study of intragroup discord,
approximately half of which occurs along social class lines. Though it is my
contention that this discord is moderate relative to black women's commitment to fostering a strong cross-class gender-ethnic community, it is certainly

common. Thus, pinpointing the specific areas where class discord is likely to occur and crudely etching out the contours of these classed patterns remains a centerpiece of this study.

Day-to-day encounters among contemporary African-American women, like the personal encounter I had with the woman in that oil-and-lube shop, relay much of the "stuff" of black sisterhood, good and bad. Through the person of Ms. Oprah Winfrey—the most renowned among today's black women—African-American women assess whether the sisterhood is on the right track. In chapter 6, "Embracing Oprah Winfrey," study women have much to say about what they know and think they know about Oprah and about what they believe she represents among the various representations of black womanhood.

Finally, chapter 7, "Restimulating the Sisterhood," provides a summary of findings from this research and my case for the need to balance the legacy of a thriving, cross-class black woman collective with the obvious challenges that persist under an expanding class structure and the impressions of black stepsisterhood. Most importantly, I share my vision for reawakening that legacy among black women and those who can appreciate that legacy's potential for helping resolve some of our nation's problems. It is my creative call to sociopolitical action and my attempt to embrace Oprah in very real terms.

Throughout these chapters, I introduce the study women by their pseudonames, ages, and occupational titles. The reader should be aware that these occupational titles can be misleading; class status and occupational title do not always match as one might expect. Table 4 is provided to inform the reader of how each woman is class identified. Also, a few of the sixteen women who were incarcerated at the time of our interview reported to have been in the paid labor market sometime during the year immediately preceding their incarceration. Reviews of these work-experience histories warranted a "middle class" designation in only one case.

My choice to not capitalize "black" in referring to African Americans is primarily to conform to the policies of a growing number of journals and book publishers. However, where the sources I cite or quote do capitalize the word, I follow suit. Also, throughout the publishing world, there are inconsistent uses of "African American" and "African-American." I prefer to use the hyphenated version as a descriptor (adjective)—for instance, "African-American women" and "African-American culture." Again, however, when quoting a source, I follow that usage. Finally, I have made virtually no alterations to the language the study women used in their interviews. Most of the changes made were to eliminate repeated use of phrases like "you know" in a single passage, to clarify for the reader the interviewee's intent, or to protect the study woman's true identity. It was important that the verity of the women's voices be preserved as much as possible.

NOTES

1. Michael C. Dawson, *Black Visions: The Roots of Contemporary African-American Political Ideologies* (Chicago: University of Chicago Press, 2001), 170.

2. Patricia Hill Collins, "What's in a Name? Womanism, Black Feminism, and Beyond," *The Black Scholar* 26, no. 1 (1996): 2.

3. An explanation of how "black," "African-American," and "gender-ethnic group" are used in this text is given in on page 6 of this chapter.

4. See Kay Pasley and Marilyn Ihinger-Tallman, eds., *Remarriage and Stepparenting: Current Research & Theory* (New York: Guilford Press, 1987); and Lawrence H. Ganong and Marilyn Coleman, *Stepfamily Relationships: Development, Dynamics, and Interventions* (New York: Kluwer/AcademicPlenum Publishers, 2004).

5. Toni Morrison, "Cinderella's Stepsisters," in *Across Cultures: A Reader for Writers*, eds. Sheena Gillespie and Robert Singleton (New York: Longman Publishers, 2001).

6. Clenora Hudson-Weems, "Africana Womanism: The Flip Side of a Coin," *The Western Journal of Black Studies* 25, no. 3 (2001): 137.

7. Sheila Radford-Hill, *Further to Fly: Black Women and the Politics of Empowerment* (Minneapolis: University of Minnesota Press, 2000), 40. Also see Reid-Merritt, *Sister Power: How Phenomenal Black Women Are Rising to the Top* (New York: J. Wiley, 1996).

8. The distinction between the terms "identification" and "consciousness" is a subtle one. Identification generally refers to one's awareness of having ideas, feelings, and interests similar to others who share important social characteristics. Race and gender have historically played major roles in the lives of African-American women, and thus they are said to be integral to both their personal and group identities. Consciousness refers to an ideology (or ideologies) arising out of identification with those sharing these similarities and nonidentification with those dissimilar. (See A. K. Burlew and L. R. Smith, "Measures of Racial Identity: An Overview and a Proposed Framework," *Journal of Black Psychology* 17, no. 2 (1991): 53–71; Patricia Gurin, Arthur H. Miller, and Gerald Gurin, "Stratum Identification and Consciousness," *Social Psychology Quarterly* 43 (1980): 30–47; and Mary R. Jackman and Robert W. Jackman, *Class Awareness in the United States* (Berkeley: University of California Press, 1983). Both of these terms are believed to influence African-American women (and men) in their appraisals of themselves and others, and some consider them to be two of the most fundamental sources of sociocultural and behavioral diversity among African Americans. Michael C. Dawson, *Behind the Mule: Race and Class in African-American Politics* (Princeton, NJ: Princeton University Press, 1994); Robert M. Sellers et al., "Multidimensional Model of Racial Identity: A Preliminary Investigation of Reliability and Construct Validity," *Journal of Personality and Social Psychology* 73 (1997): 805–15. "Solidarity" is often used synonymously with "identity" and/or "consciousness," though it is thought more to be the nourishing of identity and consciousness by the group so as to motivate and ready it to act on the group's behalf (e.g., activism, mobilization).

9. See Stephen Cornell and Douglas Hartmann, *Ethnicity and Race: Making Identities in a Changing World* (Thousand Oaks, CA: Pine Forge Press, 1997), 35, figure 2.1.

10. Deborah Willis and Carla Williams, *The Black Female Body: A Photographic History* (Philadelphia: Temple University Press, 2002). Also see Kimberly Wallace-Sanders, ed., *Skin Deep, Spirit Strong: The Black Female Body in American Culture* (Ann Arbor:

University of Michigan Press, 2002); and Michael Bennett and Vanessa D. Dickerson, eds., *Recovering the Black Female Body: Self-Representation by African American Women* (New Brunswick, NJ: Rutgers University Press, 2000).

11. Radford-Hill, *Further to Fly: Black Women and the Politics of Empowerment*, xii.

12. Collins, "What's in a Name? Womanism, Black Feminism, and Beyond."

13. Ibid.

14. Ellis Cose, "The Black Gender Gap," *Newsweek*, March 3, 2003.

15. Elizabeth Higginbotham, "Black Professional Women: Job Ceilings and Employment Sectors," in *Women of Color in U. S. Society*, eds. Maxine Baca Zinn and Bonnie Thornton Dill, 113–31 (Philadelphia: Temple University Press, 1994), 119.

16. Cose, "The Black Gender Gap," 48.

17. The source of this data is the Integrated Public Use Microdata Series, 2004. Steven Ruggles, Matthew Sobek, Trent Alexander, Catherine A. Fitch, Ronald Goeken, Patricia Kelly Hall, Miriam King, and Chad Ronnander, *Integrated Public Use Microdata Series: Version 3.0* [Machine-readable database], Minneapolis, MN: Minnesota Population Center (producer and distributor), 2004, www.ipums.org. Data are based on weighted cases. Income is reported in 1999 dollars for money acquired in 2003. Income data are also reported for total incomes greater than $0 and where total personal income is equal to or greater than that for wage and salary income. The latter restriction corrects for coding that resulted in some women having less total income than wages. U.S. census 1950 classifications were applied for occupational status. Though the IPUMS admits that "the translation of occupation codes into the 1950 classification is particularly problematic for 1980 onward," the 2000 figures here are very close to those reported by the U.S. Census Bureau, Statistical Abstract of the United States, 2001, table no. 595, "Occupations of the Employed by Selected Characteristics: 2000."

18. Dawson, *Behind the Mule: Race and Class in African-American Politics*, 35.

19. See William Julius Wilson, *The Declining Significance of Race: Blacks and Changing American Institutions* (Chicago: University of Chicago Press, 1978); and Gerald D. Jaynes and Robin M. Williams Jr., eds., *A Common Destiny: Blacks and American Society* (Washington, DC: National Academy Press, 1989).

20. Jessica Gordon Nembhard, Steven C. Pitts, and Patrick L. Mason, "African American Intragroup Inequality and Corporate Globalization," in *African Americans in the U.S. Economy*, eds. Ceclia A. Conrad, John Whitehead, Patrick Mason, and James Stewart (Lanham, MD: Rowman & Littlefield, 2005), 208–22.

21. Dawson, *Behind the Mule: Race and Class in African-American Politics*.

22. Lois Benjamin, *Three Black Generations at the Crossroads: Community, Culture, and Consciousness* (Chicago: Burnham, Inc., 2000), 2.

23. Elaine Bell Kaplan, *Not Our Kind of Girl: Unraveling the Myths of Black Teenage Motherhood* (Berkeley: University of California Press, 1997).

24. This collection of literature includes P. Lindsay Chase-Lansdale, Jeanne Brooks-Gunn, and Elise S. Zamsky, "Young African-American Multigenerational Families in Poverty: Quality of Mothering and Grandmothering," *Child Development* 65 (1994): 373–93; Lauren S. Wakschlag, P. Lindsay Chase-Lansdale, and Jeanne Brooks-Gunn, "Not Just 'Ghosts in the Nursery': Contemporary Intergenerational Relationships and Parenting in Young African American Families," *Child Development* 67 (1996): 2131–47; and Dennis P. Hogan, Lingxin Hao, and William L. Parish, "Race, Kin Networks, and Assistance to Mother-Headed Families," *Social Forces* 68, no. 3 (1990): 797–812.

25. Anne R. Roschelle, *No More Kin: Exploring Race, Class, and Gender in Family Networks* (Thousand Oaks, CA: Sage Publications, 1997).

26. See Katrina Bell McDonald, "Black Activist Mothering: A Historical Intersection of Race, Gender, and Class," *Gender and Society* 11, no. 6 (1997): 773–95.

27. Ibid.

28. Radford-Hill, *Further to Fly: Black Women and the Politics of Empowerment.*

29. "Crisis" is defined as "an unstable or crucial time or state of affairs in which a decisive change is impending; esp: one with the distinct possibility of a highly undesirable outcome." *Merriam-Webster's Collegiate Dictionary*, 10th ed. (Springfield, MA: Merriam-Webster, Inc., 1996).

30. Part of this passage (pp. 39, xxi) is a quote from a Susan L. Taylor's "Perspective" column in *Essence* magazine.

31. This sentiment was recently echoed by black public intellectual Michael Eric Dyson who wrote that the hoopla over Bill Cosby's berating of low-income black parenting was "simply the most recent" battle in "a more-than-century-old class war in black America." See Michael Eric Dyson, *Is Bill Cosby Right?: Or Has the Black Middle Class Lost Its Mind?* (New York: Basic Civitas Books, 2005).

32. cbsnewyork.com, "Oprah Joins a Very Exclusive Club: Becomes First Black Woman on *Forbes* List of Billionaires," CBS 2 New York News, 2003, http://cbsnewyork .com/topstories/topstories_story_058212927.html (accessed June 7, 2005).

33. Radford-Hill, *Further to Fly: Black Women and the Politics of Empowerment*, 48.

34. Ibid., 45.

35. Ibid., 41.

36. Ibid., xii.

37. Joyce Ladner, "Black Women Face the 21st Century: Major Issues and Problems," *The Black Scholar* 17 (1986): 12–19.

38. Patricia Hill Collins, *Black Feminist Thought: Knowledge, Consciousness, and the Politics of Empowerment* (New York: Routledge, 1990); McDonald, "Black Activist Mothering: A Historical Intersection of Race, Gender, and Class," 122.

39. Radford-Hill, *Further to Fly: Black Women and the Politics of Empowerment*, 41.

40. See Robert Cherry and William M. Rodgers, eds., *Prosperity for All?: The Economic Boom and African Americans* (New York: Russell Sage Foundation, 2000); and Joe R. Feagin and Melvin P. Sikes, *Living with Racism: The Black Middle-Class Experience* (Boston: Beacon Press, 1994).

41. Bernard R. Boxill, "The Underclass and the Race/Class Issue," in *The Underclass Question*, ed. Bill Lawson, 2–32 (Philadelphia: Temple University Press, 1992); Willard B. Gatewood, *Aristocrats of Color: The Black Elite, 1880–1920* (Bloomington: Indiana University Press, 1990); David L. Lewis, *W. E. B. Dubois: Biography of a Race, 1868–1919* (New York: Henry Holt & Company, 1993).

42. Collins, *Black Feminist Thought: Knowledge, Consciousness, and the Politics of Empowerment*; Michael C. Dawson, *Behind the Mule: Race and Class in African-American Politics*; Elizabeth Higginbotham and Lynn Weber, "Moving up with Kin and Community: Upward Social Mobility for Black and White Women," *Gender and Society* 6 (1992): 416–40; Bill Lawson, ed., *The Underclass Question* (Philadelphia: Temple University Press, 1992); Mary Pattillo-McCoy, *Black Picket Fences: Privilege and Peril among the Black Middle Class* (Chicago: University of Chicago Press, 1999).

43. E. Franklin Frazier, *Black Bourgeoisie* (Glencoe, IL: Free Press, 1957).

44. Harold Cruse, *Plural But Equal: A Critical Study of Blacks and Minorities and America's Plural Society* (New York: William Morrow, 1987).

45. Feagin and Sikes, *Living with Racism: The Black Middle-Class Experience*. Also see William Sampson and Vera Milam, "The Intraracial Attitudes of the Black Middle-Class: Have They Changed?" *Social Problems* 23, no. 2 (1975): 151–65.

46. Cornel West, *Keeping Faith: Philosophy and Race in America* (New York: Routledge, 1993); Charles T. Banner-Haley, *The Fruits of Integration: Black Middle-Class Ideology and Culture, 1960–1990* (Jackson: University Press of Mississippi, 1994).

47. West, *Keeping Faith: Philosophy and Race in America*, 287, 288.

48. Bill Lawson, *Uplifting the Race: Middle-Class Blacks and the Truly Disadvantaged* (Philadelphia: Temple University Press, 1992), 92.

49. Floya Anthias and Nira Yuval-Davis, *Racialized Boundaries: Race, Nation, Gender, Colour, and Class and the Anti-Racist Struggle* (London: Routledge, 1992); Mary Pattillo-McCoy, *Black Picket Fences*.

50. Elijah Anderson, *Streetwise: Race, Class, and Change in an Urban Community* (Chicago: University of Chicago Press, 1990); Boxill, "The Underclass and the Race/Class Issue"; Dawson, *Behind the Mule: Race and Class in African-American Politics*; West, *Keeping Faith: Philosophy and Race in America*; Wilson, *The Declining Significance of Race: Blacks and Changing America*.

51. "The Most Influential Books of the Past 25 Years," *Contemporary Sociology* 25, no. 3. See Aldon D. Morris, "What's Race Got to Do with It? Review of the *Declining Significance of Race: Blacks and Changing American Institutions* by William Julius Wilson," *Contemporary Sociology* 25, no. 3 (1996): 309–13.

52. Dyson, *Is Bill Cosby Right?: Or Has the Black Middle Class Lost Its Mind?*; Michael Eric Dyson, *Race Rules: Navigating the Color Line* (Reading, MA: Addison-Wesley, 1996), xiii, xiv.

53. Karen Anderson, *Changing Woman: A History of Racial Ethnic Women in Modern America* (New York: Oxford University Press, 1996).

54. Dawson, *Behind the Mule: Race and Class in African-American Politics*; Raymond S. Franklin, *Shadows of Race and Class* (Minneapolis: University of Minnesota Press, 1991); Robert C. Smith and Richard Seltzer, *Race, Class, and Culture: A Study in Afro-American Mass Opinion* (Albany: State University of New York Press, 1992).

55. Franklin, *Shadows of Race and Class*.

56. John L. Jackson Jr., *Harlemworld: Doing Race and Class in Contemporary Black America* (Chicago: University of Chicago Press, 2001), 126, 59.

57. Ibid., 90.

58. Pattillo-McCoy, *Black Picket Fences*, 90.

59. Ibid., 129.

60. Ibid., 210.

61. Ibid., 207.

62. Ibid., 6.

63. Jackson, *Harlemworld: Doing Race and Class in Contemporary Black America*, 238n34.

64. Cheryl Townsend Gilkes, "Holding Back the Ocean with a Broom: Black Women and Community Work," in *The Black Woman*, ed. LaFrances Rodgers-Rose (Beverly Hills: Sage Publications, 1980), 217.

65. Cheryl Townsend Gilkes, "Dual Heroisms and Double Burdens: Interpreting Afro-American Women's Experience and History," *Feminist Studies* 15 (1989): 587.

66. Collins, *Black Feminist Thought: Knowledge, Consciousness, and the Politics of Empowerment*; Paula A. Giddings, *When and Where I Enter: The Impact of Black Women on Race and Sex in America* (New York: William Morrow, 1984); bell hooks, *Feminist Theory from Margin to Center* (Boston: South End Press, 1984); Gloria T. Hull, Patricia Bell-Scott, and Barbara Smith, *All the Women Are White, All the Blacks Are Men, but Some of Us Are Brave: Black Women's Studies* (Old Westbury, NY: Feminist Press, 1982); Joyce A. Ladner, *Tomorrow's Tomorrow: The Black Woman* (Garden City, NY: Doubleday, 1971); Pamela Trotman Reid, "Feminism Versus Minority Group Identity: Not for Black Women Only," *Sex Roles* 10, nos. 3–4 (1984): 247–55; Robert Staples and Leanor Boulin Johnson, *Black Families at the Crossroads: Challenges and Prospects* (San Francisco: Jossey-Bass Publishers, 1993).

67. Frances Beale, "Double Jeopardy: To Be Black and Female," in *The Black Woman: An Anthology*, ed. Toni Cade, 90–100 (New York: Signet, 1970); Deborah K. King, "Multiple Jeopardy, Multiple Consciousness: The Context of a Black Feminist Ideology," in *Black Women in America: Social Science Perspectives*, eds. Micheline R. Malson, Elisabeth Mudimbe-Boyi, and Mary Wyer, 265–95 (Chicago: University of Chicago Press, 1988); Yanick St. Jean and Joe R. Feagin, *Double Burden: Black Women and Everyday Racism* (Armonk, NY: M. E. Sharpe, 1998).

68. King, "Multiple Jeopardy, Multiple Consciousness: The Context of a Black Feminist Ideology."

69. Leanita McClain, "The Middle-Class Black's Burden," in *A Foot in Each World*, eds. Leanita McClain and Clarence Page (Evanston, IL: Northwestern University Press, 1986), 13. Also see in Margaret L. Anderson and Patricia Hill Collins, *Race, Class and Gender: An Anthology* (Belmont, CA: Wadsworth Publishing, 1992), 121. Sadly, McClain died of an apparent suicide in 1984; see introduction to *A Foot in Each World*, and also a *Chicago Tribune* reprint in Teresa de Lauretis, ed., *Feminism as a Model for Social Change*, vol. 8, *Feminist Studies, Critical Essays* (Bloomington: Indiana University Press, 1986).

70. bell hooks, *Yearning: Race, Gender, and Cultural Politics* (Cambridge, MA: South End Press, 1990), 97–99.

71. Collins, *Black Feminist Thought: Knowledge, Consciousness, and the Politics of Empowerment*, 65.

72. Angela Y. Davis, *Women, Culture, & Politics* (New York: Vintage Books, 1989), 9. Also see Giddings, *When and Where I Enter: The Impact of Black Women on Race and Sex in America*; Gilkes, "Dual Heroisms and Double Burdens: Interpreting Afro-American Women's Experience and History"; and Collins, *Black Feminist Thought: Knowledge, Consciousness, and the Politics of Empowerment*.

73. Stanlie M. James, "Mothering: A Possible Black Feminist Link to Social Transformations?" in *Theorizing Black Feminisms: The Visionary Pragmatisms of Black Women*, eds. Stanlie M. James and Abena P. A. Busia, 44–54 (London: Routledge, 1993). For her definition of *othermothers*, James cites Rosalie Reigle Troester, "Turbulence and Tenderness: Mothers, Daughters, and 'Othermothers,'" *A Scholarly Journal on Black Women* 1, no. 2 (1984): 13–16; and Collins, *Black Feminist Thought: Knowledge, Consciousness, and the Politics of Empowerment*:

those who assist blood mothers in the responsibilities of child care for short- and long-term periods, in informal or formal arrangements. They can be, but are not confined to, such blood relatives as grandmothers, sisters, aunts, cousins or supportive fictive kin. They not only serve to relieve some of the stress that can develop in the intimate daily relationships of mothers and daughters but they can also provide multiple role models for children. This concept of other-mothering which has its roots in the traditional African world-view and can be traced through the institution of slavery, developed in response to an ever growing need to share the responsibility of child nurturance. (45)

Also see McDonald, "Black Activist Mothering: A Historical Intersection of Race, Gender, and Class"; Carol B. Stack, *All Our Kin: Strategies for Survival in the Black Community* (New York: Basic Books, 1974); John H. Stanfield II, "African American Traditions of Civic Responsibility," *Nonprofit and Voluntary Sector Quarterly* 22, no. 2 (1993): 137–53; and Nancy A. Naples, "Activist Mothering: Cross-Generational Continuity in the Community Work of Women from Low-Income Urban Neighborhoods," *Gender & Society* 6 (1992): 441–63.

74. April L. Few, Dionne P. Stephens, and Marlo Rouse-Arnett, "Sister-to-Sister Talk: Transcending Boundaries and Challenges in Qualitative Research with Black Women," *Family Relations* 52 (2003): 205–15.

75. Occupational titles and prestige were measured according to Keiko Nakao and Judith Treas, "Computing 1989 Occupational Prestige Scores," in *GSS Methodological Report*, 70 (Chicago: National Opinion Research Center, 1990).

76. The following are other relevant study statistics: 57 percent have obtained a college degree. Though the women were employed in a variety of occupations (or, for those currently incarcerated, had been in recent months)—from chief executive to forklift driver—a strong majority (67 percent) are professionals or held fairly high-level executive and administrative positions. Median family income was about fifty-two thousand dollars, and more than half of the women (54 percent) have family incomes of fifty-thousand dollars or more.

77. Roderick J. McDavis and Deborah A. McDavis, "The Fruits of Integration: Black Middle-Class Ideology and Culture, 1960–1990 (Book Review)," *African American Review* 31 (1997): 314–16.

78. St. Jean and Feagin, *Double Burden: Black Women and Everyday Racism*, 5.

79. Sandra S. Smith and Mignon R. Moore, "Intraracial Diversity and Relations among African-Americans: Closeness and Black Students at a Predominantly White University," *American Journal of Sociology* 106, no. 1 (2000): 1–39, claim that given that there are so few settings where African Americans of different social backgrounds interact, the college campus was most suitable for their research on intraracial relations and closeness. College students, however, are generally much more conscious and communicable about race and gender issues than blacks at large. Here, effort was made to identify other sites where black women of various socioeconomic backgrounds are likely to interact on a regular basis.

80. Few, Stephens, and Rouse-Arnett, "Sister-to-Sister Talk: Transcending Boundaries and Challenges in Qualitative Research with Black Women," 206–7.

81. Sellers et al., "Multidimensional Model of Racial Identity: A Preliminary Investigation of Reliability and Construct Validity."

82. These can be found respectively in Jackson S. Jackson, Wayne R. McCullough,

Gerald Gurin, and Clifford L. Broman, "Race Identity," in *Life in Black America*, ed. James S. Jackson (Newbury Park, CA: Sage Publications, 1991); Dawson, *Black Visions: The Roots of Contemporary African-American Political Ideologies*; and Janet E. Helms and Thomas A. Parham, "The Racial Identity Attitude Scale," in *Handbook of Tests and Measurements for Black Populations*, ed. Reginald L. Jones (Hampton, VA: Cobb & Henry Publishers, 1996).

83. It was determined that analyzing the survey items borrowed from Sellers et al.'s Multidimensional Model of Racial Identity (part A) by averaging the index scores for the four dimensions would convey little if any statistical variation on these dimensions because of the small sample size. Instead, data analysis involved examining these dimensions via the proportion of women who responded in the various ways to items within each set. Additionally, because "centrality" and "private regard" are generally indistinguishable substantively in the interview data, these two dimensions were ultimately combined in the analysis.

84. The small sample size warranted reducing the original five-point scale for part A and part B ("strongly agree," "agree," "uncertain," "disagree," and "strongly disagree") to a three-point scale ("agree," "uncertain," and "disagree") at the analysis stage. Table 3 displays the questionnaire items and the responses given based on the three-point scale.

Chapter Two

The Legacy of Black Sisterhood: Deep Collective Roots

It is my celebration
I will drum my drum
I will sing my song
I will dance my dance
I do not need your anemic hands
brought together in pale applause
I do not need your
"You are such musical people"
toothy smile
It is my celebration
You wonder what I have to celebrate
What does the drum tell me
If you must speculate
Watch out
One day as you throw your head back
As you gather your hearty laughter
I will change my dance
I will still sing
The drum will scream
Celebration.

—"I Will Still Sing,"
Amelia Blossom Pegram, African poet[1]

Who will revere the Black woman? Who will keep our neighborhoods safe for our Black innocent womanhood? Black womanhood is outraged and humiliated. Black womanhood cries for dignity and restitution and salvation. Black womanhood wants and needs protection, and keeping, and holding. Who will assuage her indignation? Who will keep her precious and pure? Who will glorify and proclaim her beautiful image? To whom will she cry rape?

—"Who Will Revere the Black Woman?"
Abbey Lincoln, famed singer-actress[2]

33

Black women have a history of the use and sharing of power, from the Amazon
legions of the Dahomey through the Ashanti warrior queen Yaa Asantewa and
the freedom fighter Harriet Tubman, to economically powerful market-women
guilds of the present West Africa. We have a tradition of closeness and mutual
care and support.

—*Sister Outsider: Essays and Speeches,*
Audre Lorde, black feminist writer[3]

These excerpts are but tiny fragments of a vast literature influencing the
gender-ethnic identity and consciousness of contemporary African-American
women. Much of what they understand about black women's cultural history
comes from the sharing of their own life experiences with other black women
in their families, churches, neighborhoods, and workplaces. But what is also
important is their awareness of and engagement with—be it in varying
degrees—an interdisciplinary body of literature that has sought to analyze
these very experiences from a number of "revisionist" perspectives. Unlike
the cultural history typically dictated by the dominant discourse of Western
culture (or even at times by the discourse of the patriarchal black community), this body of knowledge serves to capture the myriad of social, psychological, and political experiences of black women. It also serves to dignify
them by explicitly or implicitly correcting the narrow interpretations and
degrading representations typical in dominant discourse.

The "master" in *this* master narrative is no stranger or adversary to black
women but rather is an agent of their culture. Though certainly not fully
immune from the racist and sexist ideologies promoted by the dominant culture, this literature attempts to redocument the history of black women and
their efforts to build and sustain a socially conscious gender-ethnic community within and across class lines. I make no attempt here to encapsulate the
whole of this literature with its variety of points and counterpoints, heroines
and foes. As political philosopher African Americanist Joy James has stated,
"There is no 'master' narrative that frames the concerns of all black women
and their organizations."[4] Instead, my aim is to extract from it certain evidence showing that African-American women have long partaken in traditions that foster black sisterhood, thereby framing in greater historical detail
the impetus for my research.

LOCATING THE AFRICAN "ORIGINS" OF
BLACK FEMALE SISTERHOOD

Fierce devotion to the tenets of black women's community and maternal
activism keeps me, and many of the women whose joys and concerns are
voiced in this book, fixated on the notion of African-American women's

"deep collective roots."[5] Black women's gender-ethnic solidarity has long been vital to the material, emotional, and moral sustenance of black people. In America, this black "sisterhood" has been fostered by a common history of oppression, and it has motivated black women to preserve the centuries-old African moral authority to which they are accustomed and to protect the cultural traditions that guided their ancestors to great social wealth as accomplished educators, artisans, theologians, and political leaders. One such cultural tradition is rearing young women in the close, watchful company of their female peers. Educator Anna Julia Cooper once identified the solidarity of black women as "the fundamental agency under God in the regeneration . . . of the race, as well as the groundwork and starting point of its progress upward."[6]

But just how deep do the collective roots of African-American women go? In the first part of this chapter, I work to substantiate that the "deep collective roots" of African-American sisterhood can be traced to the pre- and early colonial contexts of West and Central Africa.[7] Like the "deep structures" questions that have been posed by many anthropologists and historians over the decades, my interest is in explaining to the extent possible the African origins of—or certain Africanisms manifest in—sisterhood traditions widely shared among contemporary black women. In aiming for the "deep," I mean to explore traditions that are derived from a set of what have been called "unconscious 'grammatical' principles" (borrowing from linguistics), "cognitive" or "common orientations," or "basic assumptions about social relations"[8] that can be traced to black women's West and Central African origins. Sidney W. Mintz and Richard Price warn that too often connections drawn between "some particular African people and some New World colony or society . . . are simply inferred."[9] Further, they suggest that particularly given the broad ethnic variations among Africans believed to have originated from a common place (e.g., West Africa), the focus of these connections should be at the level of "deep structure" rather than on the more concrete "formal elements" or "overt forms" of culture.[10] The danger in attempting to describe these more formal continuities is that one may actually create something more akin to cultural myth than convey historical fact.

Given these words of caution, some clarification is needed. First, the notion of a "sisterhood" operating among pre- and early colonial African women may be a critical misnomer. In her introduction to *African Women & Feminism: Reflecting on the Politics of Sisterhood*, sociologist Oyèrónké Oyěwùmi interrogates this term from an Africanist perspective, highlighting the lack of a comparable concept in much of precolonial, colonial, as well as postcolonial African culture (e.g., in Yoruba, Igbo, Efik, Wolof, Songhoi, Benin, Manding, and Fulani). "The languages that many of the enslaved West Africans brought to the Americas," she explains, "did not contain linguistic equivalents of the kin terms 'brother' and 'sister' because many African languages do not express gender-specificity in sibling designation. . . . In a sense then, sister indeed is a foreign relation."[11]

Gender, Oyěwùmi contends, simply was not prescribed in these cultures as a primary, essential category of family or social life. By this, she means that "the category woman cannot be isolated . . . because each individual occupies a multiplicity of overlapping and intersecting positions, with various relationships to privilege and power."[12] Similarly, Niara Sudarkasa argues that "male and female are not so much unitary statuses . . . as they are clusters of statuses, for which gender is only one of the defining characteristics."[13] Take, for example, the status of mother. The agency and power afforded mothers in precolonial African societies made ties to one's mother or mothers "the most culturally significant"[14] of all ties. One's identity is bound to mothers and to the mothering practices of one's culture. Thus, any evidence of a *collective* female identity and consciousness operating among precolonial West African women is best interpreted as *co-motherhood*, the more appropriate model of female solidarity:

> In many African societies, there is no sisterhood without motherhood. The most profound sisterly relations are to be found in co-mothering, which is the essence of community building. . . . "Co-mother" is the preferred idiom in many African cultures for expressing the relationship amongst women."[15]

Friend or peer relationships among women at similar life-course stages were (and are) also institutionalized in African culture with clear expectations, rights, and obligations, and these were likewise constructed around "experiences of shared mothering."[16]

Institutionalized relations among women are also found in such things as women's trade associations, organizations of village wives, and organizations of daughters of particular lineages. Some of the most widely discussed of such gendered institutions are the "secret" societies of women (and men) throughout many parts of West Africa, including Liberia, Cameroon, the Ivory Coast, Mali, Burkina Faso, and Sierra Leone. Michael A. Gomez, focusing on Sierra Leone, provides thick descriptions of these societies that are worth noting here:

> The societies of men and women in Sierra Leone were very complex both in organization and implementation, serving several functions. Politically, they helped resolve diplomatic and commercial differences between otherwise independent domains and villages. At the social level, they helped regulate acceptable standards of behavior and assisted individuals and families in times of crisis. Culturally, they provided formal education regarding what should be known about the world and beyond and supervised the training of males and females for the purpose of producing responsible adults. In other words, the socialization process throughout Sierra Leone, although initially and primarily the responsibility of the household, was for-

mally the responsibility of male and female societies. There were different kinds of societies according to mission, and there were various levels of achievement and status within each society. . . . The matrilineal Senufo were organized into a series of villages or settlements known singularly as the *katiolo*. Each major *katiolo* had its own Poro and Sande societies, the latter known as the Sandogo, a "powerful women's organization that unites the female leadership of the many extended household units and kinship groups of the village."[17]

But Oyěwùmi insists that the solidarity expressed through these entities in no way constitutes what is generally characterized as expressions of a black feminist politic (at least in the Western sense) or of black sisterhood:

None of these political organizations could be represented as a sisterhood in the contemporary feminist sense of a solidarity organization based on gender. In fact, in many African societies, any notions of a universal female sisterhood will immediately run up against the differing and often opposed interests of women as daughters and women as wives in the lineage and in the society at large. Gender is not viewed as a source of political identity.[18]

This point is reinforced by the contention of Olabisi Aina (a sociologist and researcher of Nigerian women's cultural and political history) that no major "feminist attacks on African traditional social structure" are recorded for the precolonial period, "and not until the colonial era did we have recorded cases of women acting as pressure groups to reject many of colonial economic and political policies."[19]

On careful examination, what Oyěwùmi is primarily concerned with is non-Afrocentric uses of the term "sisterhood" that denote a solidarity exclusive of men, and suggestions that pre- and early colonial African women's economic and political activism "[stemmed] from some notion of womanhood or gender consciousness" rather than from their roles as wives, mothers, or market women: "In African societies, the question of organizing to attain a political goal speaks to the issue of forming political alliances, and not sisterhood, since group identity is constituted socially and is not based on any qualities of shared anatomy popularly called gender."[20] Further, Sudarkasa argues that the inappropriate use of Western kinship paradigms also distorts the conjugal relation by casting husbands and wives as uneven in their acts of deference; in reality, the complexity of kinship roles was such that "overt signals of deference" were enjoyed by both men and women.[21] Notions of a black sisterhood fashioned from an awareness of gender-based discrimination and exploitation, therefore, separate the old world from the new. They reflect a cultural reality born of the new world where the cruel, racist, and sexist practices of the antebellum period and the persistence of such patriarchal practices postslavery help to recast African cultural relations among African Americans within their families and their communities. The result has been the need for African-American women to politicize black "woman" and "sister" (though not in every instance),[22] where they were once relatively benign. Over the past century, similar action has been taken by colonial and postcolonial African women who have suffered similar fates at the hands of the continent's colonizers.

Claims that pre- and early colonial African women were uninterested in or lacked a female collective conscious have not gone unchallenged, however, such as when African scholar Obioma Nnaemeka, editor of *Sisterhood, Feminisms, and Power: From Africa to the Diaspora*, suggests that claims of gender inclusiveness and power sharing must be critiqued in light of what we know have been strongholds of African patriarchy within which African women have been "compelled" to negotiate their positions.[23] For example, in societies where women were allowed to accumulate wealth, a "sense of solidarity and self-worth along with the capacity to protect female interests in the community"[24] was formed, suggesting that these women recognized that there were interests that needed their protection. Sandra Greene has shown that women of Anlo (now part of the Republic of Ghana) "who felt marginalized by the changes that had occurred in Anlo gender relations [during the second half of the eighteenth century] acted to counter their disadvantageous position," and that "their example, in turn, encouraged other women in Anlo to find additional ways to achieve" certain rights, such as the right to join the religious order of their choosing.[25] And in her reexamination of gender stratification in West Africa, Simi Afonja argues that we cannot ignore the exploitation of women inherent in "preclass societies" that were organized by other criteria (e.g., descent or political role); while Yoruba and other women lived autonomously in regard to many aspects of their culture, they were clearly subordinated in the "domestic domain," where "the rules and rites established in marriage, the property distribution laws, and the relations of production . . . clearly were adopted to the disadvantage of women."[26]

What I ultimately glean from Oyěwùmi's analysis, that of several of the contributors to Nnaemeka's edited volume (including Aina), and that of a number of contributors to *Jenda: A Journal of Culture and African Women Studies* is nonetheless extremely palatable. Their claim is that any notion of sisterhood among precolonial African women is subsumed under the broader ideal set of values that bound women to women as well as women to men in what has been called a dual-sex cultural system. Within this ideal set are the following: (1) the primacy of kinship and communalism, (2) reverence for ancestors and elders, (3) respect for and practice of spirituality, (4) the centrality of motherhood, and (5) shared power between men and women and of gendered institutional practice where it is beneficial to the self-determination and agency of family and community. It is the robustness of these ideals, then—documented by numerous scholars of African-American history and culture as pervasively held by blacks in the United States—that has helped give rise to the affinity for "sisterhood" among contemporary black women.

Class Relations among Early African Women

Many of the scholars discussed above argue that the consciousness of class among African women (and men) is attributed to the ravages of colonization. Michael A. Gomez, for instance, has argued that traditional relations among Africans were, in addition to gender, institutionalized along lines of caste (i.e., "differentiated economic and labor functions" into which one was born), where "divisions of labor had been apportioned to whole families" and "within which certain skills and economic activities were passed down from generation to generation."[27] Though class is frequently used by scholars in identifying these purported caste groups—one example being reference to a "class of women" known as the African mother-chiefs (or *ma-fo*) of Cameroon who exercise control of land and other community property,[28] and another being Gomez himself in referring to egalitarian tendencies among the "elite strata"[29]—many insist that classism was an invention of white colonialism that instituted new forms of economic relations serving to socially stratify the African populations in ways that upset the traditional division of resources and social positions. Mahmood Mamdani, in his book *Citizen and Subject: Contemporary Africa and the Legacy of Late Colonialism*, describes how it was customary for precolonial, free peasants to hold land communally; but through the strategies imposed by the invading authority, certain peasants were coerced into laboring on that land for the colonizer, creating a hierarchy among them. (Ironically, those with land [laborers] were relegated to a status lower than those without.)

Those countering such arguments about class relations in Africa say that many scholars overromanticize the precolonial era by claiming that these societies were free of class structure and of class inequality. Philosopher Charles Peterson praises Guinean revolutionary Amilcar Cabral's boldness in recognizing the "class tension and struggle within African societies," and adds that the dynamics of class relations found in the modern day are strong reflections of the "division of resources, social positions and privilege" established in the earlier eras.[30] Perhaps most relevant here is that despite the considerable influence that pre- and early colonial African women had over personal and community economic affairs (addressed further in the next section), the patriarchy governing some African societies clearly restricted the wealth status of those women in varying degrees. What remains unclear, however, is whether wealth and status inequalities among them in any way undermined their collective service to family and community life and their maintenance of cultural values.

CELEBRATING POWERFUL WOMEN
OF AFRICAN DESCENT

It is somewhat debatable, then, as to whether black sisterhood as it is typically conceived in the modern day has its roots in pre- and early colonial
West/Central African heritage, that conception being the collective awareness
of having ideas, feelings, and interests similar to other black women and
deriving an ideological stance and a sense of *political* solidarity from that
awareness. As Sara Berry, my esteemed colleague in history and anthropol-
ogy, has expressed to me, the African foremothers did not "carry around the
kind of historically imposed defensiveness that leads so many African Americans, understandably, to construct their identities in opposition to whites"
and to men. But while this fact may have strong academic import, it pales in
comparison to the well-established evidence of early African and African-
American women's cultural, economic, and political power. Today's black
women are deeply satisfied in knowing that they are descended from powerful women whom they are proud to call their "sisters." (On this point, West,
Central, or any other regional or ethnic distinction among African predecessors is irrelevant; the South African woman is as much a sister as the Ghana-
ian woman.) Black women's feelings of sisterhood with these ascendants
stem both from the valuation of ancestors and elders in African-American
culture as well as from the pride they feel in knowing that despite what the
dominant discourse would have them believe, these African and African-
American trailblazers were significant shapers of their cultures and of world
history.

African novelist Ama Ata Aidoo calls her African foremothers "some of
the bravest, most independent, and most innovative women this world has
ever known":

> We speak of the Lady Tiy of Nubia (ca. 1415–1340 B.C.E.), the wife of Amenhotep
> III and the mother of Akhenton and Tutenkhamen, who is credited, among other
> achievements, with leading the women of her court to discover make-up and other
> beauty-enhancing processes. Her daughter-in-law was the incomparable Nefertiti, a
> black beauty whose complexion was far superior to the alabaster with which she is
> not willfully painted. Again from the pharaonic era, we evoke Cleopatra, about
> whom "more nonsense has been written . . . than about any African queen . . .
> mainly because of many writers' desire to paint her white. She was not a white
> woman. She was not a Greek . . ." says John Henrik Clarke with the impatience of
> painstaking scholarship.[31]

The Suppressed Histories Archive, founded in 1970 and dedicated to
uncovering the lives of women around the world who have "been written out
of history," is among numerous sources giving praise to tenth-century Ethio-
pian religious leader Gudit Isat (Judith the Fire), who triumphed over the

Auximite empire; the legendary Queen Nanny (perhaps Ashanti or Akan) of the Windward Jamaican Maroons, who as their spiritual, cultural, and military guide "led Africans out of slavery into the Jamaican highlands"; and the beloved Nehanda Nyakasikana, who led a Shona revolt against the British conquest of Zimbabwe.[32] Queen Mother of Ejisu, Yaa Asantewaa (Ashanti, Ghana)—the woman who led an insurrection against the British around the turn of the twentieth century—is also recognized,[33] as are "the legendary powers" of Queen Amina of present-day Zaria, Nigeria, who in the sixteenth and seventeenth centuries was the warrior and architect responsible for expanding the Hausa territory to the largest borders in its history.[34]

As is signified by these and other descriptions of African heroines, pre- and early colonial women often fought alongside their men when war was waged against their aggressors, and there are accounts of "all-female battalions" (the Dahomey of ancient Benin) fighting "against invaders and internal treachery."[35] The Women's War of 1929 is one of the most highly cited examples of women's collective power in Africa, where rural Ibo market women, infuriated by the "colonial system of taxation" and "the differential integration of women into the world economic system,"[36] organized and led a major revolt for themselves and their men against the British.

The power of women to lead through spiritual ritual is embodied in the early African priestess, or by other names, the "shaman, medicine woman, diviner, spirit medium, oracle, sibyl, and wisewoman."[37] While the religious practices of the priestess are quite broad within and across African cultural groups, the priestess is a highly respected servant of her people. Gomez's description of the Sando-Mother (leader of the Sandago, Sierra Leone) suggests that she might have been a priestess. She was

> particularly powerful in that she was the individual responsible for maintaining harmonious relations with the spirit realm, calling upon powers of divination to interpret and mediate between human beings and the spirits of the bush, rivers, ancestors, and deities.[38]

Warrior Nehanda Nyakasikana of the Shona (mentioned above) was also a priestess, referred to by some as "the Priestess/Spirit-Medium Mbuya Nehandra of Simbabwe."[39] At times, the spiritual power of the priestess was transformed into political power; as historian Catherine Coquery-Vidrovitch states, such women "had a power of intercession that could change the course of events: women could make peace,"[40] both on a local and a regional scale.

African women controlled a host of economic tasks in farming, marketing, and trade, and in certain societies were securely attached to their own land, which "enabled women to command the labor and allegiance of sons and sons-in-law and facilitated access to political power. Some women even became village headwomen."[41] In his observations of Sierra Leone cultures,

Gomez is drawn to what he calls the African women's "preeminence," witnessing the exercise of "political power 'on their own'" and that the wives of rulers were routinely given charge over geographically distant domains by their husbands. He was similarly intrigued by certain elder women's "superintendence" over the women married and born to their fathers and husbands. Among the various other forms of woman power Gomez reports is that which he found essential to the operation of *male* "secret" societies:[42]

> Senufo women, as was true of other groups in Sierra Leone, were indispensable to the creation of any new Poro male society and its *sinzanga*, or sacred grove. This was because the founding of the male society required a ritual involving both a man and a woman. Glaze takes matters one step further, arguing that at philosophical and conceptual levels, it was the elder woman who was the real leader of any Poro lodge. (96)

Woman power in many African societies (such as that described here) is attributed in large part to the freedom these women enjoyed, relative to women in the West, to engage in and even control a full range of cultural activities. Anthropologist Sabine Jell-Bahlsen, expert in Nigerian culture, asserts that power in traditional African cultures had an explicit, multidimensional "female component," balanced with its male version in a "deeply democratic and religious" union of tangible and intangible rewards.[43] Comparatively speaking, African men for the most part did possess greater freedoms, power, wealth, and status; yet there are numerous accounts of women claiming and reclaiming their rights as partners in the maintenance of physical and social life.

Thus, it is the power bestowed upon and exhibited by these pre- and early colonial women that helps to provide African-American women a framework with which to imagine and exact a socially conscious gender-ethnic community necessary in the slavery and postslavery contexts. While these African ancestors may not themselves have defined their power in what are generally thought to be feminist terms—that is, specifically aimed at fostering and maintaining a shared gender-ethnic identity and at exposing the dynamics of male domination and female subordination in traditional African culture—their actions nonetheless meld with African-American women's feminist sensibilities and make them proud.

Woman power in African America has been equally honorable, and the following passage offered by Nigerian playwright 'Zulu Sofola at the 1992 Women in Africa and the African Diaspora conference (WAAD) is a fitting segue to a discussion of its tradition. In it, she exemplifies the revisionist viewpoint on African-American women's cultural history by validating the notion that certain "common orientations" and "basic assumptions" are reasonably traced back to black women's West and Central African origins, and perhaps more importantly by paying tribute to but a few of the "fearless" African-American female icons:

> And with the type of African womanhood reflected in the foregoing array of African heroines, one would have expected nothing less from women in the diaspora who themselves were undoubtedly descendants of warrior queens, monarchs, women intelligence spies, economic magnates, and powerful daughters of the land. In the diaspora of the United States of America, the Underground Railway system that got African-American slaves to escape to freedom was led by Mary Bethune and a galaxy of other fearless African American women. And it had to take another such fearless African-American woman—Rosa Parks—to resist the racial injustice and humiliation in the United States, opening the door to the Revolution of the 1960s that brought Martin Luther King, Jr., and others into prominence. For these reasons we reject the Eurocentric theory that the depletion of Afro-American men during slavery gave their women the opportunity to develop strong female presence and authority (the so-called black matriarchy). We assert that the presence of strong, black women in the African diaspora was due to the African woman's healthy psyche and heritage that they carried over to the new world. It was not brought about by a mere circumstance of being left in charge of the home during slavery. It runs in the blood.[44]

In this New World across the Atlantic (as was true during the colonial and postcolonial period in Africa), much of African womanhood was rendered subordinate or invisible, both through "changes in the mode of production whereby ideologies regulating the sexual division of labor and access to resources [resulted] in the relative disadvantage of women," and through "the inadequacies of paradigms utilized" to understand black women and their condition.[45] As a direct consequence, black women learned to employ their own cultural resources to combat the ever-encroaching devastation of racism and its ideological ally, patriarchy, and in doing so they politicized and extolled the virtues of black womanhood and sisterhood through their *activism*.

Looking back from the heyday of the African-American women's liberation crusade—the 1960s and early 1970s—we find a continuous stream of "both intellectual and activist traditions whose seeds were sown during slavery and flowered during the antislavery fervor of the 1830s."[46] But as Angela Davis—a heroine in her own right—explains, "With the sole exceptions of Harriet Tubman and Sojourner Truth, black women of the slave era remain more or less enshrouded in unrevealed history,"[47] and then even these exceptions are minimized. Like their African predecessors, abolitionists Tubman and Truth and scores of other legendary and "nameless" black women were warriors, exquisite orators, and savvy political organizers who engaged in overt and covert acts of resistance. Such acts would eventually become the cornerstone of contemporary black feminism and sisterhood in the United States, a place where black womanhood was sorely challenged by the colonizer and later also by black men anguished by racism and blinded by chauvinism.

While in slavery, black women's efforts to resist the oppression of the slave system were motivated by the necessity to preserve and protect black life, and they also were made in recognition of the fact that slave oppression had a decidedly gendered intent. In addition to the economic exploitation, physical abuse, and psychological indignation they suffered alongside their men, slave women also had to endure sexual exploitation in the form of forced intercourse with white men. (Other forms of sexual exploitation included the gross distortions of their sexuality fostered by white masters to justify their sexual coerciveness and the denial of much of their rights as biological mothers.) Slave narratives are replete with tales of black women's agency in resisting sexual exploitation by white men and refusing to conspire with them in advancing the slave system or to aid in the enslavement of their own children. This resistance has been summarized as acts of sexual abstinence, fetal abortion, and infanticide and is personified in such slave women as Harriet Jacobs, Elizabeth Keckley (seamstress for Mrs. Abraham Lincoln), Linda Brent, Ellen Craft, Margaret Jane Blake, and the infamous Margaret Garner, whose resistance inspired novelist Toni Morrison to write *Beloved*.[48]

As waves of antislavery sentiment rolled across America beginning in the early nineteenth century, black women, bonded and free, rose to prominence through their efforts to promote abolition, antilynching laws, voting rights, and gender equality. Their bold efforts were frequently branded as violations of Victorian "'true womanhood,' which stressed piety, chastity, submissiveness, and domesticity,"[49] ideals that Sojourner Truth, Harriet Jacobs, and others argued were reserved only for ruling-class white women who could sustain such an image in a racist society. Nonetheless, they worked tirelessly to promote their causes. The list of powerful black women from this era (and subsequent ones) is carefully organized and elaborated in Beverly Guy-Sheftall's anthology *Words of Fire*. That list includes Maria Miller Stewart (freewoman), believed to be the first African-American woman to speak publicly about black women's rights and about the importance of black women's personal, intellectual, and professional development; Frances Ellen Watkins Harper (freewoman, orator, and writer), antislavery advocate and race antagonist of the women's suffragist movement, who became the first black woman to have a short story published; Anna Julia Cooper (born a slave), author of the cultural feminist essay *A Voice from the South*, expounding on the virtues of black womanhood, the sexism of black men, and the racism of white women; Julia A. J. Foote (minister), antagonist of black male religious leaders, "who defied gender conventions by insisting on their right to preach";[50] Gertrude Bustill Mossell (freewoman, journalist), author of the "pioneering" feminist text *The Work of the Afro-American Woman*, correcting distortions of black women in history and bringing respectability to "true women" of African descent.

These and other women of their time initiated what to this day are challenges to the unidimensional way in which they were expected to resist their conditions, that is, on the basis of the racial oppression alone. "Certain premises" of black feminism, Guy-Sheftall explains, "are constant" and defy any simplistic notion of black women's motivations:

> 1) Black women experience a special kind of oppression and suffering in this country which is racist, sexist, and classist because of their dual racial and gender identity and their limited access to economic resources; 2) This "triple jeopardy" has meant that the problems, concerns, and needs of black women are different in many ways from those of both white women and black men; 3) Black women must struggle for black liberation and gender equality simultaneously; 4) There is no inherent contradiction in the struggle to eradicate sexism and racism as well as the other "isms" which plague the human community, such as classism and heterosexism; 5) Black women's commitment to the liberation of blacks and women is profoundly rooted in their lived experience.[51]

These premises were highly congruent with the ideals of a free and democratic society promised to human beings of whatever hue, gender, or class.

The dynamics of social class during these times would have undoubtedly been witnessed by these powerful women of the slave era and their internalization difficult to defeat. Class differentiation is described in a number of ways, including "urban or industrial slave/plantation slave," "free black/black slave," "house nigger/field nigger," and "fair-skinned/dark-skinned." In each case, the former status is shown to have afforded blacks the privilege of relatively greater autonomy. And while the two statuses are portrayed as inextricably linked, they are also often cast as apprehensive relations.[52] Nonetheless, there is also much evidence of black women crossing class lines to aid others, such as in numerous cases where free black women purchased the freedom of kin and nonkin women and their families.[53]

Despite what some analysts cite as a dry spell for feminist activity, woman power in black America continued to flourish during the 1920s to the late 1950s, especially among the women of the Harlem Renaissance who participated in promoting the "New Negro"—the symbol of racial consciousness in an era rocked by Jim Crowism and mass migration from the Southern region to "new" forms of racial practice. These women—who expressed their consciousness through the cultural media of art, dance, music, theater, poetry, and literature—and their contemporaries in other fields worked to confront the economic and gender oppression faced by black women of the World War I and II eras, as well as the continued abuse of black men by lynch mobs and the abuse of voting rights by the political system.

One of the most notable of these cultural artists and critics was the beloved folklorist Zora Neale Hurston, said to be "the most prolific black woman writer in America."[54] Hurston's *Their Eyes Were Watching God* helped to open up the possibilities for envisioning a self-pronounced black womanhood free from typical and narrow conceptions. Joining her were hosts of other black women writers, including Nella Larsen, author of a largely autobiographical novel (*Quicksand*), a second novel, and other short stories; poet, playwright, essayist, and author of short fiction Angelina Weld Grimké; poet, journalist, playwright, and novelist Alice Dunbar-Nelson; and teacher-essayist Elise Johnson McDougald. Other powerful artists and orators of this time period include playwright Lorraine Hansberry (*A Raisin in the Sun*) and pan-Africanist speaker and writer Amy Jacques Garvey (second wife of Marcus Garvey).

Many African Americans of this era and since have labeled these women (and other Harlem intellectuals) "dicty niggers" for promoting elitism by "aspir[ing] to *high* culture as opposed to that of the common man."[55] In "Blueprint for Negro Writing," Harlem Renaissance writer Richard Wright expressed this concern in stating that traditional Negro folklore—containing "the collective sense of Negro life in America"—had been neglected by the Harlem elite:

> One would have thought that Negro writers in the last century of striving at expression would have continued and deepened this folk tradition, would have tried to create a more intimate and yet a more profound social system of artistic communication between them and their people. But the illusion that they would escape through individual achievement the harsh lot of their race swung Negro writers away from such a path. Two separate cultures sprang up: one for the Negro masses, unwritten and unrecognized; and the other for the sons and daughters of a rising Negro bourgeoisie, parasitic and mannered.[56]

Others, such as Nathan Irvin Huggins, were not so harsh and argued that as these intellectuals pursued racial consciousness and/or black nationalism with great fervor, those blacks who scoffed at them "would also glow in the reflection of the honor."[57]

From this point forward into the mid-1970s, black woman power was exhibited as part of a larger "angry" power among African Americans and women in general—a relentless assault on anti–civil rights, antiblack, and antifeminist forces. Its aim was to liberate black women and their people from what should have been a long-outdated mode of backward thinking about "otherness." But at so many turns, these women were yanked in multiple directions—called to embrace the Black Power and Black Freedom struggles and downplay their desires for liberation as women, and called to embrace women's liberation even as this largely white female movement showed its propensity for racism. Particularly painful were threats to the political camaraderie of black women and men epitomized in Michelle Wallace's *Black*

Macho and the Myth of the Superwoman (1978). Wallace's work would be called "the controversial feminist polemic . . . a critique of the male-dominant civil rights and misogynistic Black Power movements, and a scathing exposé of sexual politics within the African American community."[58]

From inside this political and cultural cauldron emerged some of the brightest minds of our time, some of which were only "discovered" retrospectively: journalist and civil rights activist Frances Beale; women's liberationist Mary Ann Weathers; esteemed lawyer, professor, ordained priest, and feminist writer Pauli Murray; political activist Angela Davis; black feminist and activist Barbara Smith; civil rights activist Bernice Johnson Reagon; and Black Freedom movement leader Ella Baker. While woman power in this era was constrained by black women's exclusion from many formal leadership positions (thought to be more suitable positions for black men or white women), these women and many others were instrumental in leading the nation to a more authentic democracy.

Post-1970s woman power in African America remains a formidable force. In fact, it is exemplified in many of the women who were interviewed for this study. Among these contemporary women are many "firsts" in their fields or jobs locally, regionally, and perhaps even nationally. Many are actively engaged in the production of song and verse, in creatively revitalizing their communities, in keeping the nation's pulse on pertinent civil rights issues, and in fighting for quality education and health care for black families. In the chapters that follow, I have suppressed most of these details to preserve the women's privacy. Most who live in the Greater Baltimore Area know that it is "a very small town" where it seems that everyone knows everyone else. So I have been extremely careful not to reveal the women's personal identities, but I am certain that the reader will nevertheless feel their woman power coming through.

THE FORMALIZED PRACTICE OF
BLACK SISTERHOOD

As the preceding discussion shows, the historical praxis of black sisterhood is manifest in a wide variety of ways, each involving the harnessing of woman power for the preservation and elevation of black women's lives. In addition to that praxis being worked out through the defiance of slave masters and the slave system, the writing of politically transformative prose, and the delivery of radical oratory, it also was realized through leadership in and behind the scenes of work for community and political mobilization. Black women's participation in the abolitionist, civil rights, and women's suffrage movements are all key examples.[59] Another example—to which I have chosen to give considerable attention here—is the black women's club movement.

As was briefly mentioned in chapter 1, my academic foray into this particular area of black women's cultural history began a decade ago as I attempted to better understand the motivations and experiences of a group of black "sister-friends" I came to know at the Sacramento-based Birthing Project. Over time, my literature research, interview data, and participant observations converged on one central point: the Birthing Project was a very tangible sign that the legacy of black sisterhood was alive and well in the post–civil rights era. In 1988,[60] the project was formed with the expressed purpose of recapturing the unique cultural space once widely shared by black women. Its founders believed that by introducing that space to a new generation of women, they could become intimately and positively involved in their lives and those of their children so that they all might be "uplifted." Specifically, the project—still in operation today—offers the opportunity for young pregnant African-American women at risk for low birth weight and infant mortality to increase their chances for delivering healthy black babies. It strives to re-create kinship and communal support lacking or nonexistent for many of these young mothers, a key element in their fight to survive the despair of their poor life conditions. It was founded by contemporary black heroine Kathryn Hall.

The principles and practices of this black feminist organization were purposely designed as a modern-day version of a long line of similar strategies used by black club women. The Birthing Project was built upon a foundation laid long ago by slave women, free black American women, and later newly emancipated black women who fought hard to establish black women's clubs all over the nation in the late nineteenth and early twentieth centuries.[61] The swelling of club membership, the concerted effort to affect social change, and the official (government) recognition of the clubs' social and political significance helped to classify this broad alliance of black feminist activism as a social movement.

My appreciation for the work of black club women led to my deliberately reserving the discussion of certain pre-1960s powerful black women until now; I wanted their significance to be shown through their work in this movement particularly. Underscoring their contributions also provides another opportunity to illustrate several of the cultural ideals that have historically guided African-American women's collective action, namely the primacy of kinship and communalism, the centrality of motherhood, and gendered institutional practice beneficial to the self-determination and agency of their community. Further, because the black women's club movement was primarily led by middle-class black women determined to support "racial uplift," we can observe through their activities how social class differences among black women have fostered woman bonding, but as well how they have stymied efforts to strengthen the sisterhood.

The Black Women's Club Movement: Background

Documented evidence traces formal expressions of black sisterhood to at least 1793, with the establishment in Philadelphia of the Female Benevolent Society of St. Thomas. By World War I, the National Association of Colored Women (NACW)—the product of a black women's club merger—had grown to fifty thousand members in twenty-eight federations and over one thousand clubs; hundreds of other club women were members of clubs that did not join the NACW. Conservatively, then, more than 5 percent[62] of the black middle-class female population were participants in the black women's club movement in the early 1930s. Black club women across the country engaged in a wide variety of activities for self-improvement and racial advancement among black women and their families. Characterized as "charity work," "community development," "social reform," and/or "welfare reform,"[63] club women sought to support the most disadvantaged of the black female population (and the black community in general) by improving their standards of living. In brief, these efforts included but were not limited to organizing health relief efforts for the elderly and the infirm and establishing health clinics, developing cooperative banking institutions, providing employment services, creating homes for delinquent and/or orphaned black girls, donating food and clothing to the poor, operating local libraries, providing emergency financial support, soliciting financial support for the higher education of certain deserving black women and establishing scholarships for a range of others, and founding institutions of learning.

These activist women were particularly challenged by the devastating poverty and pervasive health problems that plagued the black community after Reconstruction, as its population became more physically mobile and scattered from one another between the North and the South.[64] Problems were particularly pressing in the urban Northern cities, but even in places like North Carolina, black activist community workers (black midwives) battled with high rates of poor health outcomes.[65] Black club women were instrumental in the laying of a black communal infrastructure of support for the health and well-being of black families, and they tried to "re-create the intimacy of village life they left behind."[66]

Black Club Women and Maternal Support

From the very beginning, it was clear that the various women's clubs took a special interest in supporting mothers in their duties and in improving the quality of home life. (As a principal target of social injustice, black motherhood has been the one social institution over which black activist women have historically felt they had some immediate, direct control and to which they have felt culturally obligated to address.) With the omnipresent threat of child morbidity and mortality, family poverty, and overt gendered racism against black mothers, African-American club women's sisterhood centered largely on the provision of maternal support. As highly religious persons, black club women saw motherhood as a sacred role bestowed on black women and as the vanguard of social uplift; every mother, no matter how dispossessed, was considered to be a "benefactor to the race."[67] Historian Paula Giddings thought that black women saw this mother role in "almost ecclesiastical terms."[68] Mary Church Terrell is well known for having stressed the importance of club women's service to mothers. She urged club women to follow through on their ideas about establishing a "mothers' congress," even on a small scale if necessary, so that black mothers could be "enlightened upon the best methods of rearing their children and conducting their homes."[69]

At its founding conference in Boston in 1895, the National Federation of Afro-American Women (NFAAW) plainly pronounced activism on motherhood as one of the primary goals of black women activists. The part of their agenda addressing this importance was articulated as follows:

> (1) The concentration of the dormant energies of the women of the Afro-American race into one broad band of sisterhood, for the purpose of establishing needed reforms, and the practical encouragement of all efforts being set forth by the various agencies, religious, ethical, educational, and otherwise for the upbuilding and advancement of the race.
> (2) To awaken the women of the race to the great need of systematic effort in home-making and the divinely imposed duties of motherhood.[70]

Another demonstration of how the primacy of motherhood issues shaped the activities of black club women was when in 1930 the National Association of Colored Women agreed that the one department of the organization that would not be eliminated in their restructuring plans was that which they called the "Mother, Home and Child and Negro Women in Industry."[71] They cited the ability of that department to continue to create a better environment for black children as their primary reason for preserving it. Also notable is that the NACW's convention of 1987 had on its schedule the discussion of at least three topics related to mothering: "Mother's Influence," "Need of Mother's Meetings," and "The Responsibilities of Mothers in the Home-Life."[72]

Succinctly stated, the black club women's philosophy was that the future of the race lay in the ability of the future generation to withstand the "inevitable battles of life which grow out of the struggle for [black] existence";[73] children needed to be reared into "virtuous, intelligent citizens" if the race was to survive.[74] It was also their philosophy that in order for black women to be accepted by the dominant culture, it was important that masses of black mothers be respectable citizens of their families in the eyes of white club women.[75] Inasmuch, then, as the "Negro home" was the center of the social and intellectual life of the masses of black women and children, that home had to provide an environment that promoted the health of its inhabitants, that was economically secure, and that was conducive to the learning and espousing of good morals and values.

It was clear that black mothers had to be built up physically in order to be successful at these tasks. The long hours of work inside and outside the home typically led to black mothers' being overworked and malnourished. Furthermore, this physical exhaustion threatened their current and future health and that of their children, particularly their young infants. Club women, therefore, supported black mothers by helping to relieve the tremendous strain on their lives so that they could concentrate more fully on their role as mothers.

In part to that end, they funded, built, and maintained public clinics and hospitals to tend to the medical needs of black families, some specifically for the health needs of mothers. In Atlanta, the health clinic established by club women through a neighborhood union offered health classes to teach the community how to care for itself,[76] and in other places, such assistance was tailored for pregnant women.[77] In addition, the distribution of an adequate and uncontaminated milk supply was important to the health of black babies. Though it is not clear from her accounting records whether they succeeded, women's studies scholar Eileen Boris noted that the Women's League of Washington, D.C., attempted to model the white women's club by establishing a "diet kitchen to provide pure milk for infants and thus curb the alarming black infant-mortality rate in the nation's capital."[78] In their efforts to teach better child care to mothers, the Women's Council of Indianapolis invited black doctors to give them instructions, and other club women offered free baby clinics and child-care courses for mothers.[79] Club women from all over the nation designed many other maternal services directed at treating or preventing various medical illnesses of women and children.

Contrary to the white club women's view of women's employment, black working mothers were looked at favorably by the club women. In recognizing that most black women had to leave home for paid work and that black family wages were severely depressed by racism and discrimination in the labor market, black club women took on labor issues as a way to make black women's work less stressful and more economically rewarding.[80] More than any other project, they sought to expand mothers' opportunities to gain or enhance their education and training to make them more marketable for higher-paying jobs.[81] As noted earlier, education-related club activities focused largely on offering scholarships and establishing schools, thus making a variety of educational classes available to black mothers. In addition to traditional academic subjects such as reading and math, there was an abundance of "industrial arts" courses on a relatively small range of topics, most having to do with homemaking.[82] Led largely by college-educated church women, these "industrial schools" were erected largely in the South (sometimes in the

homes and alleyways of neighborhood residents), where they offered some
of the poorest black mothers in the country a chance to learn a few skills to
help them clothe and feed themselves and their families efficiently and to
help them land better employment. Children, from the very young to the very
old, were also supported by club women in their educational development.
Older children often gained the same skills as their mothers in club-sponsored
schools so that they could help take some of the load off of the mothers in
their domestic chores. For the younger ones, kindergartens, nurseries, and
day-care centers were established to provide them early childhood education
and to allow their mothers more freedom to secure paid work.[83]

Promoting the improved education of black mothers was done not only to
boost their families' wage-earning potential, however. As Giddings explains,
"There was also a very pragmatic concern about the relationship among
training, the purity of the home, and economic survival."[84] Putting black
mothers in contact with educational institutions (what Evelyn Brooks Higginbotham calls "assimilating apparatuses"[85]) also put them in close contact
with educated, religiously devout middle-class women who could affirm the
virtues of true womanhood, which assisted the movement in fulfilling its
other objective of instilling good moral values in the masses of black mothers.
Although black activist women fought to change the white patriarchal structure of the nation that took the tenets of middle-class white womanhood as
the norm (domesticity, submissiveness, piety, and purity), and although they
disagreed with the inherent racism of white women reformers, they shared
many of the same values and patterns of this dominant women's culture.[86]
Bolstering black club women's tendencies toward a mainstream consciousness of the work ethic, of woman's gentility, and of religiosity was the strong
influence of Booker T. Washington's program of racial uplift through self-
help, education, respectability, and accommodation. Thus, if black mothers
were to be uplifted, then they too would have to learn and adhere to Victorian-
style morals and values. The educated female elite set forth to reform black
women and their children by promoting these "middle-class ideals among the
masses of blacks in the belief that such ideals ensured the dual goals of racial
self-help and respect from white America."[87]

Club-sponsored moral-reform activities typically came in the form of what
were called "mothers' clubs," "Mothers' Conferences," "mothers' con-
gresses," "mothers' meetings," or "mothers' training schools," where club
women went into black homes for "heart to heart talks" to "impart moral
and cultural lessons" in the development of children and the maintenance of
a clean, happy, and comfortable home.[88] Black mothers were encouraged to
take a pledge (apparently sometimes directly to the club women) to follow
various guidelines for purifying herself and her home, which included tem-
perance and chastity.

Historian Anne Firor Scott openly expressed her disdain for the club women's objective to instill moral values in the masses of black mothers. In making her point, Scott explains that these elite black women somehow lost sight of the fact that in order for these mothers to practice the values taught to them, they would first need an "economic base."[89] Granted the educational and training component of their program spoke somewhat to certain aspects of their economic needs, but surely the "endless" sermonizing on improving the nature of their home life might be psychologically counterproductive to lifting them out of their poor condition. Eileen Boris, on the other hand, saw the black activists' embrace of these high standards of motherhood as a smart way to "subvert" the gendered racism of the dominant culture.[90] But it is Scott's insight on the explicit eliteness of the club women in providing maternal support that was shared by many intellectuals of her time and of the present as well. Further concerns about class tension within the club movement are discussed in the following section.

Class Tensions in the Club Movement

The sisterhood in the black tradition was founded upon a principle of mutual respect for all black women, who, regardless of the quality of their personal and social attributes, were equally deserving of the opportunity to move forward and equally important to the survival of the race. Thus, the ideological framework for black club women mandated that the effort to promote gender-ethnic solidarity and racial uplift not be undermined by social class separatism. Unlike their white counterparts, African-American club women could hardly deny that they were, in many important ways, indistinguishable from the masses of black women: "racial unity was more important than class difference in the relation of black activist women to those they sought to uplift."[91]

Such a statement implies, however, that the black women activists were conscious of the fact that their relative social progress did in fact separate them from "those they sought to uplift." Their superiority as middle-class women was never questioned among them, and neither was the inferiority of the poor, uneducated masses.[92] At a time when the larger black community embraced the W. E. B. DuBois concept of the "talented tenth," it was fitting that educated, middle-class black women would lead the masses of black women in advancing the race, in uplifting black womanhood from the legacy of slavery, and in reclaiming black motherhood. Like their middle-class black men, these women were expected to rise to the occasion of creating the same opportunity and environment by which they were privileged for all women.

It is highly probable that because so much of the published scholarship on the black women's club movement has been narrowly focused on the creation of the most formal and nationally oriented federations of club women, we have a biased view of the movement as being one purely developed and directed by middle-class women. Historian Linda Gordon explained that the merging of local clubs into the larger, more formal national organizations like the NACW "was a landmark in class terms: It represented the attainment of a critical mass of middle-class black women."[93] But while the middle-class activist women organized clubs (the least prevalent and most secular form of black women's organization),[94] the working-class women were more likely to arrange mutual-aid programs, and the poor women were highly concentrated within church organizations. Group membership was not mutually exclusive; nevertheless, the club movement was driven by some of the most influential and talented women of the middle class: "There was a decided class bias in [certain organizations] because most of the influential and dominant members were from the emerging Black middle class."[95]

Included among these influential middle-class women were Mary McLeod Bethune, Josephine St. Pierre Ruffin, Mary Church Terrell, Fannie Barrier Williams, Janie Porter Barrett, Nannie Burroughs, Anna Julia Cooper, and Margaret Murray Washington. Middle-class black women and men of their time (about 18 percent of the black population) were distinguishable from the masses (low-income, poor blacks) by their upward mobility from slave and sharecropping backgrounds. According to E. Franklin Frazier, "middle class families depend[ed] upon wage earners in skilled and semi-skilled occupations, domestic service and the service occupations," and "the more ambitious of the middle-class families in the Negro community [sought] through education, the professions, or business to make themselves eligible for upper class status."[96]

Middle-class blacks were also distinguishable from the masses by the relative lightness of their skin. Skin color was a powerful marker for class in their day; those with the fairest skin tones were most likely to be found among the small upper class (constituting about 2 percent of the black population). Though not a perfect proxy for middle- and upper-classness, there was a strong correlation between community leadership and light-skinnedness.

It was not merely the fact that middle-class black women had the material and human-capital resources to help finance and manage the nationwide race effort that made them ripe for leadership, but rather it was the belief that they were the moral stepping-stone to the progress of all black women:

> We believe we can build the foundation of the next generation upon such a rock of morality, intelligence and strength, that the floods of proscription, prejudice and persecution may descend upon it in torrents and yet it will not be moved.[97]

The club women's conviction in morality and respectability in this effort stemmed from their deeply religious background and leadership training in the church. The black church served as an important and long-standing outlet for maternal activism. According to some contemporary observers, it was this "privileged" church work upon which the goals and organization of later club work was modeled.[98] "Steeped in the Protestant ethic" instilled by the church,[99] and fortified by Washington's popularized philosophy of self-help, black club women were determined that black womanhood should no longer be judged by the non- or counterproductivity of the "lowly," "illiterate," and even "vicious" women of the race to whom they were inextricably bound.[100] It would be necessary to "go down" among the masses, instill within them good moral values, and return them to the mainstream of the race.

Elizabeth Higginbotham's social history of women in the black Baptist church draws a distinction between the paternalistic middle-class motivations of the more prominent black club women and the cross-class cooperation and respect underlying the work of black Baptist church women. She argues that middle-class black club women conceived of lifting the race as an obligation and duty that could only be performed by middle-class women who, by virtue of their moral upbringing, could teach lower-class black women to be more like them. In contrast, the women involved in the Baptist church viewed black women and mothers as a whole to be the source of uplift for their race. Higginbotham offers the following passages from one of Nannie Borroughs's writings and speeches that explicitly expresses this distinction:

> Every mother can be a benefactor to the race. It matters not how poor the mother if she possesses a character in which sobriety, honor and integrity, and every other wholesome virtue hold sway. . . . Many of the most noted women and men of the ages have been those of the persevering poor. . . . The poor washer-woman, cook, and toiler has built up nine-tenths of all our institutions and churches. . . .
>
> . . . [Some who are] entering these organizations devoted to uplift [are doing so] for no other reason than to show her finery and to let her less fortunate sisters see how brilliantly she shines. They are insincere; they are not doing anything practical; they are full of theories on the solution of great problems, but a poor, ragged, dirty, forsaken women [*sic*] is as objectionable to them as a leper.[101]

Evidence of this cross-class cooperation in church work is also found in the post–Civil War records of the Daughters of Zion of Avery Chapel in Memphis, Tennessee. The Daughters' leaders were composed of wives of professional men along with laundresses and domestic workers. Boris also notes that the "mothers' clubs" that many Baptist club women organized to teach the masses moral values proved to be a "popular vehicle for cross-class association and for the betterment among African-American women."[102]

This distinction between the class cooperation of church club women and the class separation maintained by mainstream club women is not universally made by observers of these reformers. Ida B. Wells acknowledged that there were some mainstream club women who believed that the disadvantaged women on "State Street" were there because they had "followed their various inclinations"; but she also noted that there were others who did not believe that the masses of women were "beneath" them: "They needed State Street as much as State Street needed them."[103]

Still, a common feature of the ideology of black women activists representing both the church and the larger movement was their belief that there was a certain "latent" immorality among the masses that impeded their social advancement and personal improvement; thus, the "moral recovery" of lower-class black women from their social condition was the primary substance of black maternal activism. The club women had a sense of class "superiority," and they "feared" that their gender-ethnic commonality with the masses of black women would overshadow that superiority.[104]

In the end, however, these early black club women accomplished a great deal under the most adverse of social circumstances, proving that black women were effective social and political movers and that, to some degree, cross-class maternal cooperation could still occur in earnest. Since that time, each new decade has presented a new set of maternal-support concerns met head-on by a forceful crusade of activist women bent on preserving the race and on ensuring healthy, productive lives for black mothers and children of all social classes. As the African-American association leaders in Bette J. Dickerson's study explained, black activist women have "a continuing and changing social agenda determined by the needs of our communities and our organizational base."[105]

MOVING THE LEGACY FORWARD?

Until very recently, much of this master narrative on black women's cultural history—at least the small slice that I have chosen to highlight here—was generally outside the purview of the American mainstream. This is not because the information was unavailable, disorganized, or written in a foreign tongue; rather, it is because what we learn from it goes so much against the grain of many people's thinking about black womanhood that it had largely been silenced. But African-American women know it rather well, whether intellectually, experientially, or both, and as chapter 3 illustrates, they celebrate the legacy of black sisterhood in a variety of ways. And while contemporary concerns over Oprahs and black stepsisters mimic those of earlier eras, there is a general sense that this historical moment is in certain ways unprecedented and that the legacy is threatened like never before.

NOTES

1. Amelia Blossom Pegram, "'I Will Still Sing,'" in *The Heinemann Book of African Women's Poetry*, eds. Stella Chipasula and Frank Chipasula, 187–88 (Portsmouth, NH: Heinemann, 1995).

2. Abbey Lincoln, "Who Will Revere the Black Woman?" in *The Black Woman: An Anthology*, ed. Toni Cade, 80–84 (New York: Mentor, 1970).

3. Audre Lorde, *Sister Outsider: Essays and Speeches*. The Crossing Press Feminist Series (Freedom, CA: Crossing Press, 1984).

4. Joy James, "Resting in Gardens, Battling in Deserts: Black Women's Activism," *The Black Scholar* 29, no. 4 (1999): 2–15.

5. More commonly, "deep collective roots" is understood as the practice of communalism. Communalism, said to be common to all African cultures, is the "doctrine that the group constitutes the main focus of the lives of the individual members of that group, and that the extent of the individual's involvement in the interests, aspirations, and welfare of the group is the measure of the individual's worth." Kwame Gyekye, *An Essay on African Philosophical Thought: The Akan Conceptual Scheme* (Cambridge, MA: Cambridge University Press, 1987), 208.

6. Paula A. Giddings, *When and Where I Enter: The Impact of Black Women on Race and Sex in America* (New York: William Morrow, 1984); taken from Anna Julia Cooper, *Voices of the South* (Xenia, OH: Aldine Publishing House, 1892).

7. This period runs roughly from the 1500s through the 1880s, about the same period marking the rise and fall of the Atlantic slave trade.

8. Sidney Wilfred Mintz and Richard Price, *The Birth of African-American Culture: An Anthropological Perspective* (Boston: Beacon Press, 1992), 9–10.

9. Ibid., 14–15.

10. Ibid., 1992, 11–12.

11. Oyèrónké Oyěwùmi, "Introduction: Feminism, Sisterhood, and *Other* Foreign Relations," in *African Women & Feminism: Reflecting on the Politics of Sisterhood*, ed. Oyèrónké Oyěwùmi (Trenton, NJ: Africa World Press, 2003), 10–11.

12. Ibid., 2.

13. Niara Sudarkasa, "The 'Status of Women' in Indigenous Africa Societies," in *Readings in Gender in Africa*, ed. Andrea Cornwall, 25–31 (Bloomington: Indiana University Press, 2005).

14. Ibid., 12–13. Also see Filomina Chioma Steady, "The Black Woman Cross-Culturally: An Overview," in *The Black Woman Cross-Culturally*, ed. Filomina Chioma Steady (Cambridge, MA: Schenkman, 1981); Filomina Chioma Steady, "African Feminism: A Worldwide Perspective," in *Women in Africa and the African Diaspora*, eds. Rosalyn Terborg-Penn, Sharon Harley, and Andrea Benton Rushing (Washington, DC: Howard University Press, 1987); and Nkira Nzegwu, "Gender Equality in the Dual-Sex System: The Case of Onitsha," *Jenda: A Journal of Culture and African Women Studies* 1, no. 1 (2001).

15. Oyěwùmi, "Introduction: Feminism, Sisterhood, and Other Foreign Relations," 13.

16. Ibid., 17. Also see L. F. Rodgers-Rose, "The Black Woman: A Historical Overview," in *The Black Woman*, ed. L. F. Rodgers-Rose, 15–28 (Beverly Hills, CA: Sage, 1980).

17. Michael A. Gomez, *Exchanging Our Country Marks: The Transformation of African Identities in the Colonial and Antebellum South* (Chapel Hill: University of North Carolina Press, 1998), 95–96. Gomez explains that men and women societies in Africa were labeled as "secret" by European travelers who did not fully understand them culturally. He states, for example, "The secret societies of Sierra Leone were, in fact, functional

equivalents of social, cultural, and governmental agencies, and the secrecy within which they operated was only a means to the realization of their purpose. When placed within this context, these societies are not very different from their Western analogues, let alone bizarre" (95).

18. Oyĕwùmi, "Introduction: Feminism, Sisterhood, and Other Foreign Relations," 19.

19. Olabisi Aina, "African Women at the Grassroots: The Silent Partners of the Women's Movement," in *Sisterhood, Feminisms, and Power*, ed. Obioma Nnaemeka (Trenton, NJ: Africa World Press, 1998), 70.

20. Oyĕwùmi, "Introduction: Feminism, Sisterhood, and Other Foreign Relations," 18–19.

21. Sudarkasa, "The 'Status of Women' in Indigenous Africa Societies," 27.

22. In qualifying this statement, I mean to acknowledge that many uses of the word "sister" among African-American women are not politically charged (see chapter 3).

23. Obioma Nnaemeka, "Introduction: Reading the Rainbow," in *Sisterhood, Feminisms, and Power: From Africa to the Diaspora*, ed. Obioma Nnaemeka (Trenton, NJ: Africa World Press, 1997), 1–35. For a brief overview of opposing viewpoints on the gendered experience of African women, see Bibi Bakare-Yusuf, "Beyond Determinism: The Phenomenology of African Female Experience," *Feminist Africa* 2 (2003).

24. Jane L. Parpart, "Women and the State in Africa," in *The Precarious Balance: State and Society in Africa*, eds. Donald Rothchild and Naomi Chazen, 208–30 (Boulder, CO: Westview Press, 1988), 209.

25. Sandra E. Greene, *Gender, Ethnicity, and Social Change on the Upper Slave Coast: History of the Anlo-Ewe*, Social History of Africa, eds. Allen Issacman and Jean Hay (Portsmouth, NH: Heinemann, 1995), 6–7.

26. Simi Afonja, "Changing Patterns of Gender Stratification in West Africa," in *Persistent Inequalities: Women and World Development*, ed. Irene Tinker, 198–209 (New York: Oxford University Press, 1990), 200.

27. Gomez, *Exchanging Our Country Marks: The Transformation of African Identities in the Colonial and Antebellum South*, 15.

28. Amina Mire, "In/through the Bodies of Women: Rethinking Gender in African Politics," special issue, *Polis* 8 (2001): 10.

29. Gomez, *Exchanging Our Country Marks: The Transformation of African Identities in the Colonial and Antebellum South*, 93.

30. Charles Peterson, "Returning to the African Core: Cabral and the Erasure of the Colonized Elite," *West Africa Review* 2, no. 2 (2001): 11.

31. Ama Ata Aidoo, "The African Woman Today," in *Sisterhood, Feminisms, and Power: From Africa to the Diaspora*, ed. Obioma Nnaemeka, 39–50 (Trenton, NJ: Africa World Press, 1997), 39.

32. Suppressed Histories Archive, www.suppressedhistories.net/articles/about.html.

33. Aidoo, "The African Woman Today," 41. Wilhemina J. Donkoh, "Yaa Asantewaa: A Role Model for Womanhood in the New Millennium," *Jenda: A Journal of Culture and African Women Studies* 1, no. 1 (2000).

34. See, for example, Glo Chukukere, "An Appraisal of Feminism in the Socio-Political Development of Nigeria," in *Sisterhood, Feminisms, and Power*, ed. Obioma Nnaemeka, 133–48 (Trenton, NJ: Africa World Press, 1998). For an extended discussion of powerful early African women in history, see Catherine Coquery-Vidrovitch, *African Women: A Modern History* (Boulder, CO: Westview Press, 1997).

35. Aidoo, "The African Woman Today," 41.

36. Filomina Chioma Steady, "African Feminism: A Worldwide Perspective," in *Women in Africa and the African Diaspora*, eds. Rosalyn Terborg-Penn, Sharon Harley, and Andrea Benton Rushing (Washington, DC: Howard University Press, 1987), 3–24.

37. Suppressed Histories Archive.

38. Gomez, *Exchanging Our Country Marks: The Transformation of African Identities in the Colonial and Antebellum South*, 96.

39. 'Zulu Sofola, "Feminism and African Womanhood," in *Sisterhood, Feminisms, and Power: From Africa to Diaspora*, ed. Obioma Nnaemeka (Trenton, NJ: African World Press, 1998), 51–64.

40. Coquery-Vidrovitch, *African Women: A Modern History*, 47.

41. Parpart, "Women and the State in Africa," 209.

42. Gomez, *Exchanging Our Country Marks: The Transformation of African Identities in the Colonial and Antebellum South*, 93–96.

43. Sabine Jell-Bahlsen, "Female Power: Water Priestesses of the Oru-Igbo," in *Sisterhood, Feminisms and Power*, ed. Obioma Nnaemeka (Trenton, NJ: Africa World Press, 1998), 102.

44. Sofola, "Feminism and African Womanhood," 60–61.

45. Filomina Chioma Steady, "Women and Collective Action: Female Models in Transition," in *Theorizing Black Feminisms: The Visionary Pragmatism of Black Women*, eds. Stanlie M. James and Abena P. A. Busia, 90–101 (London: Routledge, 1993).

46. Beverly Guy-Sheftall, "Introduction: The Evolution of Feminist Consciousness among African American Women," in *Words of Fire: An Anthology of African-American Feminist Thought*, ed. Beverly Guy-Sheftall, 1–22 (New York: New Press, 1995).

47. Angela Davis, "Reflections on the Black Woman's Role in the Community of Slaves," in *Words of Fire: An Anthology of African-American Feminist Thought*, ed. Beverly Guy-Sheftall, 200–18 (New York: New Press, 1995).

48. Darlene Hine and Kate Wittenstein, "Female Slave Resistance: The Economics of Sex," in *The Black Woman Cross-Culturally*, ed. Filomina Chioma Steady, 289–99 (Cambridge, MA: Schenkman Publishing Company, 1981); Guy-Sheftall, "Introduction: The Evolution of Feminist Consciousness among African American Women."

49. Guy-Sheftall, "Introduction: The Evolution of Feminist Consciousness among African American Women," 1.

50. Ibid., 51.

51. Ibid., 2.

52. With the possible exception of the "urban or industrial slave/plantation slave" distinction, such dichotomies are said to have been institutionalized along lines of skin color by white slave masters intent on creating hierarchy and dissension among the slaves (i.e., to control them). Take for example this analysis by race commentator Lawrence Otis Graham:

When black slaves arrived on many southern plantations, they were ultimately divided into two general groups. There were the outside laborers who worked in the fields harvesting rice or tobacco, cutting sugarcane, picking cotton, or building roads and structures. . . . The second group of slaves were those who performed more desirable jobs inside the master's house: cooking, cleaning, washing, and tending to the personal needs of the owner's family around the home. While these laborers were also slaves, with no more or fewer rights than the outdoor workers, the distinctions between the slaves in the field and the slaves who served as butlers and "mammies" in the house were not at all subtle. The terms "house niggers" and "field niggers" grew into meaningful labels as generations of slaves in the master's house gained more favorable treatment and had access to better food, better work conditions, better clothing, and a level of intimacy with the owner's family that introduced the house slave to white ways, minimal education, and nonconsensual sexual relations. . . . The plantation owners began to place their lighter-skinned slaves in the house, thus creating an even greater chasm between the two groups—now based on physical appearance, not just random assignment. Because these lighter-skinned blacks were perceived as receiving greater benefits and a more comfortable lifestyle, resentment among the darker-skinned field slaves only grew. . . . Not surprisingly, both whites and "house niggers" came to consider the dark-skinned "field niggers" to be less civilized and intellectually inferior.

Lawrence Otis Graham, *Our Kind of People: Inside America's Black Upper Class* (New York: HarperPerennial, 2000), 6–7.

53. See, for example, Darlene Clark Hine and Kathleen Thompson, *A Shining Thread of Hope: The History of Black Women in America* (New York: Broadway Books, 1998).

54. Mary Helen Washington, "Zora Neale Hurston: A Woman Half in Shadow," in *I Love Myself When I Am Laughing . . . and Then Again When I Am Looking Mean and Impressive*, ed. Alice Walker, 7–25 (New York: Feminist Press, 1979).

55. Nathan Irvin Huggins, *Harlem Renaissance* (London: Oxford University Press, 1973), 5, 6.

56. Richard Wright, "Blueprint for Negro Writing," in *A Turbulent Voyage: Readings in African American Studies*, ed. Floyd W. Hayes III, 322–29 (San Diego, CA: Collegiate Press, 1992).

57. Huggins, *Harlem Renaissance*.

58. Guy-Sheftall, "Introduction: The Evolution of Feminist Consciousness among African American Women," 219.

59. For an in-depth discussion of black women's national organizations, see Deborah Gray White, *Too Heavy a Load: Black Women in Defense of Themselves, 1894–1994* (New York: W. W. Norton & Company, 1999).

60. Numerous inconsistencies were found both in printed literature and in conversation with project associates on the actual year it was established. It may have actually been 1987.

61. Stephanie Shaw, "Black Club Women and the Creation of the National Association of Colored Women," *Journal of Women's History* 3, no. 2 (1991): 10–25. Not all black activist women were members of black women's clubs, though many were associated with club women in some way.

62. Exact club membership data could not be ascertained for this study. However, using 1930 black population data provided by Reynolds Farley and black social class data provided by E. Franklin Frazier, I have estimated the population of black middle-class women to be about 1,070,000 (assuming women made up 50 percent of the total population of middle-class blacks). This would mean that the NACW membership constituted about 5 percent of the black middle-class female population (50,000/1,070,000). Reynolds Farley, "Indications of Recent Demographic Changes among Blacks: 1940 to 1970," *Journal of Social Biology* 18, no. 4 (1971): 341–58; E. Franklin Frazier, *Black Bourgeoisie* (Glencoe, IL: Free Press, 1957).

63. Linda Gordon, *Pitied But Not Entitled: Single Mothers and the History of Welfare,*

1890–1935 (New York: Free Press, 1994); Shaw, "Black Club Women and the Creation of the National Association of Colored Women"; Emilie Maureen Townes, *Womanist Justice, Womanist Hope* (Atlanta, GA: Scholars Press, 1993).

64. Jacqueline Jones, *Labor of Love, Labor of Sorrow: Black Women, Work, and the Family from Slavery to the Present* (New York: Basic Books, 1985).

65. Holly F. Mathews, "Killing the Medical Self-Help Tradition among African Americans," in *African Americans in the South: Issues of Race, Class, and Gender*, eds. Hans A. Baer and Yvonne Jones, 60–78 (Athens: University of Georgia Press, 1992).

66. Ibid., 192.

67. Evelyn Brooks Higginbotham, *Righteous Discontent: The Women's Movement in the Black Baptist Church, 1880–1920* (Cambridge, MA: Harvard University Press, 1993), 192; Higginbotham attributes this information to Nannie Burroughs, *National Baptist Union*, October 10, 1903.

68. Paula A. Giddings, *When and Where I Enter: The Impact of Black Women on Race and Sex in America*, 81.

69. Beverly Washington Jones, *The Life and Writings of Mary Eliza Church Terrell, 1863–1954* (New York: Carlson, 1990), 153. Jones notes that this is taken from Mary Eliza Church Terrell's "What Role Is the Educated Negro Woman to Play in the Uplifting of Her Race?" in *Twentieth Century Negro Literature, or, a Cyclopedia of Thought on the Vital Topics Relating to the American Negro*, ed. Daniel Wallace (D. W.) Culp, 172–77 (Naperville, IL: J. L. Nichols & Co., 1902).

70. Tullia Kay Brown Hamilton, "The National Association of Colored Women, 1896–1920" (Ph.D. dissertation, Emory University, 1978), 15. Typescript from the files of the National Association of Colored Women's Clubs (NACWC), NACWC Headquarters, Washington, DC.

71. Elizabeth L. Davis, *Lifting as They Climb: The National Association of Colored Women* (Washington, DC: National Association of Colored Women, 1933).

72. Hamilton, "The National Association of Colored Women, 1896–1920," 55–56.

73. Giddings, *When and Where I Enter: The Impact of Black Women on Race and Sex in America*, 100.

74. Hamilton, "The National Association of Colored Women, 1896–1920," 70.

75. Eileen Boris, "The Power of Motherhood: Black and White Activist Women Redefine the 'Political,'" in *Mothers of a New World: Maternalist Politics and the Origins of Welfare States*, eds. Seth Koven and Sonya Michel, 213–45 (New York: Routledge, 1993); Giddings, *When and Where I Enter: The Impact of Black Women on Race and Sex in America*.

76. Gerda Lerner, "Early Community Work of Black Club Women," *Journal of Negro History* 56 (1974): 158–67.

77. Joanne M. Martin and Elmer P. Martin, *The Helping Tradition in the Black Family and Community* (Silver Spring, MD: National Association of Social Workers, 1985); Cynthia Neverdon-Morton, *Afro-American Women of the South and the Advancement of the Race, 1895–1925* (Knoxville: University of Tennessee Press, 1989).

78. Boris, "The Power of Motherhood: Black and White Activist Women Redefine the 'Political,'" 228.

79. Hamilton, "The National Association of Colored Women, 1896–1920"; Sharon Harley and Rosalyn Terborg-Penn, eds., *The Afro-American Woman: Struggles and*

Images (Port Washington, NY: Kennikat Press, 1978); Maude Thomas Jenkins, "The History of the Black Woman's Movement in America" (Ph.D. dissertation, Columbia University Teacher's College, 1984); Martin and Martin, *The Helping Tradition in the Black Family and Community*; Neverdon-Morton, *Afro-American Women of the South and the Advancement of the Race, 1895–1925.*

80. Club women were extremely concerned about the treatment of black working mothers within the labor force. As bell hooks explains, white women were extremely hostile to black women whom they saw as a threat to their security. At times, white working women helped undermine the hiring of black women workers or would create an intimidating work atmosphere for them by demanding that black women be segregated from them. Both of these racist practices had the effect of forcing black women to accept jobs that overtaxed them physically, further depressing black women's wages and pushing them out of the central work force completely. Further, black women domestic workers often found white men menacing in their flagrant sexual harassment, a problem equally threatening to their economic welfare. Giddings, *When and Where I Enter: The Impact of Black Women on Race and Sex in America*; bell hooks, *Ain't I a Woman? Black Women and Feminism* (Boston: South End Press, 1981).

81. Boris, "The Power of Motherhood: Black and White Activist Women Redefine the 'Political'"; Giddings, *When and Where I Enter: The Impact of Black Women on Race and Sex in America*; Higginbotham, *Righteous Discontent: The Women's Movement in the Black Baptist Church, 1880–1920*; Shaw, "Black Club Women and the Creation of the National Association of Colored Women."

82. Giddings, *When and Where I Enter: The Impact of Black Women on Race and Sex in America*; Higginbotham, *Righteous Discontent: The Women's Movement in the Black Baptist Church, 1880–1920.*

83. Hamilton, "The National Association of Colored Women, 1896–1920"; Jenkins, "The History of the Black Woman's Movement in America"; Martin and Martin, *The Helping Tradition in the Black Family and Community.*

84. Giddings, *When and Where I Enter: The Impact of Black Women on Race and Sex in America*, 101.

85. Higginbotham, *Righteous Discontent: The Women's Movement in the Black Baptist Church, 1880–1920*, 28.

86. Boris, "The Power of Motherhood: Black and White Activist Women Redefine the 'Political'"; Anne Firor Scott, "Most Invisible of All: Black Women's Voluntary Associations," *The Journal of Southern History* 56 (1990): 3–22.

87. Higginbotham, *Righteous Discontent: The Women's Movement in the Black Baptist Church, 1880–1920*, 14.

88. Boris, "The Power of Motherhood: Black and White Activist Women Redefine the 'Political,'" 224; Higginbotham, *Righteous Discontent: The Women's Movement in the Black Baptist Church, 1880–1920*, 97; Jones, *The Life and Writings of Mary Eliza Church Terrell, 1863–1954*, 26; Townes, *Womanist Justice, Womanist Hope*, 90.

89. Scott, "Most Invisible of All: Black Women's Voluntary Associations," 13.

90. Boris, "The Power of Motherhood: Black and White Activist Women Redefine the 'Political,'" 217.

91. Ibid., 215.

92. Giddings, *When and Where I Enter: The Impact of Black Women on Race and Sex in America.*

93. Gordon, *Pitied But Not Entitled: Single Mothers and the History of Welfare, 1890–1935*, 118.

94. The various literature describing black women's clubs from roughly 1880 to 1940 do not clearly distinguish middle-class and upper-class club women, nor their club activities. For example, Willard B. Gatewood refers to upper-class black groups as the "colored aristocrats," "elite," and "professional class," including among them Mary Church Terrell, whom others classified as middle class (see next paragraph). Willard B. Gatewood, *Aristocrats of Color: The Black Elite, 1880–1920* (Bloomington: Indiana University Press, 1990).

95. Townes, *Womanist Justice, Womanist Hope*, 96.

96. E. Franklin Frazier, *Black Bourgeoisie* (Glencoe, IL: Free Press, 1957), 287. This upper class (about 2 percent of the black population) was relatively wealthier than middle-class blacks; they were more likely to be born free in the North, to be occupied in "outstanding" positions, to be "literary people," and to live in superior residential districts among whites (283).

97. Cited in Giddings, *When and Where I Enter: The Impact of Black Women on Race and Sex in America*, 100; from Mary Church Terrell's "What Role Is the Educated Negro Woman to Play?" 175.

98. Higginbotham, *Righteous Discontent: The Women's Movement in the Black Baptist Church, 1880–1920*, 17.

99. Giddings, *When and Where I Enter: The Impact of Black Women on Race and Sex in America*, 95.

100. Ibid., 144, from "The Duty of the NACW to the Race," originally published in the *AME Church Review*, 1900, 340–54; reprinted in Giddings, *When and Where I Enter: The Impact of Black Women on Race and Sex in America*, 139–50.

101. Higginbotham, *Righteous Discontent: The Women's Movement in the Black Baptist Church, 1880–1920*, 192, 208, 289; from Burroughs, National Baptist Union.

102. Boris, "The Power of Motherhood: Black and White Activist Women Redefine the 'Political,'" 226.

103. Alfreda M. Duster, *Crusade for Justice: The Autobiography of Ida B. Wells* (Chicago: University of Chicago Press, 1970). This particular Wells quotation is not representative of her overall stance on middle classness. She was much more likely to have been found espousing negative sentiment toward the lower classes.

104. Boris, "The Power of Motherhood: Black and White Activist Women Redefine the 'Political,'" 226.

105. Bette J. Dickerson, "Ethnic Identity and Feminism: Views from Leaders of African American Women's Associations," in *Color, Class, and Country: Experiences of Gender*, eds. Young and Dickerson (London: Zed Books, 1994), 115–27.

Chapter Three

The Contemporary Currency[1] of Black Sisterhood

I see black women, instead of being passive belles, they're women, they're vibrant, they're colorful, they're diverse. They're strong . . . even when I worked with a group of ladies now who are ex-addicts, or in the process of recovering, call it what you will. Strength. So often we have been made to feel helpless and hopeless. And yet we still not only survive, we thrive. We love, we laugh, we nurture, we still carry—the future in our hands is strength. So I, yes, I love the black woman, and I am humbled by her.

—Victoria

In their recent book *In and Out of Our Right Minds: The Mental Health of African American Women,* Diane R. Brown and Verna M. Keith engage in an empirical exercise much like that of my own. Though the data sources employed by their volume's contributors are of a very different sort than that which I have constructed for this study, we share a keen interest in the psychosocial well-being of contemporary African-American women as they struggle to make sense of and cope with the world around them. More importantly, our research endeavors begin and end similarly in pondering the "apparent contradiction"[2] between the portrayals of black women's resiliency, endurance, and progress and their high risk for distress. In essence, we search for signs of hope that black women will continue to survive and thrive within their unique gender-ethnic location and in spite of the daily "strains, stressors, and vulnerabilities"[3] it engenders. That hope, I argue, is to some degree dependent upon contemporary black women fostering and maintaining a shared gender-ethnic identity and consciousness. Encouragingly, this chapter presents ample evidence of black women doing just that. African-American women's deep collective roots and the material, emotional, and moral fortitude they have brought to black people (see chapter 2) help to inspire a fervent sense of satisfaction among today's black women. Openly and positively embracing themselves as respectable and honorable human beings is apparently quite commonplace, suggested by the vast majority of the study women—94 percent—taking great pride in the womanness and the blackness of their very existence. The women express that they feel strongly that being a black woman supports a positive self-image, that being black is important to their womanhood, and that being a black woman is an important reflection of who they are in this world. And despite whatever hardships they face, they would not have wanted to be born anything other than black and female.

This *centrality* and *private regard*[4] of black womanhood to which they speak—the extent to which they positively define themselves individually and collectively with regard to their gender-ethnicity—is shown through their daily acts of affirmation, whether they be black womanist mantras spoken in the mirror each morning; the receiving of "soul food" (both literally and figuratively) from the breakfast and dinner tables of significant elder black women; or the sharing of stories of their foremothers' major accomplishments, contributions, and advancements. Acts such as these are repeated across the millions of black women in America, whatever their social backgrounds, and they have encouraged not only strong individual self-esteem but collective self-worth. It is this, the most immediate of ideas to emerge from this study, that I contend considerably undermines any potential for a pervasive and polarizing black stepsisterhood.

CENTRALITY, PRIVATE REGARD, AND THE SALIENCE OF SISTERLY ATTACHMENTS

Strong gender-ethnic centrality among black women is reflected primarily in the attachments they pursue, secure, and sustain with other black women. These attachments are fueled by a strong sense of belonging to one another. Both the survey questionnaire and the women themselves tend to characterize this sense of belonging as "feeling close" to other black women, to "race" women with whom they share common "feelings and ideas" across a number of domains. These strong intragroup connections were reported by nearly 90 percent of the study women, and for many, such bonds of black sisterhood occur "naturally" from their "subconscious" realization that others "like them" exist. Gwynn, a twenty-three-year-old social worker, expresses the ease with which she identifies with and relates to other black women:

> I don't think it's something, like, I think about every day; it's more so like some of the same issues that we share, like on a job, or in relationships, and [how you] express yourself as a black woman and as a woman at the same time, that double-

bond thing. So I think I feel really connected. I don't think I've ever felt disconnected from black women.

Joanne, a forty-six-year-old probation agent, expresses similar ideas and
adds that the connections black women hold to one another are essential to
their psychosocial health:

> I just think we share so many qualities, characteristics, experiences that it kind of
> bonds us together. We have a lot in common. I think that African-American women
> have always felt that they needed to be connected to one another, 'cause we really
> don't have a lot of opportunities to express, like, what's really inside. Those emo-
> tions, those feelings, so much is suppressed because they're superceded by roles that
> we have to play. . . . So connecting and bonding with women affords an opportunity
> to open up a window or open up a door for the real person who is inside to come
> out.

When asked on the survey questionnaire to consider whether they feel
close or not so close to black women from various subgroups, an overwhelming majority of the study women (about 81 percent) responded that in particular they feel strongly attached to religious, churchgoing women. In fact, this
represents the highest proportion for any of the subgroups. Though a number
of the study women admitted that they are not, at least currently, churchgoers
themselves, it is the combination of black women's deep devotion to spiritual
life, the frequency and quality of black women's church involvement, and the
particular style with which black women approach church life that helps fuel
their adoration of and connection with such women. In general, the black
churchgoing woman is lovingly portrayed as a grandmother type ("older")
who is passionately spiritual and who is devoted to the religious training of
her children and other community children, toting them to church with her as
regularly as she totes her hymnbook and Bible. And she always sports a
smart, dressy hat.

"Can I Get a Witness?" from Charisse Jones and Kumea Shorter-
Gooden's book entitled *Shifting: The Double Lives of Black Women in
America*, explores the fusion of religion, church life, and black womanhood
and the strong attachment to religious, churchgoing women that rests upon
it:[5]

> Houses of worship have long been havens for African American women, places
> where they felt they could lay down the burden of shifting,[6] briefly forget about the
> myths of color, and be accepted for who they are. They could leave the lily complex
> on the church steps and with their flamboyant hats and going-to-church clothes feel
> regal, beautiful, and embraced by a distinctly African American world. For Black
> women, developing spiritual practices and getting involved at church have provided
> significant resources for coping with the challenges of being Black and female—for
> managing the myths, negative stereotypes, and discrimination of the outside world.

For many African American women, the church has been crucial for their very survival. (259)

Alice, a thirty-eight-year-old staff specialist at a state corrections facility, wants us to be cautious, though, not to reduce this honorable woman to a stereotypic caricature, "because the churchgoing woman has more substance than just that. She uses the church as her filling station to help her get through what her calling really is." Fifty-four-year-old public school teacher Taylor concurs and offers this as the content of black "church ladies'" character: "strong, faithful, family-oriented, assertive—maybe even aggressive, but definitely assertive—nurturing, loving."

In recent months, religious, churchgoing black women have been an especially important part of Phyllis's life. When we met, this twenty-five-year-old mother was being held in detention by the state corrections administration on murder charges. Though she claims to have come to sorely distrust many other black women, she apparently has reserved some trust in churchgoing women:

> Field notes: Phyllis says she was raised in "the church," so in that sense she feels very close to churchgoing women. And she talked about how the women at her church have been very supportive of her since she's been in the jail, that they have written to her, that they have prayed for her. I don't know that she said they ever visited, and I don't know exactly how long she's been there, but she said she was very much aware that they were caring for her, and that she has no problem going back into that environment once she's released. She doesn't feel that they'll ostracize her or what have you. So she feels very grateful to have had the care of these church women.

Naturally "connecting and bonding" with other black women generally happens very subtly and through simple interactions women have with each other in everyday social spaces. It often occurs in the moment that black women "discover" each other in institutional corridors rarely graced by their presence; they are relieved to not only find each other but to witness their mutual survival. As a mathematician for the government, Latrice (age twenty-nine) knows that sense of discovery all too well:

> It happens because I work with a lot of white persons, [and] when I'm going down the hall, and I happen to see [a woman of color], it's like, "Oh, hi." It's just an immediate thing. I can smile, no matter what's going on. I can smile and actually benefit. There doesn't have to be a spoken word there; it's just that when it happens, it's just a general "it's good to see you." You know, it's just that type of thing.

There was further evidence that workplaces and work-related environments may be particularly conducive to naturally bringing black women together:

Aurora (public school administrator, age sixty-two): I can go to a conference, and
most of them I go to are predominantly white. Well, if there are black women there,
I am going to migrate to them, because I want to know what they're doing, why did
they attend the conference, and usually there is a conversation, and sometimes it
ends up being a friendship, where later we are contacting one another about something. So I do feel a sense of connectedness to black women.

Monique, a sixty-year-old retired college administrator (now a GED
instructor), reminds us, however, that finding other black women in work and
other everyday institutional spaces is both relatively new historically and, in
a sense, a luxury not afforded to black women coming of age in the pre–civil
rights era.[7] The racial segregation endemic to that period made it virtually
impossible for black women of her generation to bond with women of other
races/ethnicities, and hence she offers a slightly different slant on the foundation for naturally occurring bonds of black sisterhood:

I grew up in a time when we only had each other. There were basically no white
people in the picture, in terms of neighborhood, in terms of friendship, in terms of
school, community. . . . So that's who my friends are, black women, and that's who
my family is.

Given the popularity of the term "sister" in black feminist/womanist discourse and in popular black media, literature, and folk talk, I anticipated that
the women I interviewed would use "sister" more often than they did in
referring to and characterizing these non–biologically related black women
(i.e., fictive kinswomen) with whom they have a strong gender-ethnic attachment. In retrospect, my own use of the term during the interviews—in quoting other women's comments as illustrations, in further elaborating the
survey vignettes, and in providing personal anecdotes as a means to building
good rapport with the women—may have curtailed the women's need to
evoke it themselves. But though occurring less often than expected, there are
still multiple and independent evocations of "sister" during thirty-two of
these interviews (about 36 percent); further, it is clear that where the term is
absent, the substance of "sister" is intended. Quite often, "sister" was spoken
simply as a general marker for other black women, "obvious" members of
the gender-ethnic family. More often than this, however, "sister" was intentionally used as a term of endearment to signify a more purposive attachment
to other black women and/or to specific others with whom they share the
same values, ambitions, priorities, and intentions.

Names of specific women were sometimes attached to persons they may
never have actually met but who have had a profound positive impact on their
concept of black womanhood. These references tended to be to what Patricia
Reid-Merritt in her book *Sister Power* calls "phenomenal black women"—
"sisters so visible at the top of the American power ladder [that they] must

be exceptional."[8] In this category are placed women like Congresswoman Maxine Waters, Secretary of State Condoleeza Rice, Bennett College president Johnetta Cole, author and activist Alice Walker, African Methodist Episcopal bishop Vashti McKenzie, former surgeon general Dr. Joycelyn Elders, performer and author Patti Labelle, *Essence* magazine editorial director Susan L. Taylor, author Terri McMillan, and of course talk-show host extraordinaire Oprah Winfrey. While the study women as a whole reported feeling only moderately attached to such renowned black women,[9] some found certain of these women to epitomize the black "sister."[10] Pamela, a thirty-year-old technical writer for a research firm, expresses her kinship with women of this caliber:

> When I see them on television, and when I see them interviewing or being interviewed, I believe with all of my heart that I could have a conversation, and I wouldn't feel nervous, and I wouldn't feel uncomfortable. I'd just feel that they are women who are real. . . . Oprah and Angela Bassett and Alice Walker and Maya (Angelou) and Gwendolyn Brooks, these are women who have come up from nothing, or not a whole bunch. . . . They've worked hard, they had goals, and they achieved those goals. These are women who have crossed the bridge I'm trying to build. They are role models, and I don't see them as that far off from where I am.

Donna Marie, a fifty-four-year-old college professor, is unique in that she *has* had a direct, close attachment with an "exceptional sister." One of her very good friends is a performer with Sweet Honey in the Rock, a highly successful, Grammy-winning African-American female a cappella ensemble with a social activist agenda: "When I'm in her presence, I'm in the presence of greatness." That greatness, she suggests, is representative among those like her friend who have found meaningful and successful venues for expressing black womanhood.

Names of other specific "sisters" with whom study women mentioned having a direct, close attachment are clearly less well-known than Donna Marie's friend, but these women are likewise characterized as significant long-term girlfriends, that is, *sister-friends*—special life partners who have shared in celebrating (and sometimes lamenting) black womanhood over the years. According to Laura, a thirty-eight-year-old hairstylist and entrepreneur, sister-friends share a special commitment to one another even when time and geography separate them for some time. After ten difficult years of marriage, while on the road home from a trip to Georgia, Laura questioned whether she should even bother returning home to her husband. By reconnecting with her sister-friend from high school, a woman then living in Georgia and who had taken a "different path" in life than Laura had ("she decided to go the wrong road"), Laura was helped in thinking more clearly about what she needed to do with her marriage.

The term "sister-friend," though used only occasionally during the interviews, has a fairly recent and universal meaning among African-American women. Its origin is unclear, though I was told some twelve years ago by a woman I interviewed for the Sacramento-based Birthing Project study that the term seems to have originated sometime in the early 1980s with Byllye Avery, founding president of the National Black Women's Health Project.[11] As the story goes, Byllye decided that she and her girlfriends had simply grown too old to be called "*girl*friends" anymore, and "sister-friend" seemed much more appropriate and specific to the intimate relationships currently shared among black women of their generation (then roughly aged thirty-five to sixty). Whatever its source, "sister-friend" as a reference to close friendships among black women is extremely popular.[12]

Other specific references to intimate "sisters" were reserved for those with whom a rewarding mentor-mentee relationship had developed between them. Kitty (age twenty-eight), for example, is a successful hairstylist and says that she owes much of her professional success to the guidance she received from her current shop owner, Laura, while she was in training, whom she says has been a "mentor and big sister" in her life for some while.[13] Similarly, Charlene, a twenty-seven-year-old job coach whose strongest nonbiological black female attachments have been with her work supervisors, says that she is grateful that these women have lovingly taken here aside to "correct her attitude" on the job. Mentoring other black women is described by Desiree, a fifty-seven-year-old attorney, as one of the most intimate forms of social uplift, and she feels strongly that mentoring is something that black women like herself, who have acquired prestigious degrees and occupations and who have gained access to a wide range of beneficial resources, are particularly obligated to give:

> Because if we don't help each other, in these so-called positions we have, where we have contacts and the ability to help people, then . . . what's it all about?

Slightly more than 80 percent of the women reported that they were currently affiliated with a local organization such as a church, church auxiliary, lodge, sorority, civic league, or professional organization, and 75 percent of these affiliations were with organizations comprising primarily black women. Thus, it is not surprising that references to specific "sisters" as a term of endearment also include those with whom study women serve in one or more black women's organizations. And, given that about 24 percent of the study women were recruited from Baltimore chapters of two national black sororities—Alpha Kappa Alpha and Sigma Gamma Rho—it is also not surprising that the organizations noted most here are national black sororities. Trisha, a twenty-two-year-old program assistant for a nonprofit group, left New York City to attend college in Baltimore County. There, as an undergraduate, she became a member of her sorority and soon after continued her active membership by joining the local graduate chapter (i.e., a chapter composed of postbaccalaureate women). Trisha describes her association with the sorority as her lifeline to other African-American women:

> Well, three years ago, I would have told you no, I'm not attached to black women at all, but I mostly deal with black men, and most of my friendships have been with black men. But since I joined a sorority, there's like an automatic bond with African-American women, from all age groups. So, right now in my life, and probably for the rest of my life, I will feel really connected. . . . With me being in a sorority, I've found that I've been able to connect with women there that are in other sororities. . . . I share a sisterhood with my sisters, and they share their sisterhood with their sisters, so somehow there's a common bond.

Currently, more than half a million women grace the rosters of the four national black sororities.[14] These formal Greek-letter sisterhoods were established between 1908 and 1922, three at Howard University in Washington, D.C., and one at Butler University in Indianapolis, and they rapidly expanded to other colleges and universities. Each was created "out of the desire to form social bonds with like-minded students,"[15] with young black women committed to academic excellence, social responsibility, activism, and service. They have been particularly instrumental in providing much needed support to black female students on "heavily paternalistic,"[16] predominantly white campuses, such as in sometimes supplying the only campus housing open to or affordable to black women. Early on, the racism and sexism pervading their campuses and the world around them fueled a strong "sense of urgency,"[17] which then drove and still drives them in advancing a number of significant social and political causes, such as women's suffrage, educational reform, economic development for African nations and African-American communities, and sheltering the homeless. Lawrence Otis Graham, in his book *Our Kind of People: Inside America's Black Upper Class*, finds that it is sorority sisters' extensive involvement in such activities after graduation that sharply distinguishes their organizations (and black fraternities) from their white counterparts:

> For my aunt, my uncle, and many other blacks, their sororities and fraternities are a lasting identity, a circle of lifetime friends, a base for future political and civic activism. . . . For many of them, these black Greek-letter organizations provided a forum, postcollege, through which some of the best-educated blacks in America can discuss an agenda to fight racism and improve conditions for other less-advantaged blacks.[18]

The work of black sororities is now carried out within and among the thousands of chapters that have been established at predominantly white and historically black colleges and universities across the United States, as well as in some parts of Africa, the Caribbean, and Europe. Some of the most renowned black women in American history have joined and served these sororities over the years, among them author and Nobel laureate Maya Angelou, opera diva Leontyne Price, radio executive Cathy Hughes, and writer and anthropologist Zora Neale Hurston.

The twenty women from this study currently active in sorority life (24 percent) are clearly an overrepresentation of the proportion of black women who are sorority sisters in the Greater Baltimore Area.[19] Nationally, about 43 percent of the black female population over the age of sixteen is eligible to apply for membership—full-time undergraduates and those currently holding college degrees.[20] That proportion decreases dramatically as other stringent criteria, based on academic, social, and personal characteristics, are applied. The proportion ultimately accepted to pledge and then promoted "across the burning sands" is relatively quite small. These organizations (and their male counterparts), while very well-known and highly respected throughout the African-American population, are unmistakably elite institutions. Opportunities to form attachments to other black women via sorority membership, then, is limited to a select few, though the pool of prospective members continues to grow as the number of black female college attendees and graduates increases. There are potentially thousands of nonmember women, however—affiliates to the sororities' social, political, and economic projects—who are in various ways regularly brought into that sisterhood.

Though not formally active for many years, I myself pledged Alpha Kappa Alpha Sorority, Inc., in the spring of 1981 with two other women from Mills College (one on exchange from Howard University), and three from San Francisco State University where the chapter was based. Since that time, people—usually those who shun or lack reliable information about black Greek-letter organizations—frequently ask me why I chose to become a member of that or *any* sorority. My response has been that while coming of age, it was AKA women—in the form of my junior high school vice principal, my high school counselor, my middle-class girlfriends' mothers, and certain women of my church—who went to great lengths to make sure the world knew that I was an aspiring violinist, a well-trainer singer, and, most importantly, a strong student. They sacrificed hours of their time shuffling me to music auditions, arranging for me to play my violin at sorority luncheons, pointing me to prospective colleges, and nominating me for college scholarships. (Special thanks to my aunt Precious Bell Craft; to the mothers of my friends Yvonne Giles, Vanessa Jackson, and Kimberly Scott; and to my high school counselor Archalene Martin.[21]) I pledged AKA as an undergraduate to honor the extraordinary black sisterhood those women had shown me. All of the other numerous benefits of joining the world of sororities—such as my excellent training in organizational leadership—were revealed in time, but I had been very narrowly focused in my decision to become an AKA woman initially, which speaks volumes about the impact that black sorority sisters can have on young black women.

Oftentimes, the impetus for establishing a predominantly black female organization, be it formal or informal, is the need to provide an alternative, supportive, and "safe" space for women battling for inclusion in traditionally male-dominated environments. This same impetus has prompted organizing among a fairly new (in its "official" recognition, anyway) and growing sisterhood of black women: black female Christian ministers. Though the primary purpose for their forming "sister circles," "women in ministry" auxiliaries, and "circles of love"—in the real world or in cyberspace—is to guide black women to spiritual growth and fulfillment, there is also a strong commitment to eliminating sexism from the pulpits of black churches,[22] a commitment, Alice explains, that has encouraged a special bond among those she specifically calls "sisters." Alice has begun serving on the ministerial staff of a local church where she is learning just how difficult being a woman minister can be and why sistering among black women ministers is vital to her survival:

> Since we're talking about sisterhood establishment, let's talk about this one. I'm in the ministry, and most of the females, even though I don't know them personally, the ones that I have talked to (within the ministry) tell me about the struggle. And the struggle is it's a male-dominated field. It's worse now, even more so than it was. It's hard. . . . I have friends outside of my church community that are ministers themselves, evangelists themselves. And there's one of them that I said, when you become reverend, you go back and you ordain your sisters.

She goes on to speak of the special gifts she finds that black women bring to the ministry—even former drug abusers like herself—and the intimidation these gifts tend to evoke:

> They just don't want to let us in! Because a woman is a powerful vehicle. When the woman is ill in the family, the whole family structure stops. She's the one that loves and nurtures, and when she's not together, you have dissension through the whole family. And as much as they say, when the head's sick, the body's sick, the man is placed at the head, but who is actually the backbone and the structure of the family? The woman. We can reach more, because the majority of the church is what? Women. And they've made it very hard for us. They do not want to let us in. We study harder. When you get there, we come, and we're prepared. We come, we're prepared. My pastor told me when I first started out, you're gonna have to have double the education that your male counterparts have. The educational goals don't reach them [men]. And that's why he has a bachelor's; I have a master's now. So I'm surpassing him. And the average female minister has reverend doctor so-and-so in front of her name, so that means she's going up and beyond and ahead of her male counterparts. And they don't like that. . . . It's a evil thing.

In one chapter of Johnetta Betsch Cole and Beverly Guy-Sheftall's book *Gender Talk: The Struggle for Women's Equality in African American Communi-*

ties, the authors provide an extensive discussion of black women's struggle against traditional biblical interpretations of (and prescriptions for) gender, and for full participation in the "black church," including the right to ordination. Equally compelling is Bishop Vashti M. McKenzie's *Not Without a Struggle: Leadership Development for African American Women in Ministry*, Renita J. Weems's *Just a Sister Away: A Womanist Vision of Women's Relationships in the Bible*, and a portion of Charisse Jones and Kumea Shorter-Gooden's *Shifting: The Double Lives of Black Women in America*. This literature, like that focused on other social, professional, and political spheres, balances its detailing of the nature of sexist oppression within black Christian culture with tales of passionate and often successful challenges to it.

Foundational to all other strong attachments that black women have formed with one another are those modeled in the black home, where bonds of sisterhood are forged through both practical and affective relations among female kin. The study women express that much of the positive self-image they possess and the importance they place on their black womanhood was and continues to be instilled in them by their biological mothers, grandmothers, aunts, and sisters and by working together with these women to build a life worthwhile. As feminist scholar bell hooks explains,

> In our young minds houses belonged to women, were their special domain, not as property, but as places where all that truly mattered in life took place—the warmth and comfort of shelter, the feeding of our bodies, the nurturing of our souls. There we learned dignity, integrity of being; there we learned to have faith. The folks who made this life possible, who were our primary guides and teachers, were black women. . . . This task of making homeplace was not simply a matter of black women providing service; it was about the construction of a safe place.[23]

Elizabeth, a twenty-eight-year-old financial services specialist, expressed that while "male figures" were plentiful in her family growing up, her family was unquestionably "dominated" by women who were clearly the "stronger of the two" gender groups, and that this led to her becoming more firmly attached to her mother, grandmother, and extended female kin.

Whether or not black families are dominated—in whatever sense—by black women, it is evident from the study women's testimonies that there is often a unique and powerful "connecting and bonding" that occurs naturally among black female kin. These "key black women" are described as intimate allies on the home front. Two young professionals, Nancy, a software engineer, and Naomi, a teacher, explain:

> Nancy (age twenty-nine): I guess it all goes back to family, when you're a child growing up. All the women in my family were very strong. I was very close to all the women in my family. And then I had strong friendships with people. I guess that's the way I thought of it. I mean, nothing negative; I never felt negative things

about black women. I always had a common bond. They gave me very good self-esteem. They gave just positive; I just felt love; I never felt afraid of anything. I don't know, I just think that it's a great part of who I am today. . . . I was very close to my grandmother and my mother, and we just did a lot of special things together. And just, you know, [it] always made me feel good about myself.

Naomi (age twenty-six): My grandmother and my mother are probably my best friends. . . . And they've been such wonderful role models for me, and looking at them interact with other women has helped me to kind of, I don't know, develop a schema, some type of picture of how I want my social life to look, and my interactions with other people to look.

Further, as other study women attest, there is a valuable spillover effect to having close and mutually respectful relationships with female kin; one gains access to an intricately woven security net of sisterhood stretching from the ties each of these black women has to yet another black woman. "Clearly," then, Brittney (a clinical social worker) says, "my strong sense of connectedness with African-American women started with my family." Now at age thirty-five, she demonstrates a commitment to that connectedness in her current work with her sorority and with the local chapter of a predominantly female black social workers organization.

However, just as we have been forced to acknowledge that traditional African-American networks of biological and extended kin are not universally available or beneficial to members of the black community, so too must we acknowledge that for some contemporary black women, opportunities for modeling black sisterhood could not be found at home. Appreciation for sisterly bonding and for the virtues of black womanhood in such cases had to be acquired through relationships negotiated with black women elsewhere, either because other black women were simply absent from the home for one reason or another, because there was some degree of strife or disconnect among those who were there, or both. Judy, a forty-nine-year-old nurse, and Hattie, a thirty-year-old computer systems analyst, are two such cases:

Judy: In my own immediate environment, kinship with black women has been limited because my mother died when I was ten. I do have a sister. We had a rocky relationship. . . . So the extended family, so to speak, has not been there in terms of relationship with other females. So basically I grew up kind of having to determine what a woman was on my own, per se. But the people, the females, I think that I have had strongest attachments with, the females within my life that I feel as though I love, and they mean something to me, have all been black women [and] I guess my contemporaries.

Hattie: Growing up, I grew up in a family that had lots of females but not a lot of close ties. So I could never resolve in my mind why [I had] such a large family, with X number of cousins and X number in [my] age group, but because of issues at other levels that we had nothing to do with. . . . I mean, we had family reunions and all that stuff, but I mean intimate bonding? My strong connection with black women came through the people I met in high school, the people I met in college, my friend relationships, you know? Certainly my sister and my mother were a sensible role model, but not when I was younger.

But as other evidence clearly shows, even when the essential black "homeplace" fails to indoctrinate black daughters, granddaughters, and nieces sufficiently with a sense of attachment to the world of black women and of worth within it, other spheres of sisterly influence serve to emulate that experience.

(DIS)REGARD FOR BLACK WOMEN
IN THE PUBLIC MIND

What other human being absorbs so much virulent hostility and still functions?

—*Sister Outsider*, black feminist writer and poet Audre Lorde[24]

There is serious doubt among black women as to whether they are viewed in a positive manner, are respected, and are viewed as a societal asset by *others*, that is, those outside the black female community. In their delineation of the various dimensions of African Americans' racial identity, Robert M. Sellers and his colleagues describe the two ways that scholars have tended to incorporate the role of the larger society's view of black people, each assuming a *negative public regard*.[25] One understanding—and I move immediately here to making the point relevant to black *women*—is that others' devaluation of African-American women can have "a deleterious influence"[26] on how they view themselves, thereby undermining their gender-ethnic identity. The other is that negative evaluations of black women, which are reflections of the larger society's racist and sexist mentality, only work to fuel "healthy" gender-ethnic identities among them by providing opportunities for black women to sharpen their defenses against oppression. What has been revealed by this study so far appears to substantiate the latter more so than the former: black women generally exhibit strong gender-ethnic centrality in nourishing close sisterly ties with one another despite, and perhaps because of, perceived poor public regard for them.

This is not at all to say that the serious doubt that black women have about the public's regard for them—a doubt expressed by 46 to 60 percent of the study women—is insignificant, however. First, black women are generally well versed in the history of black women's oppression, and their doubt is well-founded on this historical evidence. Some even believe this evidence constitutes a "conspiracy to destroy black women."[27] In her highly acclaimed book, *Black Feminist Thought: Knowledge, Consciousness, and the Politics of Empowerment*, Patricia Hill Collins covers much of the terrain of black women's oppression.[28] This terrain is marked by black women's exploitation in the labor economy, beginning, of course, with their forced physical and reproductive labor during the antebellum period. In slavery, black women and the children they bore were mere property and were vehemently denied ownership of their own labor and therefore of a major aspect of their traditional West/Central African roles in the family-based economy. Motherhood was plagued by racist ideas about racial purity, which effectively bound *black* children only to their *black* mothers, and by that design to an indefinite lifetime of enslavement. In the years immediately following emancipation, black women were thrust into paid labor of the southern agricultural or domestic-service type, where, having been denied the choice of doing anything else, they continued to endure exhausting work under the foot of economically and sexually exploitive white men. Later, service and manufacturing work that could be found in the North was only marginally less dehumanizing, with undue deference to white employers and filthy, dangerous work conditions the norm. The post–World War II economy has brought about new economic opportunities to some black women and has depressed old economic opportunities for others, leading to a still-growing class diversity among them. Nonetheless, each class strata of black women is wrought with specific socioeconomic vulnerabilities: poor wages, job insecurity, and poor working conditions for the working and working-poor classes, and "glass ceilings" and limited marital prospects for the middle classes, to name a few.

The terrain of black women's oppression is further marked by a complex mythology about black women, "controlling images" born from the fertile imaginations of former and contemporary "elite white men and their representatives,"[29] the need to set black women apart as inferior human beings, and the desire to exercise power over them. As Collins explains, the obedient, asexual "mammy"; the castrating, unladylike "matriarch" (failed mammy); the child-breeding "welfare mother"; and the whorish "Jezebel" have been the most popular images of black women and are wedded by the common theme of sexuality. Together, these—and all the varieties in which they come—serve as "effective ideological justifications"[30] for the oppression waged on black women over the years. In the words of Annette (a thirty-two-year-old nurse and research associate),

> It's like we're not too far from slaves. I mean, it's just that there's a question there about African-American women, and do people think we're good or whatever. We were the workhorses, from the bedroom to the fields, and [still] I think that people have that overall sentiment.

Second, augmenting their knowledge of black women's history of oppression is experiential knowledge gained from their direct personal encounters with others. Lillian, a nineteen-year-old youth organizer, shares her assessment of the public's regard for black women, which is enlightened by a variety of sources:

> I think we still have the stereotype of the black woman as being a welfare queen
> who wants to lay up and have babies and collect the welfare check. And I think our
> bodies are not . . . just us as women, I don't think we're valued, because the ideal of
> beauty in this society is a white woman with, you know, narrow hips. And every-
> thing that's us is not valued, our broad behinds, our big thighs—not to say that that's
> what every black woman looks like, but the average black woman's body, I don't
> think, is valued. Or even, I think, when black women receive positions of power, I
> think a lot of times they still don't get as much respect as they should, as educated
> people. . . . One of my black professors, for instance, was talked to by a white pro-
> fessor as if she was, like, a child. And I don't know how often that happens, but I've
> seen it, whereas the black women who obviously have been well educated and have
> worked their way, or tried to work their way, up the social ladder, and are still not
> looked at as respectable, you know. . . . And it's just become so acceptable until it
> seems almost normal.

Lillian, Annette, and other of the study women in essence express that they
are sadly and keenly aware that it takes a rather fierce distaste toward black
women for society to persistently generate and regenerate flagrantly misogynistic images, casting them as bitches, hos, and welfare queens, Jezebels and
mammies; they know it takes a great deal of resentment to deny them the
professional rewards they have worked so hard (and by the book) to earn; and
they know it takes a great deal of irrational fear to constantly blame black
women for so many of society's ills.

Third, the salience of sisterly attachments among African-American
women and the strong gender-ethnic centrality that undergirds it does not
immunize them from internalizing the public's negative sentiment entirely.
While others' devaluation of African-American women may not have a "deleterious influence" on how they view one another—that is, on their *private*
regard and contentions regarding black stepsisterhood—it does appear to
have some effect. One consequence that emerges from my discussions with
the study women is the "beauty discrimination" that black women often
inflict on each other, accepting and rejecting certain women from their inner
circles on the basis of such things as skin tone, body type, wardrobe, and
hairstyle:

> Joanne: We are just so divisive. We do it with hair, we do it with figures, and we
> discriminate against one another based on so many stupid things. . . . You have per-
> ceptions about people without trying to actually get to know them. We just divide
> ourselves on just the most ridiculous [things].

Even though the range of images depicting black beauty has widened considerably over the years, there is still a tendency for women to retreat to those
that meet the more externally defined standards of beauty (i.e., whiteness) in
choosing an image for themselves and in regulating the relations they have
with other women. And as my friend Judy Ford (public health advocate and

philanthropy specialist) frequently points out, the "hierarchy of style" is dictated by black women who by virtue of their class position can materially afford to be discriminating.

Another effect is the competitiveness that often erupts among black women in the paid labor market. The fact that opportunities for jobs and career advancement are plentiful now more than ever, at least for most segments of the black female population, presents a peculiar problem. There is a sense that those who are "making it" must remain highly competitive so as not to be displaced by the next black female rising star. Though many anti–affirmative action types have promulgated inventive tales of black women's privileged position in the labor market (i.e., their providing a two-for-one gender/race deal for employers), black women know from experience that workplaces are highly unlikely to hire more than one or two at their rank at any given time due to the persistence of race and gender discrimination.[31] Then on the other side there are those who are battling to get their first foot in the door, scrounging together meager funds from their low-paying jobs to take a college course here and there in order to increase their chances of some day landing one of those one or two positions at the top. Certainly, strategic cooperation among black women, such as fostering the number of occupationally relevant sisterly mentor-mentee relationships, helps to temper the tension that exists here. But like the beauty myths that undermine the quality of interpersonal relationships among African-American women, the pervasive myth of the aggressive, man-eating, stubborn black matriarch and the general perception that "blacks don't know what to do with success when they get it" help to sustain this uneasiness in the labor market. Exacerbating this tension further is the fact that those "making it" have greater access than those "trying to make it" to the supplies and services needed to meet dominant beauty standards, fusing together beauty success with high occupational status.

Lastly, the study women are particularly concerned that the socioeconomic success of some contemporary black women coupled with the larger society's sanctioning of their "inappropriate independence" and the "negative imagery" of the castrating black matriarch[32] may together have had the consequence of further fueling the "shortage of good black men" problem. Some believe that competitiveness among black women in the dating and marriage market may be fueled in part by an effort to help dispel the notion that "black women don't need men." African-American women are generally viewed as intensely engaged in securing a mate, and sometimes at the expense of sisterly respect among them. Madison, a forty-six-year-old government program analyst, says of occasions when she observes black women being unsupportive of each other, "I guess the main thing has to do with women and how we behave with men," that behavior being too often related to "letting guys walk all over them." Further, because beauty plays such a significant role in the dating and mating market, black women are yet again confronted with conforming to the dominant model.

The tensions among African-American women that appear to have arisen from the internalization of negative public regard, from the perception of ever-growing heterogeneity among them, and from other potential sources are explored at length in chapter 5 of this book. Here, the main idea is that in the midst of such tensions lies evidence of a bountiful pursuit of self-love and a determined devotion to collective affirmation.

SHARED GENDER-ETHNIC IDEOLOGY

The strong gender-ethnic centrality and private regard evidenced among today's African-American women are also apparent in their espousal of a shared black feminist "standpoint."[33] Also described as "historical tendencies"[34] in black women's political thought, these tenets capture complex constellations of black women's beliefs, opinions, and attitudes. In his book *Black Visions: The Roots of Contemporary African-American Political Ideologies*, Michael C. Dawson contends that the "adherents of black feminism exhibit more agreement on what constitutes the political core of their ideology than the adherents of any other black ideology,"[35] an observation that resonates with what is revealed from the study women's elaborations on *ideology*-related topics. In virtually every case, the women gravitate more readily to tenets of black feminist thought than to those of any of the other ideologies explored. Further, they speak certain aspects of that standpoint in virtual unison: the black woman's condition is best defined as a unique "double" and even "multiple" burden born historically from the gender, racial, and other forms of oppression, and relieving this burden requires that society acknowledge her complexity and join with her in combating her oppression on multiple fronts simultaneously. Their strong conviction that multiple forms of oppression—racial and gender oppression, foremost—uniquely intersect to shape their social location is well versed, highly salient, and resolute.

To be fair, the very subject of this research and the methodologies that were employed to examine it are themselves black feminist or black "womanist" (the preferred term for some women) in nature, and the study women knew in responding to my request for an interview that we would be focusing almost exclusively on issues related to black women. Nonetheless, it was clear that before having ever joined this study, these women had actively fashioned and practiced feminist ideas regularly over the course of their everyday lives. These ideas are in part inherited from their foremothers' experiences of slavery and other violent forms of racial and gender segregation, and in part are shaped from modern-day forms of racist and sexist oppression, both of which together constitute what Dawson would call their "indigenous" political thought.[36]

It was typical for the study women to raise the issue of black women's standpoint in the course of explaining why they generally feel estranged from white women. For example, Charlene expresses that while black and white women share some of the same issues, "being woman and being black, it's a double minority, so there are some different things." Naomi says that, with the exception of her white lesbian coworker friend ("which made us both minorities"), she finds that she is "not attached to their feminism" because it is not adequately sensitized to black women's priorities: "It's really a different struggle for me. Like I said, I prioritize race; they prioritize gender." In a fashion not uncommon among black feminists and African Americans in general, Jessica, a thirty-eight-year-old special education teacher, fastens her multifaceted condition to her humanity: "I'm human first, and then I'm part of the spiritual body, and from that, then I'm female, and then I'm probably African American. That would probably be the hierarchy." Despite the fact that Naomi and Jessica "package" their multiple identities differently, they both communicate the importance that black women place on being viewed holistically, which helps support black feminists' claim that the battle against oppression is multifaceted.

Also typical are the specific contexts in which the study women find racially divergent standpoints to be most readily revealed: at home and at work. Many of the women argue that black women and white women are superficially similar in their desires for quality of life in family and work (i.e., they genuinely care for their children, value marriage, and want to be recognized on the job for their hard work); however, white women have had a much shorter history of balancing family and work outside of the home and have faced fewer challenges to achieving that quality of life. Judy's reflections on this topic speak much like the analyses put forth by such scholars as Jacqueline Jones, Patricia Hill Collins, and Elizabeth Higginbotham, who have contributed significantly to our knowledge of how race and gender have intersected historically to shape different work-family dynamics:

A lot more white women have to work now than many years ago. I remember, when I first started in nursing . . . took me three days to realize I was the only black woman. And I was like, wait a minute. And most of my counterparts were white women working part time, because their husband said they could come. There wasn't a lot of they had worked and reared families, like black women had. And I think that's been more of the traditional experience for black women, in that they've had to rear their families by themselves; they've always had to work. Not a whole lot of them, at that point, or still, even, I would say, are in that traditional relationship where a man is taking care of them, and they don't have to work, and they can stay home and be Mom, and that doesn't happen for us a whole lot. Some, yes, but not a lot; it's not the majority, by any stretch of the imagination. I think black women are more often the matriarchs of the family, much more often in our family than white women, which I think has created a different view, different perceptions, once you get beyond the basic wants, needs, and desires, like I said.

Monique grounds her black woman's standpoint regarding family and work in words that very closely parallel those of Judy, particularly where she alludes to the difficulties that black women have faced securing black marital partners with whom to share their lives and their heavy loads:

> I would say [the differences lie in] the role as wife, 'cause a lot of white women aspire to be housewives, where we, we have to work. . . . We can't count on a black man to be there forever.

Another work-related social reality that helps to establish the black woman's standpoint is that, compared to white women, "having to work" places them disproportionately at risk for workplace abuse of various kinds and, more importantly, uniquely at risk for both blatant and hidden forms of racism there. Here, two story lines emerge, both, interestingly, implicating white women in a particular way. In one example, black women are portrayed as having to carefully navigate white women's discomfort—an apparently racially motivated discomfort—with having to work side by side with and possibly compete with black women. Rosalee, a thirty-one-year-old administrative assistant at a corrections facility, describes this as the "fear factor of me trying to take what's theirs, or trying to disrupt their, I guess, day-to-day operations." Their fears, she suggests, are particularly acute when they see the potential for black women to meet or surpass white women's employee status. In the other, more frequent example, white women are portrayed as conspirators or coconspirators in suppressing black women's job advancement. At the time of our interview, Madison was contemplating leaving her government job where she witnessed black women (herself included) being regularly denied advancement despite their strong work experience and credentials:

> She [the branch manager] is the type . . . she has to like you to pick you up. Now, she's white, but she's from the South, and she's definitely racist. She's definitely. And it's not like you could file a EEO complaint, because you really can't, because you don't have anything concrete except that you've seen what they're doing. I mean, it's obvious.

Leah (age fifty-three) says that she feels compelled to educate the "younger generation of black women" on how to survive the gendered racism she and other women her age have had to endure. In particular, she is concerned that they not be lulled into believing that the playing field is even, but rather that the "white man ultimately is the decision maker" and that more often than not he will give white women the first choice at the best jobs, to white women's delight. "Attractive black women" may come in second, she says, but those who are not as attractive or perhaps are less skilled in their jobs will have to work much harder to advance. In sum, Leah, like most other study women, conveys a consciousness of black women's social position "at the bottom of an often brutal American hierarchy of power."[37]

Proclaiming a unique black woman's standpoint, particularly the "double jeopardy" with which they must contend, does not mean that the study women grant themselves superior social status over other gender-ethnic groups, however. On the contrary, a good majority of these women also coalesce around a *humanist* ideology, where persons of all racial, ethnic, gender, class, and other backgrounds are viewed as equally human and equally deserving of human rights protection; where similarities among people are emphasized over social differences; and where it is believed that the pursuit of any one group's interests should be consistent with their humanity and that of others. Agreement is particularly strong around the humanist survey-questionnaire item stating that "it should be socially acceptable for African-American women to marry outside of their race" (92 percent), and where the subject emerged during the interviews, it was clear that their acceptance extended to all gender-ethnic groups.[38] A good proportion (40 percent) of the study women agree with the humanist idea that "being an individual is more important than identifying oneself as a black woman." This suggests that these women (and perhaps others also) believe that it is their right to assert a strong gender-ethnic identity and to make that an important aspect of their humanity and of their sociopolitical practice, and, further, that this assertion should not be interpreted as inherently contradicting their commitment to the freedom and liberation of other groups. The merging of these ideas is highly consistent with a black feminist agenda.

While black feminism and humanism are the dominant ideologies among the study women, there is a high degree of consensus around certain elements of other ideologies, again suggesting that what might at first appear to be internal inconsistency may actually be a healthy integration of ideas owing to the complexity of their black feminist standpoint. Evidence supporting *assimilationist* tendencies among the study women is sorely uneven across the two bodies of data. While less than half of the women were found to drift toward the full set of assimilationist ideas presented in the survey, there was strong enthusiasm for most of its principles during the interviews. As might be expected from their expressions of strong centrality and private regard, on the whole these women find the fact that they have now entered the American socioeconomic and political mainstream more than ever before quite significant, and they take great pride in that accomplishment. This they believe is one sure sign of their gender-ethnic progress:

Christina (retiree, age eighty-nine): When they get up in the Congress, or when they get up in these large organizations, and they say, "Introducing Miss So-and-So,"

and she's black, ooh, it makes me feel so happy! Because I have come so long and
so far from the time when you just didn't have that.

In all, 76 percent of the study women concurred that they should continue
to strive for full membership in the American political system by using that
system to pursue their political and economic goals. Keeping close watch
over the ascension of black women to political office was seen as a vital
means to that end. (Several of the women had political aspirations of their
own.) Granted, many of the women admitted that they generally neglect to
keep abreast of political happenings, but many did say that when there is a
black woman on the ticket, at whatever level of government, they tend to
zoom in. For Wynona (quality review technician, age thirty), focusing in on
prospective and elected black women officials reflects her enthusiasm and
appreciation for black women's "finally being recognized" as viable,
respectable political colleagues, even if the progress these women are able to
make for their constituencies may be slow in coming. Lillian believes that
such "gradual" ascension into political rank is smart politics: she wants to
protect black women in office from being accused of being "too blunt" and
of "making too many demands."

Most agree that black women benefit from their "sisters" being in elected
office, if for no other reason than to bring their standpoint into the discussions
that affect their lives:

Aurora: [It matters that they are in these positions] because our issues, the things
we're concerned about, we need someone there to voice them, or work on commit-
tees or whatever they do, to make sure that our issues are addressed.
    Naomi: [These women should] feel free to represent their own views and their
own issues; we just need them there.

Melanie (currently incarcerated, age twenty) says that she views black wom-
en's participation in such discussions as their long-overdue "entitlement."

It was concern for *structural* assimilation, then, that was central among
the assimilationist issues raised among the study women. Issues of *cultural*
assimilation generally surface in tandem with structural assimilation concerns, such as when the women suggest that exploiting improved interpersonal relations with other racial/ethnic groups[39]—that is, with white men and
women—can be vital to providing black women access to elected office and
to higher positions in the workforce. Opportunities to exploit such interpersonal relations with contemporary white women (generally imagined in society as potential political allies), however, appear to be quite limited. Strained
relations with white women certainly are not universally experienced among
the study women, but the often edgy interracial associations between these
women frequently came to the surface during the interviews, though a large
majority of the study women reject the black *nationalist* suggestion that black

women and white women can never truly trust each other or be friends.[40] Natalie, for example, an eighteen-year-old college student, tended to gravitate equally to humanist and *oppressed-minority* ideologies, including when discussing her relationships with white women. But when pressed to consider whether black women and white women could ever truly be friends, she said that she is "uncertain." Ashley, a fifty-seven-year-old health scientist with the federal government, acknowledges that despite the similarities she recognizes between herself and the white women who heavily populate her workplace, "I don't invite them home or anything like that." And many of the women say that white women simply "don't get it," are "not on the same page," and are "completely unaware" in reference to their knowledge and understanding of the black woman's condition. For example, Brittney says,

> For the most part, I think that there are more similarities than there are differences. I do, however, see a clear divide when it comes to the economic perspective on subjects like teenage pregnancy, poverty issues, lower socioeconomic kinds of situations, and how people respond in crises, when perhaps they . . . they've come from a family where there's never been modeling of how to kind of get out of generational cycles. But when I get into conversations like that with some of my friends of, especially the Caucasian cultures, they don't seem to get it. . . . I wouldn't say baffled. I would say clearly just clueless.

As a result, Brittney says that while it is important to her work as a medical clinical social worker to feel comfortable and speak effectively with white women in advocating for her patients, she would not actively pursue a personal relationship with them.

There is also a tendency for the women to adhere to certain oppressed-minority principles, mainly those aligned with a black feminist/humanist agenda. Here, the women support the idea that some of the same forces that have led to their oppression have also led to the oppression of other groups—that there are other people who experience racial injustice and indignities similar to those experienced by black women. And most believe that black women who support racial separatism (a black nationalist idea) are just as racist as whites who do so. Thus, they believe that black women should learn more about the oppression of these other groups and involve themselves in their causes. It is worth noting that the combined proportion of women uncertain and disagreeing (66 percent) "that the struggle for black liberation in America should be closely related to the struggle of other oppressed groups" may have suppressed the number shown to embrace an oppressed-minority ideology overall. Since the notion of "struggle" proved to be so highly salient among the study women (explored in depth in chapter 4), some of them may have felt compelled to reserve this term exclusively for their own group. Also noteworthy is that the women are somewhat hesitant in equating the sexism that black women have experienced with that experienced by nonblack women, as well as in embracing the idea of forming coalitions with other oppressed groups as a viable strategy for helping to ameliorate the problems that black women suffer. This all suggests that while there is strong empathy toward those who have been the target of social, political, and economic subjugation, the women may still see the need to particularize the "struggle" of black women.

On the whole, the study women believe that a thorough knowledge of black history is very important to black women today; that it is important for black women to surround themselves and their children with black art, music, and literature; and that whenever possible black women should purchase goods and services from black businesses—all black nationalist in sentiment. Of particular concern was the need to promote meaningful connections to Africa, the motherland. This was illustrated in part by many of the women expressing a desire for a stronger connection to black women in Africa—with three out of four study women stating that their personal and/or sociopolitical ties are uncertain or nonexistent—and to African women in America. Lillian, for example, says she desires a stronger relationship to African women than she currently has, and she knows she must overcome barriers that have been systematically placed between her and them:

> I think a lot of African-American women that I encounter don't consider themselves to be connected in any way to African women. And I think this society has encouraged us to do that—white people in America—to disassociate ourselves from black people in Africa. But I think that there is a relationship there, and it should be nourished, and it should be encouraged, for us to see ourselves as one.

Tia, a thirty-year-old certified forklift driver currently serving time, says she has found a connection to African women "on the level of strength." By this she is referring to their attendance to family and community needs and to the values and moral principles upon which that maternal practice is built:

> For me, that's where I draw my strength from. Because the adversity, and the things that black women in Africa have overcome over the years, it makes you say, who am I not to be able to stand up to this? Who am I not to try that much harder to achieve this?

Of the particular issues analyzed in this chapter, one observation remains—a puzzling one. Despite all of the evidence intimating that the basis of black sisterhood is the women's sense of shared (or linked) fate, fewer than half of the study women feel that their "destiny is tied to the destiny of other black women." Previous research leads us to anticipate a proportion approaching 80 percent. Much of that research measures linked fate by asking, "Do you think what happens to [black men, black women] in this country will have something to do with your life?" Those who respond affirmatively are then asked, "Will it affect you a lot, some, or not very much?"[41] I believe my seemingly contradictory observations may simply reflect a difficulty for at least some of the women in interpreting what the survey questionnaire intended by "destiny," a word used nowhere else in the survey or by the study women. On the other hand, it may signal something more substantively real, that for most of the women the term "shared destiny" suggests something too deterministic about gender-ethnic identity and consciousness. The women's word of choice appears to be "plight," or something akin to it, and what they seem to be communicating is that black women undoubtedly experience individual life *journeys* burdened by common needs and problems—that is, the "plight of happiness, strong spiritual life, you know, just the basic needs . . . the need for love, belonging" (Alice). These life journeys, however, are not believed to necessarily lead to common *destinies*.

As has been demonstrated at different points throughout this discussion, it is not uncommon for black women (African Americans, and people in general, for that matter) to espouse ideological beliefs, opinions, and attitudes that at times appear internally inconsistent. This stems largely from the fact that ideologies do not form "a neat, separate set of ideas and values."[42] For example, the women's rejection of the humanist idea that "being an individual is more important than identifying oneself as a black woman" might be construed by some as potent enough to suggest a strong black nationalist leaning among the women. But there is little support (about 6 percent) for nationalist ideology overall. This is very likely because such ideology is dedicated to advocating race as *the* fundamental category of social difference, effectively negating the interdependency of the social categories that define black women's experience. In sum, the women of this study adhere most tightly to black feminist and humanist ideologies, and other ideas generally subsumed under other ideological labels are fairly easily reconciled with their black feminist/humanist postures.

This, then, is a good portion of the evidence undergirding my claim that the potential for a pervasive and polarizing black stepsisterhood is considerably undermined. Taken together, these observations of strong individual self-esteem and collective self-worth shown across these four dimensions of black women's gender-ethnic identity—centrality, private regard, public regard, and shared ideology—suggest that contemporary black women's commitment to sisterhood is impressively salient across the spectrum of socioeconomic backgrounds, and that numerous healthy patterns of relations among black women abound.

NOTES

1. "Currency" is defined here as the widespread acceptance of an idea and practice.
2. Diane R. Brown and Verna M. Keith, eds., *In and out of Our Right Minds: The*

Mental Health of African American Women (New York: Columbia University Press, 2003), xiii, 278.

3. Ibid., 283.

4. See chapter 1, note 83.

5. Also see "The Black Church: What's the Word?" chapter 4 in Johnetta B. Cole and Beverly Guy-Sheftall, *Gender Talk: The Struggle for Women's Equality in African American Communities* (New York: One World/Ballantine Books, 2003).

6. Reference mine. Jones and Shorter-Gooden define "shifting" as what Black women do—"[m]ore than any other group of Americans"—to "serve and satisfy others" and to accommodate "differences in class as well as gender and ethnicity." In doing so, they unconsciously "change their outward behavior, attitude or tone, shifting 'White,' then shifting 'Black' again, shifting 'corporate,' shifting 'cool.'" Charisse Jones and Kumea Shorter-Gooden, *Shifting: The Double Lives of Black Women in America* (New York: HarperCollins, 2003).

7. Approximately 15 percent of the women were age fifty-five and older at the time of the interview, and it is these women who are most likely to have experienced the kind of stark racial segregation and discrimination Monique describes.

8. Patricia Reid-Merritt, *Sister Power: How Phenomenal Black Women Are Rising to the Top* (New York: J. Wiley, 1996), xiv.

9. Further discussion of the study women's feelings about this class of renowned black women is provided in chapter 5.

10. An in-depth discussion of what the study women convey as the epitome of black womanhood or authentic black womanhood is provided in chapter 4.

11. In 2002, the National Black Women's Health Project was renamed the Black Women's Health Imperative. See www.blackwomenshealth.org.

12. Its appeal is much wider than this, however. The Birthing Project, for example, uses it in naming the middle- and working-class black women who volunteer there to lend maternal support to disadvantaged young women (though the intent here is to stimulate close friendships between them); and at least two cybernewsletter/forums use it to call not only African-American women but women of color to dialogue around issues relevant to them.

13. See Adia M. Harvey, "Becoming Entrepreneurs: Intersections of Race, Class, and Gender in the Black Beauty Salon," *Gender and Society* 19, no. 6 (2005): 789–808, for a discussion of the common practice among shop owners of mentoring newcomers to the hair-care business.

14. These black sororities are labeled "national" in that each has 100,000 members or more worldwide and is a member of the National Pan-Hellenic Council (NPHC), the ruling body of black Greek-letter organizations. They are Alpha Kappa Alpha Sorority, Inc.; Delta Sigma Theta Sorority, Inc.; Zeta Phi Beta Sorority, Inc.; and Sigma Gamma Rho Sorority, Inc.

Public policy scholars Theda Skocpol and Jennifer Lynn Oser, in their study of African-American fraternal organizations, describe these sororities, their male counterparts, and their non-NPHC parallels as "elite . . . enrolling only college-educated African Americans," and, therefore, in many ways quite distinguishable from the dozens of "fraternal groups recruiting men and women across class lines"; Theda Skocpol and Jennifer Lynn Oser, "Organization Despite Adversity: The Origins and Development of African American Fraternal Associations," *Social Science History* 28, no. 3 (2004): 425n1. Examples of these latter groups—founded as early as 1775—are the Prince Hall Masons, the Grand United Order of Odd Fellows, the Knights of Peter Claver, and the gender-integrated American Woodmen.

15. Paula A. Giddings, *In Search of Sisterhood: Delta Sigma Theta and the Challenge of the Black Sorority Movement* (New York: William Morrow, 1988), 18.

16. Walter M. Kimborough, *Black Greek 101: The Culture, Customs, and Challenges of Black Fraternities and Sororities* (Madison, NJ: Fairleigh Dickinson University Press, 2003), 21.

17. Giddings, *In Search of Sisterhood: Delta Sigma Theta and the Challenge of the Black Sorority Movement*, 18.

18. Lawrence Otis Graham, *Our Kind of People: Inside America's Black Upper Class* (New York: HarperPerennial, 2000), 85.

19. These twenty women are those clearly identified as such, recruited directly from the two sororities. There may have been one or two other sorority members unbeknownst to me. Also, because they are all college-educated women, their proportion in the study sample effectively inflates the proportion of women from the middle classes.

20. This crude figure was computed from two 2002 U.S. census sources, one on school enrollment reporting 26 percent of black women age sixteen to twenty-four enrolled full time in four-year colleges, and the other on educational attainment reporting 18 percent of black women age fifteen and over holding a bachelor's degree or higher.

21. My mother, Gladys Bell, would very likely have been an AKA during this time. Being the lioness of a mother she was, she postponed her own college education to support me during my high school and undergraduate years. She only recently qualified to join a graduate chapter—having obtained her BA at age sixty-two after part-time student status from approximately 1993 to 2003.

22. Cole and Guy-Sheftall explain that by "the black church," we generally are referring to "organized Christian religious institutions to which African Americans have been attached since slavery," institutions "forged from the retention of complex African beliefs and rituals that were reinterpreted in a 'New World' setting." Cole and Guy-Sheftall, *Gender Talk: The Struggle for Women's Equality in African American Communities*, 105.

23. bell hooks, *Yearning: Race, Gender, and Cultural Politics*, 41–42.

24. Audre Lorde, *Sister Outsider: Essays and Speeches*, The Crossing Press Feminist Series (Freedom, CA: Crossing Press, 1984).

25. A full discussion of Sellers et al. can be found in the introduction.

26. Robert M. Sellers et al., "Multidimensional Model of Racial Identity: A Preliminary Investigation of Reliability and Construct Validity," *Journal of Personality and Social Psychology* 73 (1997): 805–15.

27. See, for example, the book by this very name: Michael Porter, *The Conspiracy to Destroy Black Women* (Chicago: African American Images, 2001).

28. Patricia Hill Collins, *Black Feminist Thought: Knowledge, Consciousness, and the Politics of Empowerment* (New York: Routledge, 1990). Similar discussions of the history of black women's oppression can be found in the work of Leith Mullings, "Images, Ideology, and Women of Color," in *Women of Color in U.S. Society*, edited by Maxine Baca Zinn and Bonnie Thornton Dill (Philadelphia: Temple University Press, 1994); Paula Giddings, *When and Where I Enter: The Impact of Black Women on Race and Sex in America*

(New York: William Morrow, 1984); and Jacqueline Jones, *Labor of Love, Labor of Sorrow: Black Women, Work, and the Family from Slavery to the Present* (New York: Basic Books, 1985).

29. Ibid., 68.

30. Ibid., 78.

31. For an overview of black professional women's employment status, see Elizabeth Higginbotham, "Black Professional Women: Job Ceilings and Employment Sectors," in *Women of Color in U. S. Society*, eds. Maxine Baca Zinn and Bonnie Thornton Dill, 113–31 (Philadelphia: Temple University Press, 1994).

32. Leith Mullings, "Images, Ideology, and Women of Color," in *Women of Color in U.S. Society*, eds. Maxine Baca Zinn and Bonnie Thornton Dill (Philadelphia: Temple University Press, 1994), 274.

33. See Collins, *Black Feminist Thought*, for discussion of standpoint theory.

34. Michael C. Dawson, *Black Visions: The Roots of Contemporary African-American Political Ideologies* (Chicago: University of Chicago Press, 2001), 10.

35. Ibid., 140.

36. Ibid., 140.

37. Ibid., 138.

38. Among the study women, Taylor was alone in her objection to black men marrying white women, a very strong objection.

39. Cultural assimilation in these discussions was narrowly defined as the improvement in black women's interracial/interethnic relations over time. Little attention is given to cultural assimilation as a process toward the adaptation of the dominant society's cultural value system, though some of the women intimated during their interviews such things as that today's black women having taken on too many of "white's people's ideas," and they do so using very vague language.

40. It is unclear how the study women differentiate "trusting" white women from being "friends" with them. In the survey, the percentages tending toward trust and friendship were 80 and 90 percent, respectively. I am inclined to believe that the difference between these percentages (albeit relatively small) may be due to the fact that issues of distrust are primarily job related, where interracial contact is more frequent and less voluntary. Black women have greater control over with whom they form close personal relations at work and elsewhere.

41. See, for example, Evelyn M. Simien, "Race, Gender, and Linked Fate," *Journal of Black Studies* 35, no. 5 (2005): 529–50.

42. Dawson, *Black Visions: The Roots of Contemporary African-American Political Ideologies*, 22–23.

Chapter Four

"Struggle" as a Marker of Authentic Black Womanhood

Struggle[1]
~ a strenuous effort
~ an energetic attempt to achieve something
~ an open clash between opposing groups (or individuals)
~ to exert strenuous effort against
~ to make a strenuous or labored effort
~ to be engaged in a fight; carry on a fight
~ to be a black woman.

Library bookshelves, academic journals, popular magazines, and Internet websites house scores of references to works and events about African-American women. A good many of their titles include a certain word, "struggle," that has become virtually synonymous with their subject. Among them are the following:

"Black Women and the *Struggle* for Liberation" (article, 1970)
"Slave of a Slave No More: Black Women in *Struggle*" (article, 1975)
The Afro-American Woman: Struggles and Images (1978)
"Facing Our Common Foe: Women and the *Struggle* against Racism" (book chapter, 1989)
The Rhetoric of Struggle: Public Address by African American Women (1992)
Uncivil War: The Struggle between Black Men and Women (1996)
"*Struggle* among Saints: African American Women in the YWCA, 1870–1940" (book chapter, 1997)
How Long? How Long? African American Women in the Struggle for Civil Rights (1997)
African American Women in the Struggle for the Vote, 1850-1920 (1998)

Between Sundays: Black Women and Everyday Struggles of Faith (2003)
*Gender Talk: The Struggle for Women's Equity in African-American Com-
   munities* (2003)
"Sisters in *Struggle*" (a program in celebration of Black History Month,
   Sacramento, California, 2004)

It would be difficult to determine whether the popularity of the term "struggle" within the general population of African-American women has led to
the proliferation of such titles or whether such titles have led to the term's
popularity in everyday folk talk. Whatever its evolution, the salience of struggle is quite clear. As Patricia Hill Collins explains, "The legacy of struggle
against racism and sexism is a common thread binding African-American
women"[2] one to another and is a core theme of the black woman's standpoint.
It is no wonder, then, that so much scholarly and popular material on the
black woman prominently features her struggle.

   The contemporary African-American women of this study are likewise
committed to the notion of struggle and to embracing it as relevant to their
gender-ethnic identity and consciousness. Its historical significance resonates
so powerfully among them (and among others who study them) that it easily
ranks alongside the idiomatic notions of black "sister" and "sisterhood." On
close examination of the ways in which these three concepts intertwine, one
is led to the conclusion that without the idea of collective struggle for its
sustenance, the meaning of "black sister" and "black sisterhood" would be
vacuous.

   Granted, the notion of struggle is by no means unique to the discourse on
African-American women. The liberation ideology that feeds the discourses
of feminist, antiracist, working-class, and antihomophobic movements of various kinds also strongly provokes the idea of struggle and calls upon it as an
organizing principle. Struggle helps to accentuate the long, drawn-out, and
difficult task of "eliminating the chains of various social oppressions and
with creating much more just and egalitarian societies."[3] Following suit,
black feminist ideology, to which these study women strongly adhere, is by
and large a call to the acknowledgment of black women's struggle, past and
present, and within multiple spheres of social life. It is the *cumulative* toll
that gender-ethnic oppression has had on African-American women's well-
being—more so than that with which they must contend on any given day—
that is reflected in their notion of struggle. This cumulative toll is also understood as an intergenerational phenomenon, something passed on from one
generation of black women to another. As forty-two-year-old Tamara
explains, "We come from struggle and should not be surprised that many of
us still struggle."

   Coming to this understanding of struggle through my conversations with
the study women helped to clarify why only 31 percent said that on a day-to-

day basis they find being a black woman difficult (a survey questionnaire item). The women seem to say that they make out fairly well in immediate contexts, winning one small battle after another on the home front, in the job place, and in other areas of social interaction. But when they step back from these smaller victories and take stock of the whole, their lives are viewed through the lens they call struggle. Moreover, struggle for black women is not only something *done* but also something they feel they have come to uniquely *personify*. My interpretation of this sentiment is that consciousness about the experience of struggle in one's own life is the primary mark of authentic black womanhood.

The contemporary black women whose voices are reflected in this text have partaken frequently in the kind of "kitchen-table" folk talk about the current state of black sisterhood I described earlier.[4] That folk talk highlights the everyday performance of "boundary work"[5] among black women to establish who among them is "real." Boundary work is the process by which one group works to establish its own authentic identity and its own intragroup practices, and to then use that information to draw boundaries between it and other groups. Common to all racial, ethnic, and gender-ethnic groups, authenticity is socially constructed from "complex foundations . . . pieced together out of [a group's] history, tradition, experience, myth, and a host of other sources" including that which is imposed on the group by outsiders.[6]

I learned from my interaction with the study women that it did not matter whether she had attained a Ph.D. or was incarcerated with no postsecondary education; her views on a particular black woman or a group of black women ultimately came down to whether authentic black womanhood was conveyed to her. The contours of authentic black womanhood can be articulated in either very concrete or very abstract terms; in either case, they are understood to be the embodiment of that which is believed to be "the" black woman's way of life. In general, authenticity may be expressed (knowingly or unknowingly) through such things as style of dress, speech, dating and marital practices, property ownership, child-rearing practices, economic practices, educational achievement, and political ideology, packaged together in such a way as to make the bearer "real," and it guides the acceptance or rejection of one woman by another as they interact within the family, at work, among neighbors, and at community events. When these unwritten rules of gender-ethnic expression are obeyed—such as conveying a consciousness of struggle in one's life as a black woman—they are believed to signify that the woman is aligned with the "true" meaning of black womanhood and can therefore be counted "in" as an authentic black woman.

These symbols of authenticity are comparable to what *Shifting* authors Charisse Jones and Kumea Shorter-Gooden call "home codes." They are "complex behavioral codes" and "rules of comportment" that together constitute the cultural content of African-American community.[7] Much of that content is fashioned from the cultural ideals that the black community has historically fought to uphold, namely (1) the primacy of kinship and communalism, (2) reverence for ancestors and elders, (3) respect for and practice of spirituality, (4) the centrality of motherhood, and (5) shared power between men and women and of gendered institutional practice where it is beneficial to the self-determination and agency of family and community. Home code content is also fashioned, however, by the racial ideology of the dominant culture as well as by its gender and class ideology, providing a distorted basis for assessing blackness, womanhood, and the relationship of poverty and wealth to both. Internalizing these distortions is likely to result in a rigid "either/or" dichotomous orientation[8]—white/black, light/dark, feminine/masculine—that at its worst is exhibited in bigotry, one African-American woman against another:

> [When] a community is buffeted with negative stereotypes by a more powerful, dominant group, it is inevitable that some of the biased perspectives seep in. Social scientists call this "internalized oppression." Sadly, when this happens, the victimized group becomes a partner in discrimination.[9]

As Marilyn M. White points out in "We are Family! Kinship and Solidarity in the Black Community," to be called "sister" is not indiscriminate; the person to whom it refers must "earn the rights and privileges" of the black sisterhood and prove that she is "worthy of the trust and status bestowed by the term."[10] The women with whom I spoke suggest that it is the "real" black woman who earns the title "sister." While some of the women are aware that they might be perceived by certain other women to be inauthentic, most are very confident that they possess the qualities worthy of a real sister, particularly the quality of struggle.

ARTICULATIONS OF BLACK
WOMEN'S STRUGGLE

The study women's recurrent attention to the idea of black women's struggle also reveals their tendency to articulate the nature of that struggle in different ways: (1) the struggle for economic and physical well-being, (2) the struggle to hold black families together, (3) the struggle to not "forget where you come from," and (4) the struggle to endure negative public regard. While not mutually exclusive in their content, each of these articulations accentuates a particular set of problems the study women believe exemplifies contemporary black women's oppression. For the most part, this attention to struggle is spoken in a language that tends to minimize the effect of social class and its ability to variegate the experience of struggle among black women: "We all struggle the same way" (Stephanie, twenty-four-year-old accountant). Twenty-seven-year-old nonprofit employment advocate/job coach Charlene's commentary on the universal roots of black women's oppression is representative of such language:

> The struggle. Just the different things that black women had to face. I mean, if you really want to go deep, I'm thinking about how children were taken from us—you understand what I'm saying—our identity of being great being taken away from what [we] know. Treated differently because of your color and then being that you're a woman, that struggle. I mean, it doesn't matter how much money you make, it doesn't matter how much education you get, how do you forget that? When you look in the mirror, how do you forget that, you know? So that's what I mean when I think of struggle—really dealing with real life, some serious issues, and being able to say, hey, but I can make it another day.

Black women have developed a common language reflective of their being highly cognizant of society's negative regard for them, and it is the universality of that language and the areas of social life to which their struggle is most frequently attached that are the primary subject of this chapter. But as this evidence unfolds, there are also glimpses—some subtle, some more blatant—of the way in which class can produce particularized challenges for black women in their struggle, both from outside and within the black community, the full analysis of which will be presented in chapter 5.

The Struggle for Economic and Physical Well-Being

Black women's struggle to improve their fundamental material and health conditions is one of the four articulations of struggle identified as salient. Amidst the flurry of reports regarding contemporary black women's ascension into the middle class—measured primarily by proportional increases in professional, managerial, and executive status and in higher-degree attainment—lies the sobering reality that meeting life's basic needs remains a frequent concern for many. The latest census reports show that one in four African-American women subsists below the poverty line, and among families headed by black women alone (43 percent of all black families), the poverty rate is a staggering 35 percent, significantly higher than that for their Hispanic and non-Hispanic counterparts.[11] Though improved over the past twenty years, black women's high poverty rates are in large part reflective of the low pay they receive for their work in the labor market relative to black men, white women, and white men. Their poverty also reflects their proportionately high representation among single-headed households.

Currently employed as a social-security insurance specialist, Michelle (age forty-two) had once faced the difficult struggle of raising her three children on very little money. She was pregnant at the young age of sixteen by an older man (the father of her oldest child) with whom she was cohabiting and that she says physically beat her regularly. After finally wrestling herself away from that abusive relationship, she was determined that she would care for her children alone. Her pride did not keep her from accepting public assistance, but she relied on that assistance minimally by working as many as three jobs at a time to meet her family's basic requirements. As is frequently the case, Michelle learned along the way the irony of social-services agency policy, finding the agency unable to assist her in creating a balance between the receipt of public assistance and what resources she could garnish for herself: "I was discouraged from working." Eventually, the part-time work she was able to sustain led to her current full-time occupation. As Charlene says, "A lot of us came from nothing and made something. And that's when I think of struggle."

Lillian, a nineteen-year-old youth organizer, would say that Michelle's story is far more common than most people know given the widespread negative imagery surrounding welfare mothers in recent decades. In her work, she frequently encounters young black teenage mothers faced with very difficult choices in solving their poverty dilemmas:

> I think it could go two ways. I think some kids who have teenage mothers, or who have teen parents in a situation where they were about to become young parents, I think either they would get rid of the child in some way, because they would be so scared of their child struggling and growing up in poverty the way they did, either they would be so scared of that happening to their kids, and they wouldn't want their kids to have to go through the struggle, or I think they would have it and deal with it, and try to be as strong as their parents were.

From this experience, she has found that poor black women, often out of fear that their children will suffer as they have suffered, will take whatever steps are necessary to ensure their family's survival. She also finds that despite what the public tends to assume, the strategies that poor black mothers employ are more often than not lawful, as in Michelle's case.

Many of the study women seem certain that if not true of the present, financial struggles are a familiar feature of every black woman's past. They are even more certain that the mothers of today's black women have known poverty well. In fact, the experiences most vivid in some study women's minds are that of their own mothers and of their childhoods. These memories frequently include the absence of an income-generating male partner in the home:

> Maisha (incarcerated, age twenty): Before, it was just a struggle for us, period. You know, 'cause I remember when my mother was coming up. And she was raisin' me and my sister by herself, and the job that she was working at, she was goin' to school, and then she wasn't getting paid a lot of money.

Charlene (employee advocate, age twenty-seven): My mother was a single parent, and for me, I'm struggling with trying to get my education and trying to achieve some things so that when I have a family, that I can be able to provide and give them the things that I didn't have, so that they can have more of a chance for success. So I think about that struggle.

Adrienne (incarcerated, age fifty-two): I was brought up with a mother and a father. . . . And the father worked; our mother worked. And my father left my mother, and my mother struggled. And I knew she was struggling, you know, with her five kids. And two of her sister children, that two of her children was out of wedlock. And my mother saw [how the fathers treated the children], so she took her niece and nephew. And, you know, I looks up to my mother. My mother's still living. I looks up to my mother because she struggled with all of us and working.

For some study women, the financial strain experienced by their own mothers helps them to identify and empathize with black women today who are less fortunate than they are. Sometimes these less fortunate women are in close reach—a biological sister, a cousin, a client, a neighbor, or a coworker—and find themselves in much the same condition as the study women's mothers had been in, spreading their meager resources thinly across various clusters of family members and floating month to month on one income.

Among black women who have suffered little or no material poverty or who have managed to rise above poverty over time, the struggle to stabilize one's economic status is common. Research on the "strangely fragile" black middle class highlights the weak wealth portfolios such women possess relative to middle-class whites (i.e., lacking in savings accounts, investment accounts, and other income-producing assets) and, therefore, their financial vulnerability when personal and family crises hit or downturns in the nation's economy occur.[12] Furthermore, as sociologists Melvin Oliver and Thomas Shapiro explain, while the lack of desirable human capital among middle-class blacks helps to explain their economic fragility, this problem "can be traced, in part, to barriers that denied blacks access to quality education, job training opportunities, jobs, and other work-related factors"[13] historically. There is plenty of evidence that these and other forms of discrimination against African Americans continue, limiting their ability to acquire the wealth needed to secure their futures and those of their children. Institutional discrimination in the real estate and mortgage-lending industries are particularly significant given that middle-class blacks tend to invest most in housing. Because the status of middle-class black households—single-headed and married-couple ones alike—hinges on the sizeable income contributions that black women make,[14] African-American women share a sizeable portion of the black middle-class burden. Thus, the struggle of many contemporary black women to maintain or increase their economic resources is clearly structured by the intersection of race, class, and gender.

Dorraine, a sixty-seven-year-old social worker, says she knows firsthand the challenges middle-class black women face in meeting their socioeconomic objectives. She also knows that the obstacles encountered while working to meet those objectives are frequently revealed through racist and sexist institutional practices. For women like herself who have managed to acquire a college education (and even more so for those less educated), the doors to further opportunity are often closed. To support this, Dorraine tells of a time in her life when she desperately needed a paid job to support her transition from one college to another. The job she targeted and for which she was clearly qualified suddenly slipped away:

> I went in and took a test, and I got something like ninety-eight [out of one hundred], and there were only ten people taking the test. And there were eight positions, they told us. And I was the only black woman there. And I didn't get the job.

As a result, Dorraine stressed for some time over how to continue her education and meet her financial obligations to her family. She was convinced then (as she still is now) that the organization offering that job erred by prejudging her as somehow ineligible or even unfit for the job because of her gender and race. Such encounters throughout her life and those of other black women close to her, she says, have led her to conceptualize black women's struggle as "mainly about economics." Thus, she presses on in her quest to become "stronger economically" so that she can "have something substantial, enjoy my life more, and have something substantial to give to [my son], for the people, my son, and his family."

In this articulation of struggle, black women's difficult economic plight is coupled with the dilemmas of black women's health. In a recent statement published by *Ebony* magazine, Lorraine Cole—president and CEO of the National Black Women's Health Project—reported, "The deplorable state of Black women's health in this country has relegated Black women to the bottom of nearly every health index compared to other women and, in some cases, when compared to Black men. Too many Black women are dying too soon, too often and needlessly. Too many others suffer unnecessarily from preventable conditions."[15] Complex social phenomena negatively impact the health status of black women across the socioeconomic spectrum, some of them understood far better than others. While material poverty and unaffordable health care are considered prime suspects in the poor health outcomes of impoverished and working-class black women,[16] this "poverty-driven paradigm"—pervasive in public health and policy research—insufficiently captures the specific pathways through which the disadvantages of race, gender, and class materialize in the form of poor health for other black women.

My first professional encounter with the black women's health care quandary came by way of research on black women's poor maternal health outcomes, specifically on the high rates of low birth weight and infant mortality.[17] In the mid-1990s, I joined with other black maternal activists and with the interdisciplinary social research community in voicing our concerns about the theoretical paralysis hindering the advancement of black women's health.[18] We argued then (as we still do now) that by narrowly focusing on poverty-related issues, the impact of noneconomic factors is unduly deemphasized. Since that time, consensus has grown over the lack of attention paid specifically to the underlying psychosocial condition of black mothers in the United States—the impact of everyday struggles with racism, sexism, and class inequality on the quality of their maternal health—and to the biomedical translation of psychosocial stress to increased susceptibility to maternal health problems.[19] That is, before that time, little conceptual work had been done in explaining black women's overall health status as directly or indirectly impacted by the unique historical and contemporary social environment within which they must cope physically and psychologically. Fundamental to the paradigmatic shift that occurred is the acknowledgment of the failure of a structural interpretation to capture the psychosocial nuances affecting health that can be traced to the fundamental corrosive power of oppression and that are experienced in the lives of black women throughout the social class spectrum.

Several of the study women shared stories of struggle with health problems of their own, while others told of how they have nursed or counseled other black women battling a variety of diseases and debilitations. By and large, their focus is on coping with black women's affliction rather than on trying to pinpoint its psychosocial or other causes (e.g., environmental or genetic). When I met Monica (nanny, age fifty-four), for example, she was battling through her war with the leading cause of death for black women her age: cancer. Though statistics show that her form of cancer—breast cancer—is less prevalent among black women than among white women, it has proven more aggressive in black women due in part to the more advanced state of the cancer at the time of diagnosis.[20] But doctors admit that little else is known about why outcomes are poorer for African-American women. Monica knows, then, that she is a medical exception in having now survived nineteen years longer than her doctors predicted. (They had only given her six months to live.)

But Monica also recognizes that psychosocial stress invades her cancer-survival process in ways she would not have predicted. In particular, she describes an incident when her severe reaction to a morning of cancer treatment was assumed by white bystanders to be a reaction to alcohol abuse:

> The reason, I was down here at the market, and I had had my treatment, and I was throwing up. And my son and I were in the market, so I left out, rather than throw

up in the store. And then these two ladies called me a alcoholic, first thing in the morning. . . . And I'm, like, I was throwing up to the point that I couldn't turn to tell these ladies, no, it's not like that. But then they went on. My son was in the store. He was kind of frantic, because he didn't know that I had left out.

Monica was horrified that these women would draw such a conclusion based on stereotypes they held about her as an urban black woman rather than offer her compassionate assistance. She credits her deep religious faith and the love and care of her extended family for sustaining her through the disease and for defending her against such psychosocial trauma.

Ashley's experience with the diagnosis and treatment of black women's health problems has been from within the federal government. At age fifty-seven, Ashley (federal government regulatory health scientist) has become a strong advocate for educating black women about advances in medical technology that could one day save their lives and the lives of those whom they serve as caregivers. Her church community is where she performs much of her advocacy work, and she recognizes that the relatively little formal education beyond high school that these churchgoers have is an obstacle to engaging them in discussions about black women's health. Such obstacles frustrate Ashley's ability to convey the seriousness of the health problems they face and the gross inequality that exists among populations benefiting from the new technologies:

> I think that they're important for us to know, because it appears as if they have identified black women as being number one in almost every disease you can think of. You know? Every disease you think of, they've identified us as at the top of the list. So it's really been a struggle, and I guess I think that it's been difficult for me to relate, to talk to people about what I do, and how important it is.

Like Ashley, Gwynn (methadone clinic social worker, age twenty-three) is highly committed to health advocacy work on behalf of African-American women. As a social worker for a Baltimore methadone clinic, Gwynn seizes the opportunity to help arrest the growing black female epidemic of drug addiction. The special circumstances shaping the life struggle for economic and health stability among these addicts are deserving of analyses devoted solely to that purpose, something that extends far beyond the scope of this book. Suffice it here to say that since the 1980s, the number of black women in the United States being supervised by the criminal justice system (in jail, in prison, on parole, or on probation) has increased substantially—according to some reports, by as much as 78 percent—and that increase largely has been attributed to the zero-tolerance policies and mandatory sentences established as part of America's "war on drugs." Hosts of women are convicted for nonviolent drug-related offenses and for crimes related to their drug addiction, namely theft and prostitution.

Lula A. Beatty, who provides an overview of these trends in her chapter "Changing Their Minds: Drug Abuse and Addiction in Black Women," shares Gywnn's concern about this troubling health problem:

> Traditionally women have been a stalwart, stabilizing force in Black communities, providing financial, emotional, spiritual, and social support to kin and friends and to community organizations such as the church. What makes a Black woman—mama, sister, daughter, friend, wife—voluntarily take a substance into her body that alters her perceptions and feelings of well-being? Why does she seek to literally change her mind, change the way she sees, thinks, and behaves?[21]

Beatty goes on to explain that there are a number of complex microlevel conditions that give rise to drug abuse among black women, many of which appear to be related to "the interaction of stress and trauma and family and interpersonal relationships,"[22] for example neighborhood violence, parental influences, child loss, and sexual partner influences. Many experts, however, implicate more macrolevel factors, namely the relatively recent and massive infiltration of cheap and highly addictive substances among highly vulnerable members of the African-American community. They note that prior to the introduction of crack cocaine in the early 1980s, upper- and middle-class men (disproportionately white) were the primary users of illicit drugs, and this fact fueled the widespread notion that their drug activity was merely recreational. Pre–crack cocaine statistics show that men addicts outnumbered women addicts five to one. Beginning in the 1970s, however, heroine and marijuana use by women steadily increased, followed by a devastating and "unprecedented" number of black women—primarily from poor urban neighborhoods—becoming addicted to crack.[23] Nationally, crack cocaine and heroin are the drugs of choice in the African-American community due to their low cost and the intense high they create.[24] (In the Baltimore area, heroin is reported to be the leading drug problem, but with cocaine and crack cocaine running close behind.[25]) As of 1993, about 10 percent of African-American women reported having used cocaine, heroin, or some other illicit drug in the past year, and the negative health, financial, family, and neighborhood consequences of drug use and addiction have been heavily documented.[26]

Study woman Gywnn says it is the fierceness of drug addiction and the variety of dependencies it spawns that estranges her from the black women she serves. While she admits that every woman (including herself) suffers from relationship dependency in some shape or form—"I've been told that sometimes in relationships, when you search for certain things, you seem to be dependent on things that are abstract things you probably can't control"—it is the frighteningly close association of drug addiction and the woman addict's dependency on men to finance that addiction that is unique. Many of these women turn to prostitution as a means of maintaining a steady intake of drugs. Their desperation puts them in highly precarious positions with the men in their lives—men who often rely on the women's addiction, for profit or for sexual gratification. As Gwynn explains, "They're afraid that they will lose them [the men], or they would lose that security or financial stability." One example of how such fears are exploited is the "emergent sex-for-crack-cocaine barter system"[27] in which addicted women trade their bodies for drugs. This in turn puts these women at risk for a host of other health problems, such as HIV and AIDS, unwanted pregnancy, and poor childbirth outcomes. Still, as one black woman to another, Gwynn clearly feels some connection: "They have, you know, they have jobs, they have children, they have families. I mean, they're just normal."

Ironically, though inmates (male and female) generally report that drug rehabilitation during incarceration is not provided in a manner that maximizes their chances for success—a problem that criminologist Andrew J. Chishom says will ultimately lead to the demise of African Americans—black women still look to the criminal justice system for help.[28] As Irene C. Baird's work with incarcerated women in Pennsylvania reveals, drug-addicted women often speak of "their inability to handle their habit and exercis[e] agency by deliberately putting themselves in situations where they would be apprehended, hoping incarceration would provide them treatment."[29] While study women Tia (unemployed certified forklift operator, age thirty) and Candice (incarcerated, age thirty-three) do not appear to have committed crimes deliberately to become imprisoned and receive drug treatment and counseling, they do find that incarceration serves as a refuge from an addictive life and as an opportunity for personal growth:

> Tia: I gotta be here. I guess this was a blessing from God, because even in my weakest states of mind, I was still strong. I stayed, and drug addiction just whooped that part of me out that I was afraid to let out in the beginning. See, now I can stand strong and firm, and I'm clean. I can stand strong and firm, because I believe what I believe in, and I know who I am. I've accepted my faults, I've accepted my weaknesses, and I'm trying to turn my weaknesses into strengths, to go with the strengths I already have.
>
> Candice: And since we're on the drug situation, I'm gonna tell you something. There is really nothing that is productive that's gonna come out of drugs. Anything that you do concerning drugs, it's like we learned in stress management, if you do what you always did, you're gonna get what you always got. You can't expect to do the same things and get different results. If you continue in the roll, if you continue on the roll that you're on, you're gonna be led to the same, the same thing. You have to change people, places, and things. You have to want the wantingness and the willingness to change. You know? You have to have that. And that's what I've learned. You understand?

The fight to overcome drug addiction and to recover economically from the havoc that addiction wreaks is a fairly common theme among the incarcerated black women with whom I spoke during the course of this research. These women were intent on helping me understand the seductiveness of illicit drugs, how health and personal finances are undermined by that seduction, and how being incarcerated (usually for abusing or selling drugs or for closely associating with those who do) can be both a godsend and a curse for the addict. During the time I spent interviewing at one correctional facility, I found these women particularly drawn to black women visitors who had some tangible experience with drug abuse. In one instance, the facility invited a black woman physician to offer a motivational speech as part of a daylong informational program for the women inmates. She was an extremely inspirational speaker who talked to the inmates about their ability to turn their lives around. Most importantly, she explained that even though she had a medical degree and had not herself struggled with drug addiction, she most certainly understood the disease indirectly through members of her own family, having raised a niece and a nephew as a result of her sibling's drug problems. The doctor also suggested that she was no better than they were, that she very likely was raised in the same kind of black family as they had been, but that she had been blessed not to have fallen to the lure of drugs. The inmates' frequent and rousing applause for this woman was reflective of how strongly they relate to those who openly articulate drug addiction and its consequences as a significant part of black women's struggle for economic and physical well-being.

The Struggle to Hold Black Families Together

Throughout my interview with Brittney (clinical social worker, age thirty-five), she put a good deal of emphasis on the struggle of black women as members of a family—being spouses and daughters and sisters and mothers. And she also emphasized the need to work through all of the murky water around how black women somehow emasculate black men and make it impossible for them to play the roles that fathers should. She felt that there needed to be healing around those issues. So a lot of the struggle had to do with finding a way to excel as black women without damaging the psyche and self-esteem of black men in the process. She also said something to the effect that the type of black family one comes from obviously varies somewhat from person to person, but she believes that fundamentally we all defer to "the black family-value system." Brittney also said that she is distressed by the fact that so many people fail to reach back to the positives of what they learned in being raised by both biological and extended kin, and fictive kin even. She says we fail to draw upon the strength of that training for the training of our children today.

These notes sketched immediately following my interview with Brittney provide indications of a complex web of family issues facing black women today. As was true of their African and African-American foremothers, black

women play pivotal roles individually and collectively as keepers and watch-
ers of black family members as they navigate the complexities of family life
and life in general. Brittney's sentiments and those of other study women
constitute another articulation of black women's struggle that emerges from
this research, that being the struggle to hold black families together.

Numerous scholars have identified the last four decades as a time of significant change in the structure and stability of African-American families,
and they focus heavily on the association of economic issues with low incidence of marriage, high incidence of single-headed households, and highly
disproportionate poverty for women and children.[30] As discussed earlier,
because the black woman generally earns a substantial portion (if not all) of
the black family's income, she sits squarely at the center of the struggle for
the family's economic and physical well-being. But there are also other ter-
rains of family-related struggle that were raised by study women.

In addition to the struggle of raising physically healthy black children
under stable economic conditions, for example, black community blood
mothers and othermothers[31] desire that their children live lives free of the
suffering they see around them every day. Tabitha (emergency-room physician, age forty) and her husband both have secure jobs that pay well, so meeting the basic daily needs of her family is not an exigent problem. Her biggest
challenge, she says, is much like any other working mother: she struggles to
balance her work life with her responsibilities to her husband and her three
sons. Raising her boys to be strong independent thinkers—intellectually and
spiritually—is clearly a priority, and to this end she meticulously researches
for the best schools and churches for her children to attend.

For Sabrina (single mother and community-college administrative worker,
age forty-something), successfully raising her daughter meant helping her to
avoid the difficulties that often accompany unwanted or premature pregnancy, and at a minimum to complete her high school education:

> I'm trying to help my daughter understand things. She's twenty-three, and you try
> to steer 'em up the right way, but they don't see what you see, you know? You've
> already struggled. You're trying to make something easy for them. I mean, it's really
> hard to be a single parent. I mean, but I'm proud of myself. I mean, I look at it like
> this. She has no children. I mean, a lot of people wish they could sit back and really
> say these things. And graduating, she graduated from high school; I mean, I feel
> good behind that. And she has no kids. I mean, I feel good. And if somebody asks
> me what did I do, I just told them, I said, look, she took part of it, and I gave part
> of it. And if she really wanted to go out here and have some kids, I mean, look at
> her friends. She's got a bunch of friends that got some children. And I'm very much
> proud of that, yeah.

Her colleague and friend Megan (education administrative assistant, age
forty-two) also expressed how proud she was of Sabrina's accomplishments

with her daughter and how much Sabrina's efforts reminded her of how much her own tenacious mother valued education for her children and for herself:

> I look back at my mom raising her children by herself, and coming where she came from, where she didn't even have a high school diploma, and she went back to school, she worked two jobs, plus went to school and got her GED. Then she came here, she graduated from here with an AA, and went to Morgan State.

Unfortunately, despite meeting most of her goals as a mother, Sabrina says that she feels estranged from her daughter, who does not fully appreciate the sacrifices that her mother and countless other black women knowingly and unknowingly have made for her, who has not yet found her independence, and who insists on "running the streets" with her friends rather than actively pursuing a secure future for herself. Laura (hairstylist and entrepreneur, age thirty-eight) describes a parenting process much like Sabrina's:

> I tried so many different things to get [my daughter] to that point [high school completion]. I just wanted her to be a success. It's like she just wanted to choose to go the wrong way, no matter how many positive values I instilled in her. So it was a struggle, you know?

Both mothers hope that they have at least laid a foundation for their daughters that will help them live strong in the long run.

Desiree (corrections attorney, age fifty-seven) similarly worked tirelessly to raise a daughter who would not get sidetracked. As an attorney with the state corrections administration, Desiree knows all too well how drugs, crime, and the men who peddle them can divert young black women from fulfilling the destinies their families have in mind for them. She says that actively and consistently focusing on building up a black daughter's self-esteem is essential:

> When [my daughter, now age twenty-eight] was coming along, I didn't . . . I didn't say this is right or this is wrong. She knew what was right and what was wrong. But I said, if you care about yourself, you won't get pregnant. If you care about yourself, you won't have unprotected sex. I never gave her a curfew to come in. But she came in at a reasonable time; then we went with it. I spent my time building her self-esteem.

Desiree was particularly determined to teach her daughter how to be independent by modeling that independence herself: "[The] biggest thing that I struggled with in raising a daughter was to strike the balance between depending upon some man to take care of her and being a bitch." The "bitch" that she harbored within herself helped to deflect the notion that she and other black women could not survive on their own. She now sings high praises of her daughter, who is now an avid world traveler and who followed in her mother's footsteps by recently completing law school.

Terry (senior drug policy analyst, about whom you will hear much more in this chapter) is a shining example of traditional black othermothering and of informal adoption in the black community. At age thirty-nine, she is raising her younger drug-addicted sister's five children—ages seven, eight, nine, fourteen, and sixteen—and they all share a home with her mother. At the time of our interview together, Terry's sister had once again fallen back into addiction, part of a pattern that at each turn increases Terry's commitment to provide a stable home environment for her niece and nephews. This commitment has also deterred Terry from marrying and having children of her own. Terry gave no indication that she regrets the commitment she has made to mother these young relatives, and she is often frustrated by other black women who complain about their responsibilities under much less stressful conditions:

> I have been able to achieve my goals regarding education and all, and that has been a sacrifice. . . . Some other women [bemoan their situations], where they may be raising one child, and it's like, you're saying you have so many problems; [try to] raise five, and then you can talk.

According to sociologist Robert Hill, informal adoption is "the process by which dependent children are informally reared by adults who are not their natural or formally adoptive parents,"[32] and it historically has been a cultural resource upon which the black community relies, particularly in times of parental crisis. The prevalence of such kin care cannot be known; estimates place it currently at about 13 percent of black children.[33] What we do know is that women—grandmothers, churchwomen, or other fictive-kin women—become the primary caregivers.[34] Given the rise in single-family households and the epidemic of cocaine, crack, and heroine in recent decades, drug problems and incarceration among single black mothers are among the usual circumstances. That the practice of informal adoption among African Americans has survived for so long speaks to the numerous positive benefits it brings, namely the provision of caring and secure homes for children in need and fostering a sense of belonging to and continuity within a kinship network. There are some who are concerned, however, that adoptions of this sort may negatively impact black families by helping to create or sustain a cycle of dependency for the birth mother and her children; others claim that the heavy stigma attached to formal adoption in the black community may prevent a needy child from being placed permanently in the best home possible. The disproportionate representation of black children placed in institutionalized care clearly indicates that the need for informal adoption is greater than the black community's capacity to offer it. Still, the cultural imperative to absorb the black community's needy children within itself is strong nonetheless, as demonstrated by Terry's devotion to her kin.

The struggle to fulfill one's responsibility as a black othermother sometimes extends to adult children of the kinship group. In Judy's case (nurse,
age forty-nine), the black women she wants so badly to guide to full maturity
are her thirty-three-year-old and thirty-six-year-old nieces. These two women
were raised by her sister, "a gun-totin', shootin' niggers, sellin' drugs gangster," in a Baltimore area federal housing project where they learned that
there was little more to aspire to than the gangster life. Now mothers themselves and living in a similar fashion, the nieces are unaware of or indifferent
about the potential repercussions their lifestyle can have for the next generation. Judy's primary concern is for her great-nieces and great-nephews:

> I would have to go down into that environment, because that's where [my sister]
> was. I ran into my first realization of . . . when they talked about black kids who
> only knew Negro dialect, [that would apply to] two of my nieces' children. Had no
> idea. They say "nuffin" [meaning "nothing"], so they'd be trying to spell "nuffin."
> And "muvva" [meaning "mother"], and would try to spell "muvva." And wonder
> why they couldn't read, you know? Got my first experience of it in my own family.
> In my own family.

Judy indicated that the physical location in which these family members
live is the same as or is in close proximity to the area in which she was raised.
But the "ghetto" she once knew as a child is nothing like the inner-city
neighborhood her nieces and their children must endure:

> I didn't know I lived in the ghetto until the white people told me. Didn't know. I was
> like, ghetto what? Where's that at? Didn't know it was my neighborhood. 'Cause we
> didn't; that was not our perception of where we lived at all.

To help counter the poor self-concept she sees played out by her nieces on a
daily basis, Judy frequently makes suggestions to them about how to rise
above their condition, drawing on her own success in personal development.
Rarely, however, do the women follow.

Of all the women I interviewed for this study, Molly (incarcerated, age
eighteen) is undoubtedly the saddest case. She suffers tremendous obstacles
in her struggle to pull her young family together—two boys (one infant and
one "older") and one child on the way. Her children are scattered about—one
with his father, the other with her grandmother, and the one she was carrying
is likely to end up in someone else's custody. Molly is a functionally illiterate
tenth-grade dropout, and a detainee at a woman's correctional facility. Her
father and mother died when she was very young, of AIDS and of a drug
overdose, respectively. She was brought to the correctional facility after being
indicted for allegedly assaulting another black woman with a gun. The victim
was a young woman pregnant by Molly's boyfriend, who had recently been
shot along with Molly's aunt. (The aunt died just prior to our interview.) I
tried very hard to sort it all out with her:

Molly: A girl lied on me, because we was . . . my aunt got shot; the boy that got shot with my aunt, I was going with him, and a girl found out, and now that [girl] be pregnant by him. And she got mad, and she called the police. I don't know, somebody had to do something to her. They must have had this, I don't know, must have made it like it was me or something. I don't know. The girl just went nuts and came in the house with the police.

She said that you were the one who did the shooting or something?

Molly: No, she said I was the one that beat her with a gun.

Beat her with a gun?

Molly: Uh-huh.

And it wasn't you?

Molly: No, it wasn't me.

And you think she's doing that out of jealousy, 'cause she's pregnant now, or are you?

Molly: I am.

You think she's maybe upset about that, that that's what prompted her to do it? Why were you here [at the facility] before?

Molly: For stabbing my boyfriend up.

For stabbing him? What'd you stab him for?

Molly: 'Cause he was tryin' to kill me.

While it is certainly rare to have so many issues converging upon one individual black mother—teenage pregnancy, illiteracy, violence, and incarceration—some mothers do face more than one serious life difficulty at a time, making their struggle to hold their families together particularly acute.

Another example of family-related struggle among black women is the "man issue." The health of the relationship between mothers and fathers is extremely vital. Brittney's concern is that fathers may be performing below the level expected, in part because of the tension that exists between them and the women who "emasculate" them—that is, who provide income and authority in ways "traditionally" bestowed to fathers—and she may be right. In Annette's case (registered nurse and academic researcher, age thirty-two), her husband feels emasculated from having just recently put himself through college for a baccalaureate degree while his sister's education was apparently financed by his family, scholarships, or a combination of both. She says that "it's a struggle in our household" to have him still suffering from low self-esteem issues related to this, and perhaps from Annette's currently making "significantly more money" than he does.

According to Robert Staples and Leanor Boulin Johnson, authors of *Black Families at the Crossroads: Challenges and Prospects,*

Because Black females have been more economically independent, many developed attitudes of freedom and equality unknown to most nineteenth-century and even many twentieth-century females—attitudes that predated the modern women's liberation movement. The consequences of this independence for Black marriages are of concern. While African men consider economically independent women an asset, it is unclear whether such women are considered in the same light among Afro-Americans. Messages received from the media strongly indicate that Black males are threatened by the accomplishments of Black women.[35]

While it is unclear in what historical period the authors are placing "African men" and just how "modern" women's sense of "freedom and equality" truly is among them, most black women would agree with them about black men generally not embracing gender egalitarianism in their relationships. But as Brittney indicates, black women are somehow expected to remedy this problem, a formidable challenge indeed (if they should choose to take it on), given the internalization and societal reinforcement of hegemonic masculinity among black men. This is not to say, however, that black women cannot or should not participate in the process to heal wounds between black men and black women; the benefits for the next generation of black mothers, fathers, and marital partners could be significant. But a great deal of "shifting" on the part of women to accommodate the needs of black male egos would be necessary in that process, something known to create psychological stress for the women.[36]

Some of the study women also spoke of the difficulty in holding their families together in the aftermath of their husbands' infidelity, another "man issue" in the struggle. While infidelity is certainly not exclusive to men, a University of Chicago study reports that black men are more likely than black women to admit to having an extramarital affair (a proportion that may be as high as 50 percent).[37] Leah (age fifty-three) was the most revealing on this issue. She became pregnant, gave birth to a son, and began raising him on her own when she was about twenty-three years old. Later on, she married her current husband, who after a few years began having children with another woman, unbeknownst to her. Once she learned of the affair and the children, she realized that the little baby girl she saw on a few occasions at her mother-in-law's house was actually one of those two children. Her biggest struggle has been with forgiveness, with the understanding that her husband had been an adulterer. For the sake of the family, she chose to stay in the marriage; she said that God had shown her that it would not have been best to leave her husband. That decision angered Leah's mother (actually the great-aunt who raised her), who refused to have anything to do with Leah for a solid year because she had not sought a divorce. A prayer group to which she was introduced by a friend helped her endure the pain of that adultery. In retrospect, Leah says she takes great pride in her now thirty-year-old ex-marine son whom she managed to continue raising and supporting throughout her marital trauma.

Adrienne would likely have a negative reaction to Leah's decision to reconcile with her husband and would say that such a reaction represents the majority of black women. She says that black women's personal and collective strength makes them much less tolerant of men's infidelity and other marital shortcomings than white women are, and that the centrality of motherhood to black women's gender-ethnic identity leads them to prioritize the well-being of the their children over their desire to remain in a marriage:

> A lot of white people, their mothers and fathers stay together to keep the family name. You know what I'm saying? They [say], I'm still with my [spouse] 'cause of the children. You hear a lot of white people [say that]. When I used to work on my job, that's all they ever talked: I'll be glad when my child turn eighteen, so I can leave him! Whereas, though, a black family is just different. If you're not happy, y'all ain't gonna stay together. Where you got some women that's afraid of a man, and they stay with him. And you got some women, they're, hey, I ain't got to put up with this. I'm workin' every day, and I ain't got to do that. See you later. Bye. And it's on to the next thing. . . . You gotta be strong out there.

Some women and men blame the pervasiveness of male indiscretion on black women's refusal to walk away from the marriage when the indiscretion is revealed, but experts say that genuine remorse by husbands and genuine forgiveness by wives can help save a marriage, stabilize family life, and even make both the marriage and the family better than they were before.[38]

Stories of resentful "emasculated" black men and of the pain inflicted by adultery are troubling to black women seeking black male partners and the chance to form families of their own. Dating and marriage markets for African Americans have become nearly infamous. Black women all around the country say that there is both a quantity and a quality factor working against their chances for meeting "good black men," let alone developing and sustaining a romantic relationship. The quantity factor is the imbalanced sex ratios that exist virtually everywhere. Nationally, there are about ninety black men for every one hundred black women, and in the Greater Baltimore Area, those aged twenty-five to forty-four find that there are about eighty-one black men for every one hundred black women.[39] Neither of these statistics takes into account black men who are gay, who are confirmed bachelors, who are involved in interracial relationships, or who are institutionalized, so the prospects for heterosexual black women are not particularly strong if they are seeking black men. Add to these the additional qualities that black women generally desire, such as stable employment, spirituality, and fidelity, and the prospects grow even dimmer. Further, research indicates that while "most unmarried persons desire to marry . . . black males are the least desirous of marriage" among gender-ethnic groups, in part because they find no significant improvement in their sex lives or in their same-sex peer relationships by doing so.[40]

For Pamela (research-firm technical writer, age thirty), who has desires to marry someday, her lack of success in the dating and marriage market has become a constant theme. Confiding in other thirty-something single black females about how best to improve her chances, she says, is equally frustrating. Their strategies for securing a black husband, "or even just a man," are of the sort she would never employ:

> I do not enjoy being single. I want a husband; I love babies; I want my own. That's what I want. But I just feel that hunting for him, there's something wrong about that. And what happens is, the younger women, they don't have a connection to anything other than how can I get this man. And there's more. There's more there than finding the man, or hunting, you know, and doing whatever you can, and all the dirty games. I understand why men are fed up with women. There's all these dirty games, and she's trying to help me, and I was thinking, I . . . there's no way in the world I'm gonna take this advice, you know, and . . . it's a lot of sex, sexual, and, you know, that's the only way I can get him is through seducing, and this . . . I'm not into that. I'm an old-fashioned gal. I want someone to introduce me to a nice fellow, we date for a while, I get my roses, he gets his foot rubs, it all works out, and, and you develop a relationship and a life together. I don't want to hunt him down, because I don't want to go to a club and hunt him down and, I got him 'cause I was the drunkest but could still walk, or whatever. And that's what's happening. I don't get that. I don't understand that. And I don't believe in showing all my stuff . . . all of it. So, the younger women, poop on them.

I did not detect a sense of desperation among the single study women about marriage, though as Pamela indicates, most knew other black women who were somewhat consumed by the matter. What I did experience on several occasions, however—generally among the incarcerated women—were interviewees commenting on the fact that I was wearing a wedding ring, after gazing at it for bit. They would say something like, "Oh, wow, you're married! That is so nice that you have someone. And he must really love you." In those moments, I realized how much I take for granted the fact that I "have a man" (for sixteen and a half years now, ten of them in marriage) and what little experience I have had navigating the increasingly turbulent waters of the black marriage pool.

In the passage regarding Brittney that leads this section, I note her concern that family-related struggles among black women in part reflect the degeneration of at least some aspects of the black family-value system. Tabitha expresses similar concerns, particularly in regard to the welfare of black sons and ultimately of black men, and she rejects that this problem is unique to the less advantaged social classes:

> It's on all levels. It's not just lower class; it's on all levels. Something's falling away. We're not teaching them something. I mean, I look at my own son, and it's like, okay, sit back and let's think, what am I leaving out? You know, you have to consciously give them everything . . . that's going to make them strong fathers or strong husbands or whatever. I think as black women, we are pretty supportive of each

other. We support each other, but then what happens when it comes down to our
relationships and keeping a strong family. Something . . . something's wrong there.
And it's probably a circle. Whatever's missing, it's affecting everything. 'Cause
black men, for sure, had to get the way they are because we helped them.

Where I earlier stated that the disproportionate representation of black
children placed in institutionalized care clearly indicates that the need for
informal adoption is greater than the black community's capacity to offer it,
women like Brittney and Tabitha might argue that this issue is about lacking
both the capacity and the sense of cultural obligation for women to do so.
The failure to carry on such cultural traditions has serious consequences for
holding black families together; therefore, teaching black women the significance of these traditions and how to actuate their legacy as cultural leaders is
a necessary step toward stabilizing black family life. Of course, the regeneration of black women's power in this area also requires eliminating socio-
structural impediments to their economic and physical capacity to exact it.

The Struggle to Not "Forget Where You Come From"

Two other ways that black women's struggle is articulated by the study
women focus on concerns about "forgetting where you come from." The
pressure to demonstrate to other black women, black people in general, and
at times even to themselves that they have not "forgotten," or to defend themselves against accusations that they have "forgotten," is enormous. In most
interpretations, forgetting where you come from means the black woman is
"acting white" in some way.

Authentic black women do not act white—they do not fling their hair, they
know how to talk among the homegirls, they do not hesitate to discipline their
children, they never leave the house with their hair unkempt, they never talk
negatively about any black person in front of white people, and so on. Furthermore, real black women have been so immersed in black culture that
avoiding such things comes naturally. It is not so surprising, then, that Hannah (community-college training program manager, age thirty-three), raised
in the suburbs, educated at a predominantly white college, and married to a
white man, says that she has had "an internal struggle with being black
enough" and with determining whether she has had a sufficient "black experience." Though her history is much different from Hannah's, Paula (teacher,
age twenty-seven) has also wrestled with being fully accepted as authentically black:

> I think partly because of just how I've grown up, and how I've been raised, at some
> times I get a lot of making fun of how I talk. Or I get the, oh, but you're light. You
> don't understand. I kind of made a joke out of it, but I always used to say, I didn't
> become black until ninth grade. Before then, I could . . . I mean, I'm the greatest at

Trivial Pursuit; I could tell you any Def Leppard song, and any other song, any other group you want to know, and I'm humming to commercials and singing the real words, and everybody's like, how do you know that song? But then I had to think, and I'm like, who else can I refer to? . . . And then, you know, when I came to Baltimore at first, I'm originally from New York, I started at Morgan [State University], and my first thought was, wow, there are so many other people who look like me. I had not seen other people who were as light as me. I've seen, you know, you have light skin, or brown, but, but not this tone . . . you know, light. And I . . . so that was even a relief to me, to see, you know, that it was okay, and I could still be black. I didn't have to justify or explain.

Neither do authentic black women "look white," whether they can help it or not. Virtually every study woman had experienced or witnessed the cultural phenomenon known as *colorism* operating among African-American women. Colorism is defined as intraracial tests of authenticity based on skin color and other "phenotypic features" known to be "highly correlated with skin color,"[41] and it is one of the most blatant forms of internalized racism and sexism. Rooted in colonialism, in the racialization of human and social life during slavery, and in the institutionalization of racial stratification in later decades, colorism is a practice that assigns high or low status to black women who carry certain physical markers.[42] Exacerbating this practice is evidence that in the United States (and in other places around the world), women of lighter hues, with thinner noses and lips, straighter hair, and the like, are more likely to enjoy greater socioeconomic success than those on the other end of the continuum; that is, they are more likely to have higher educational and occupational attainment, better incomes, and better physical health.[43] Colorism is perhaps most oppressive when inflicted on black women by members of their own family, particularly by mothers or grandmothers:[44]

Georgia (incarcerated, age thirty-one): [My mother] said, you was a white ugly baby. She said she put that black grease [on my hair]—you know, that black grease. When I came out of her, she said, "That ain't my child. Get that baby out of here. That is not my baby." She said, "Call security, 'cause that is not my baby." They said, "Miss Jones, that's your baby." She said, "That ain't my baby."
Did she react that way, did she react that way to your other brothers and sisters?
Georgia: No! Just me! They said, "Now, look at that baby real good." She [told me], "I turned you all upside down, and just like my friend do, everybody." She said, "I turned you upside down and around and only thing that made me almost sure that you was my child is you had a head like your father." So I said, "Why do you say that?" And she said, "Well, you was the ugliest baby. You was white, and you had no hair." She said, "I used to take you outside and put you in a walker and put some grease on your head and on your face, on your skin, and sit you outside in a walker," and you know how our mothers, when they sit, they all sit out on the steps, and she said when her and her girlfriends set down the street and she put me in the walker with a long rope on it and put me up on down the other side of the

street, not across the street, but away from her. And I said, "Why did you do that; why did you do that, Ma?" And she said, "'Cause you was a ugly child. I didn't . . . I didn't want you near me," she said. "You was ugly." She said, "I set you in the sun so you would get a little . . . some color to you."
So how did you respond to that, growing up?
Georgia: I cry every time she say that.

In contrast to Georgia's mother's reaction to her looks, Maris's grandmother tried (granted, in a questionable way) to protect her from what she knew would be fierce colorism hurled at her during childhood. Maris (incarcerated, age forty-four) explains that her grandmother would preach regularly to her about her not being any better (i.e., better looking) than anyone else simply because she was light skinned and had long hair. But despite Maris's attempt to internalize these messages, she said it was very difficult not to feel oppressed by the glaring looks by other black girls and by their assuming that Maris "thought she was cute." She also says these glares and assumptions have continued throughout her life, even into the facility where she is incarcerated.

Tests of authentic black womanhood become particularly disturbing when they tend to "dumb down" black culture by suggesting that the ability to speak in fluent English or to successfully complete a high school or college program (even in predominantly black environments) is a code of whiteness: "They always used to say, 'Oh, you talk proper, you act white,' growing up, 'cause I'm in school with white people" (Alexis, thirty-five-year-old teacher). Georgia says that her fellow dorm mates at the women's correctional facility frequently call her a "white girl" because of her efforts to encourage interracial and interethnic cooperation among the inmates, a label by which she is particularly offended given how it haunted her so badly during her childhood. Other study women gave similar examples of how, often, when they felt they were doing the right thing by increasing their human and social capital—for instance, learning to speak well, extending their scope of friendships, and performing well at school—their status as authentic black women was challenged:

> Shelley (database administrator, age twenty-three): And I think that's where people get it confused. The first thing that they [say is], "She thinks she's better than us; you think you're hot." "You're too uppity." I'm like, wait a minute; just because I like to treat myself a certain way, or I won't degrade myself in [a certain] way, or I set certain standards for myself does not mean that I'm not blacker than anyone else.

The "Black-Culture" Vein

In the women's articulation of the "forgotten" struggle, emphasis is generally placed either on "coming from" black culture or on "coming from" the lower classes, but because people often conflate black culture and lower-class status (i.e., they assume that all African Americans are born into poor families), it is not always clear which of the two kinds of concerns is operating at a given time. Nonetheless, these two veins of the "forgotten" struggle appear to be somewhat distinct. Each of the examples provided just previously, for example, fall under what I call the "black-culture vein" of the "forgotten" struggle.

The other concerns that are raised within this vein focus on the significance of staying in touch with family and supporting the needs of the black community. Numerous scholars contend that the most enduring feature of African and African-American culture is the strong ties among biological and extended kin, and black women have been central players in the maintenance of these kin relations. Frequent and meaningful contact among black family members is highly encouraged, as is witnessed by the popularity of annual family reunions, Sunday after-church dinners, and random family cookouts. To neglect engaging in these and other family rituals or to deny that one belongs to one's family group would be seen, then, as taboo, something that white people often take to doing. Thus, as the study women explain, some black women are accused of forgetting where they come from when they avoid contact with their family, their "people." In Kitty's words (hairstylist, age twenty-eight), black women should not forget "the closeness that their families have and what their grandparents had to go through in order to bring their children on what they did, as far as morals, values, and togetherness."

There may be a number of reasons why a black woman chooses to avoid interacting with her family members, but choosing to do so because she finds their ways annoyingly "black" is considered quite distasteful. Sarah (information-technology software engineer, age thirty-two) acknowledges that she sometimes falls into patterns of avoidance when encountering certain of her family members:

> I know sometimes, because I'm from Charleston, I always said my family was ghetto. Oh lord, you know, you can take them out the country, but you can't take the country out of them.

Here, Sarah suggests both a class ("ghetto") and a cultural ("Southern") basis for her reaction, and thus she also conveys—owing in part to her professional status and residence "up North"—that she sees herself as detached from what these family members represent. As she continues, however, she demonstrates how her resistance to contact with family can be only temporary; in the end, her identity is nourished by black family fellowship:

> But actually, when they come here, I almost, I can almost like say, whew. I can almost breathe. I can put my scarf on, walk down the street; I can do that when

they're here. And you know, act the way I wanna act, you know, talk country. . . .
When they come here, it's like, it's a relief, and I actually enjoy myself.

It is likely that for Sarah the next encounter, even with these same family
members, will be a repeat of this cycle, hence the nature of her "forgotten"
struggle.

Kitty also notes how significant owning family members is for remember-
ing where a black woman comes from. Black family togetherness, she
explains, allows for the intergenerational transfer of the morals and values
that serve as the foundation for black culture. Family togetherness also provides black women access to the affirming tales of their foremothers' difficulties in raising their children and supporting themselves. A black woman
who "perceives herself to be much higher [in her] standards than the normal
black woman" (i.e., supposes herself to be more "white"), and thereby distances herself from certain family members, threatens her ability to remain
connected to her roots. Her struggle, then, is to remain grounded in spite of
herself.

Much like the taboo of disowning family members, several ideas within
the "forgotten" struggle theme speak to the taboo of black women having
appeared to have abandoned the black community. For some women, the
appearance of abandonment comes from their having physically moved away
from the poor neighborhoods in which they were raised to working-class
neighborhoods. In describing her relocation experience, Terry first clarifies
that her family was middle class, though they had lived for years in a relatively poor neighborhood area, and because of this, "where she comes from"
is often misunderstood:

> We were middle class, you know? (But) everything in Park Heights is not standing
> on the corner with them all. Well, we were middle class, and even then, even then I
> didn't go to Mondawmin [a popular local shopping mall] at all, thinking about it. I
> don't know whether it's just a personal preference; there are some places in the city
> that I would never go, and I didn't go there when I lived in Park Heights. I think
> I've only been to Lexington Market a couple times.

Despite her departure from some of the cultural practices of that neighborhood, Terry still formed a strong bond with the community. Today, Terry
wrestles regularly with the decision she made to relocate her extended family
to another neighborhood. She never says this new neighborhood is a better
one (though by most socioeconomic indicators it clearly is), but rather that it
better serves her need to help raise her sister's children and to provide housing for her mother. So as not to feel estranged from these roots or be accused
of disowning them (she asks herself, "May I have taken [my kin] away from
their blackness?"), Terry maintains her membership with the church in which
she was raised and patronizes several of the establishments that have served

her family over the years. In doing so, she exposes her nieces and nephews to aspects of urban black culture that are not exhibited in the predominantly white neighborhood where they all now live:

> [It is likely] due to my preference that I don't go to these places. They're going through [a phase] where they want to buy the big pants, and because of the schools they went to [in our current neighborhood], the oldest one always wore khakis, and when he went into high school, he declares his independence because he could wear jeans, and that's the first time he could wear jeans, you know, and now he wants to wear the baggy things.

Struggling to balance remembrances of where a black woman comes from with steering young family members away from certain aspects of the culture can be extremely difficult, but Terry knows that rebuilding old and establishing new connections to the old neighborhood also helps teach the children about people's tendency to generalize the black urban experience as dysfunctional. Though amused by her young niece's attempts to be socially conscious about race—"she wants to be a minister, talks about she wants to be like Martin Luther King, to overcome racism not only between whites and blacks, but also the racism between blacks"—Terry frequently has to reel her young niece back from declaring black folk inappropriate:

> If we see kids out at night, [she'll say], why are these kids out this time of night? That's how they act in the city. The people in the city don't know any better.

Terry usually responds by reminding her niece that she and the rest of the family are also "from the city" and that how black people act varies. But she finds that argument a hard sell since what the niece observes appears fairly homogenous.

The "Social Mobility" Vein

The other thread of the "forgotten" theme stems from the fact that, historically, African-American women (and men) have found that along with the achievement of higher social status comes the obligation to "give back to the community." Giving back is believed to be demonstrative of not forgetting where you come from. As has been pointed out in previous chapters of this book, the obligation of black women to dedicate themselves to the uplift of other blacks has been prevalent in the African-American community practically since its inception. Bill E. Lawson, in his chapter "Uplifting the Race: Middle-Class Blacks and the Truly Disadvantaged," notes that the "races as families" analogy promoted by the race school of thought and founded upon the philosophies of W. E. B. DuBois and Booker T. Washington has been an extremely palatable political device in the black community and that it is from within this framework that racial obligations arise. Individuals are held "morally culpable" if they do not live up to this expectation. While black women of all social classes are called to give to their communities in various ways, this is particularly true for the more successful black women whose community-related activities, or lack thereof, may at times be highly scrutinized.[45]

Over a meal we shared together one evening, Charlene illustrated beautifully one form that she believes the struggle to give back to the community can take, and the boldness, selflessness, and wisdom that is required of more advantaged black women to accomplish it:

> To me, I think that [giving back] looks like when you can be able to talk about [the struggle] and take it back and share with kids. I read this book called *Pot Liquor*, by Millicent Thompson Hunter, and . . . and she was talking about . . . pot liquor is that stuff that's at the bottom of a pot of collard greens. And it's like, it has all the nutrients and all the juice, and it's when you can share that juice and those details with your children, and they can share that with their children, and you can share it with other children, you can give them strength to help build them. And when you can go in the community and not be afraid regardless of where you may be living now . . . I'm not afraid to go in East Baltimore, I'm not afraid to go in West Baltimore, in the hood, in the ghetto, and go back and work with those same people where I came from, and be able to look them in the eyes and say, hey, I had some real issues. Sure, I may talk proper now, I may have a house, a two-car garage with two nice cars sitting in the garage—I have a educated husband, children going to private school—but I can go back and still be a part, a intricate part of their lives, and not be afraid, not . . . not afraid to share. That, to me, is what it looks like.

Charlene and other study women say that the act of giving back presupposes an acknowledgment that one's own social mobility is owed to the sacrifices of black women who have gone before her, women who modeled the woman power that is now required of her. Mariah (public school guidance counselor, age fifty-six) is especially concerned that black women not lose sight of those earlier sacrifices—some made long ago and others in the more recent past. And like Charlene, she uses a food analogy to make her case, telling of black women's roles as purveyors of "soul food":

> Well, for me, it is always remembering that I got here on the shoulders of somebody else. And don't forget that. It's my responsibility to put . . . to put somebody on my shoulders, too, so they can get somewhere. I think we forget that, some of us, when we get to where we want to be; we have arrived, quote, unquote, and then we look back, and we don't want to help anybody do anything, and we just got here. Now, how'd you get there? I think it's important for us to remember that we can't do this by ourselves. It's a struggle that we have to do. And however we can add to the pot, then go ahead and add it. You may think a dash of salt is not gonna make a difference

in the soup, but if you leave the salt out, it's gonna make a big difference. . . . Just tell the story.

Naomi (age twenty-six), a Harvard-educated schoolteacher who from what I gathered has enjoyed a fairly steady middle-class existence, is no less compelled than those whose social mobility has been more dramatic to participate in the uplift of African-American people. Naomi says that giving back to the community is a "passion" and not merely a middle-class obligation; passion, she says, drives the community activism of all black women. Naomi's struggle to give back is complicated by the fact that she is generally viewed as practicing quite the opposite by other African-American women, and thus much of her struggle involves justifying her actions. Naomi is a teacher at an elite, predominantly white private girls' school in Baltimore, just feet away from a predominantly black public school. She explains that in the private-school environment, African-American girls—most of whom do not come from privileged backgrounds—have little opportunity to be educated by black teachers, and she feels that through evoking her power as a black woman in that space, she can be an important asset for the personal development of these girls. What is more, Naomi also believes that giving of herself to the white students has the potential indirect effect of improving the climate within which the African-American and white students interact, now and in their future as adults. By helping to give white students a view of black womanhood (and black people in general) that they might not otherwise have, Naomi believes that she is helping to fulfill the humanist vision of black women's activism:

> I chose to do it at [a local elite private school for girls], where, you know, those black kids didn't have any black teachers. I mean, there are only two of us in the upper school. And also I chose that job as a way . . . because I'm alert to Oprah, to educate all the white kids who have never had a black teacher, and who had never, or they may have had a black teacher. . . . So yeah, I do; I struggle with that, and you know, even now, sometimes I say maybe I should try to get a job in the [predominantly black] Baltimore City public schools. I think they're really struggling.

The Struggle to Endure Negative Public Regard

As was pointed out earlier in chapter 3, today's African-American women feel strongly that despite improved socioeconomic advancement and improved visibility in certain professions, the public generally views them as problematic. They understand that the public's views continue to be highly influenced by popular images that distort black women's sexuality; demonize their maternal character; and devalue their physical, intellectual, and spiritual attributes. They also recognize that the public's buying into this imagery leads to black womanhood's being cast as something to control. In the end, black women feel they have received just a pinch of what they rightly deserve. In collectively cultivating strong gender-ethnic centrality among them, black women have managed to ward off the fatality of this oppression. Famed poet Nikki Giovanni has said,

> We, black women, are the single group in the West intact, and anybody can see we're pretty shaky. We are, however (all praises), the only group that derives its identity from itself. I think it's been rather unconscious but we measure ourselves by ourselves, and I think that's a practice we can ill afford to lose. For whatever combination of events that made us turn inward, we did. And we are watching the world trying to tear us apart. I don't think it'll happen.[46]

Still, their having to endure this oppression and resist internalizing the stigma attached to black womanhood is worrisome. Thus, what constitutes this last articulation of struggle is their constant awareness that black women think far more of themselves than others do.

I met up with Annette (age thirty-two) as she was settling into her new office from which she was managing an intervention program to assist people with diabetes 2. She had cleared her calendar to spend the entire morning with me exchanging about her favorite topic: African-American women. She was particularly anxious to speak her mind on this particular theme of black women's struggle: the public's lack of positive regard.

> When I think of struggle, I think clearly that black women have been the last to get anything, in terms of rights in this country. And I think that that's the gist of our struggle. And so we're still, in my mind, thirty to fifty years behind in getting our piece of the pie in terms of what's rightfully ours. And any place you go, it's like we're second-class citizens. And I think just recognizing that that is our foundation in this country, that's the struggle. And then, where we came from and we're still coming from there, from my perspective, it's like, we're not too far from slaves. I mean, it's just that there's a question there about African-American women and do people think we're good, or whatever. And I think that people still have the same mentality about African Americans in general, but specifically about African-American women, because we were the workhorses, from the bedroom to the fields, and I think that people still have that overall sentiment.

The suffering that comes from having been socially deprived as black women on the basis of their gender-ethnicity is exacerbated further by the strenuous work involved in trying to combat the racist and sexist ideologies that feed that deprivation. Many of the women are highly cognizant of the fact that in order to begin changing people's minds about them, they must diligently project the best of what they have to offer. Doing so is terribly burdensome and can have debilitating consequences for those committed to taking what Rochelle (physician, age fifty-three) calls "the higher position" on this matter:

Every single day, from the people who clean the floor all the way up to people that I deal with, you have to figure [it] out, as an African-American woman, in a positive fashion, because my whole thing is about how do I best behave to reflect a positive image of us as a people. And I don't like it sometimes. In fact I get very tired of it, having to be representative, because it's a big burden; every day, you're having to, to be the example. But you don't have a choice. Now, there are others who feel different, but I feel that because we are just beginning to make some inroads into the larger society, and into our own lives, we don't have a choice but to be examples. And that's tough. And I don't always make it, but that's my objective.

Despite the women's basic contention that no black woman, whatever her class status, can escape the indignation of the public's negative regard for her, many accede to the fact that the women of the middle classes fare better than those from the lower classes. Most of their comments focus on black women's participation in the paid labor force. Some of the blue-collar study women, and others who empathize with them, see their group as highly vulnerable to struggles with human resource administrations and requests for upgrades, promotions, and new job responsibilities, struggles that are fundamentally about the lack of respect for them as intellectuals. Still, as Tanya (health care contract specialist, age thirty-five) says, the professional black women with whom she works also have difficulty "getting their just rewards" and "being accepted" by others. Recall, for example, that Dorraine's efforts to improve her occupational and income status were met by what she viewed as a biased recruitment process that rendered her ineligible for the job to which she applied.[47] Opportunities to participate as full partners with men and white women in their professions are frequently blocked because black women are perceived as undeserving of or unprepared for full partnership. At times when such opportunities are extended, those whom the black woman must supervise or share power with give her an unnecessarily difficult time.

Mariah, like so many other seasoned working black mothers, tried to prepare her daughter (now age thirty) to confront the negative public regard that she was bound to confront in the workplace. After completing college, her daughter's first job was serving as an intern, where she performed well and was eventually offered a regular paid position. It was then that she was reminded of her mother's warnings:

She said to me, "Mom, I know what you mean by racism and all," because I don't think she ever really truly experienced it full force until she went there. She was a scholar-intern, and so when she came out of college, she got the job, and she rotated around, and then finally they offered her a position. And she said it was really hard because of, like, especially elderly white women that had been there for years, maybe come out of high school and went there and worked up; they really resented her. She said, "They really don't like me because I'm a higher position and I make more money, but that's because I went to school and did that." So she had a hard time with that at first. She said, "Now I know what you mean by, it's not dead, it's just in another form." . . . She said, "You know, I really try real hard to be friends with them, and for them to like me, but they really don't, because I'm just a young black woman coming in there trying to give orders."

Mariah also explained that her daughter sought to extend her social circle to women of all racial/ethnic backgrounds at that workplace, something she is naturally inclined to do. But with there being so few African-American women there and with many of the other women unwilling to embrace her, life on the job for her could be rather lonesome.

The women of this study seem a bit reluctant to implicate African-American men in feeding the misogyny toward black women, at work or in any other context. For the most part, they have great sympathy and even empathy for the struggles of African-American men in this country, and this tempers somewhat their condemnation of them. These are their cultural partners—their fathers, husbands, sons, and friends—and they have witnessed firsthand how little the world thinks of them as well. A number of the women, like Madison (government program analyst, age forty-six), even firmly believe that black men suffer a good deal more than black women do. Here, she shows her support for a black male colleague who has struggled for recognition on the job:

> I just think it has to go all the way back to slavery; the black man is a strong man, 'cause he survived the Middle Passage. He survived them during slavery, the master and everything. It's just, black men had it rough. They really did. I see how . . . a friend that just called me, he's real smart. He's real smart. He should be in charge; he's a contractor; he should be in charge. But he's not in charge. He's like down the totem pole. And they have all these Caucasians in charge, and I'm just like, we know he should be in charge. He's very intelligent and very articulate. My friend who— she's a contractor too—we talk about it all the time, but there's nothing too much we can do about it. We just know it.

But there are a few specific concerns. Contemporary black women certainly decry black men's participation in and promotion of music videos and other popular media that portray black women as hypersexual, conniving vixens. (The "hoochie mama," they say, is a black man's invention.) But they are equally if not more frustrated with black women's willingness to lend their bodies for these images, with how they internalize their oppression and conspire against their own well-being. The women are also frustrated by how they are castigated by black men for being strong black women, when their strength is necessary in order to take care of things that black men neglect. "I have a real disdain about taking care of men, period," says Rose (assistant high school principal), a fifty-something-year-old divorcee, who, like other women, finds that taking care of them often means regularly giving them money, food, and shelter and covering the men's share of their children's needs. But, again, many of the women feel that black women are enabling black men to neglect their responsibilities by continuing to allow them to drain their finances and their energy.

Concerns about black men's contributions to the public's poor regard for black women are closely aligned with black women's struggle to hold black families together, where we also observe black women burdened by black men's resistance to genuine gender egalitarianism, by their sexual indiscretions, and by their general resentfulness for having been "emasculated" by black women's historical power. And, because black women clearly view black men as their cultural partners, men's displays of poor regard for them may be the most difficult for black women to endure. But the women are also highly cognizant of the fact that black men, like others in this society, have been programmed to subjugate the black woman.

THE JOY AND PAIN OF
BLACK WOMEN'S STRUGGLE

In *Yearning: Race, Gender, and Cultural Politics*, bell hooks (and Cornel West, with whom she is in dialogue) reminds us that there is "a joy in struggle."[48] What some might view as an oxymoron is to many black women an affirming proclamation: there is joy in having survived and not succumbed to struggle thus far. Personally and collectively embracing a gender-ethnic identity wrapped around the notion of struggle helps in undermining a pervasive and polarizing black stepsisterhood.

What is gained through black women's struggle does not come without a cost, however. Melissa Harris-Lacewell, author of "No Place to Rest: African American Political Attitudes and the Myth of Black Women's Strength," is particularly concerned that, ironically, black women's lived experience in the struggle helps to reinforce the "continued transmission of [the] cultural myth" of the "strong black woman" that loops back and constrains the black woman.[49] Testimonies to black women's strength are pervasive and are of the sort that Alice (corrections inventory control specialist, age thirty-eight) gives about the black mother:

> A woman is a powerful vehicle. When the woman is ill in the family, the whole family structure stops. She's the one that loves and nurtures, and when she's not together, you have dissension through the whole family. And as much as they say, when the head's sick, the body's sick, the man is placed at the head [by God and society], but who is actually the backbone and the structure of the family? The woman.

Harris-Lacewell argues that the powerful symbol of the strong black woman lies in direct contrast to the dominant culture's master narrative, replete with a language of historical myth stereotyping black women in such negative caricatures as Mammy, Sapphire, Jezebel, Matriarch, Welfare Queen, Baby Mama, and Chicken Head.[50] Attributed primarily to the practices, beliefs, and vestiges of antebellum slavery, these mythical images have helped to rationalize the sexual and physical abuse of enslaved black women by white men, and have then "provided the roots for contemporary, externally imposed, controlling images"[51] of African-American women:

> [The strong black woman] is a deeply empowering symbol of endurance and hope. Her unassailable spirit is uplifting. Her courage in the face of seemingly insurmountable adversity emboldens black men and women when facing their own life challenges. But in her perfection the strong black woman is also harmful. Her titanic strength does violence to the spirits of black women when it becomes an imperative for their own daily lives. When seeking help means showing unacceptable weakness, actual black women, unlike their mythical counterpart, face the ravages of depression, anxiety, and loneliness.[52]

Thus, Harris-Lacewell and others warn that the revisionist pro–black woman agenda can itself produce distortions of black women's truths. Yes, the black woman is strong and possesses enormous personal and cultural power, but neither she nor the sisterhood to which she belongs is invincible.

NOTES

1. With the exception of the last, these definitions of "struggle" were provided by OneLook Dictionary Search (www.onelook.com).

2. Patricia Hill Collins, *Black Feminist Thought: Knowledge, Consciousness, and the Politics of Empowerment* (New York: Routledge, 1990), 22.

3. Joe R. Feagin and Hernan Vera, *Liberation Sociology* (Boulder, CO: Westview Press, 2001), 1.

4. See chapter 1, pp. 1–25.

5. Michele Lamont, *The Dignity of Working Men: Morality and the Boundaries of Race, Class, and Immigration* (New York: Russell Sage Foundation, 2000), 3.

6. Stephen Cornell and Douglas Hartmann, *Ethnicity and Race: Making Identities in a Changing World* (Thousand Oaks, CA: Pine Forge Press, 1997), 92.

7. Charisse Jones and Kumea Shorter-Gooden, *Shifting: The Double Lives of Black Women in America* (New York: HarperCollins, 2003), 83.

8. Collins, *Black Feminist Thought: Knowledge, Consciousness, and the Politics of Empowerment*.

9. Ibid., 83.

10. Marilyn M. White, "We Are Family!: Kinship and Solidarity in the Black Community," in *Expressively Black: The Cultural Basis of Ethnic Identity*, eds. Geneva Gay and Willie L. Baber (New York: Praeger, 1987), 25.

11. Jesse McKinnon, "The Black Population in the United States: March 2002," in

Current Population Reports, Series P20-541 (Washington, DC: U.S. Census Bureau, 2003), 3, 6, 7.

12. Dalton Conley, *Being Black, Living in the Red: Race, Wealth, and Social Policy in America* (Berkeley: University of California Press, 1999); Richard Miniter, "Why Is America's Black Middle Class Strangely Fragile?" *American Enterprise*, November–December 1998; Melvin L. Oliver and Thomas M. Shapiro, *Black Wealth/White Wealth: A New Perspective on Racial Inequality* (New York: Routledge, 1995). One recent report now also cites the high and rising rate of job loss among black workers in long-standing jobs as a new labor market vulnerability suffered by middle-class black women and men. John Schmitt, "Recent Job Loss Hits the African-American Middle Class Hard" (Washington, DC: Center for Economic and Policy Research, 2004).

13. Oliver and Shapiro, *Black Wealth/White Wealth: A New Perspective on Racial Inequality*, 37.

14. Robert L. Harris Jr., "The Rise of the Black Middle Class," *The World and I* 14, no. 2 (1999): 40; Robert Staples and Leanor Boulin Johnson, *Black Families at the Crossroads: Challenges and Prospects* (San Francisco: Jossey-Bass Publishers, 1993).

15. Lorraine Cole, "National Black Women's Health Project," *Ebony*, October 2002, www.findarticles.com/p/articles/mi_m1077/is_12_57/ai_97997705 (accessed October 10, 2004). The National Black Women's Health Project was recently renamed the Black Women's Health Imperative.

16. For example, see Thomas A. LaVeist, Verna M. Keith, and Mary Lou Guiterrez, "Black/White Differences in Prenatal Care Utilization: An Assessment of Predisposing and Enabling Factors," *Health Services Research* 30, no. 1 (1995): 43–58; and Johan P. Mackenbach, Karien Stronks, and Anton E. Kunst, "The Contribution of Medical Care to Inequalities in Health: Differences between Socio-Economic Groups in Decline of Mortality from Conditions Amenable to Medical Intervention," *Social Science and Medicine* 29, no. 3 (1989): 369–76.

17. James C. Cramer and Katrina Bell McDonald, "Kin Support and Family Stress: Two Sides of Early Childbearing and Support Networks," *Human Organization* 55, no. 2 (1996): 160–69.

18. See Katrina Bell McDonald, "Black Activist Mothering: A Historical Intersection of Race, Gender, and Class," *Gender and Society* 11, no. 6 (1997): 773–95; Katrina Bell McDonald, "The Psychosocial Dimension of Black Maternal Health: An Intersection of Race, Gender, and Class," in *African Americans and the Public Agenda: The Paradoxes of Public Policy*, ed. Cedric Herring, 68–84 (Thousand Oaks, CA: Sage Publications, 1997); and Diane Rowley and Heather Tosteson, eds., "Racial Differences in Preterm Delivery: Developing a New Research Paradigm," *American Journal of Preventive Medicine* 9, no. 6 (November–December 1993): supplement.

19. For example, see Richard Rothstein, "Lessons: Linking Infant Mortality to Schooling and Stress," *New York Times*, February 6, 2002.

20. Office of Women's Health Centers for Disease Control and Prevention, "Leading Causes of Death by Age Group, Black Females—United States, 2001" (Atlanta, GA: Centers for Disease Control and Prevention, 2001), www.cdc.gov/od/spotlight/nwhw/lcod/01black.pdf (accessed October 24, 2004); National Cancer Institute, "Breast: U.S. Racial/Ethnic Cancer Patterns" (Bethesda, MD: National Cancer Institute, 2004), www.cancer.gv/statistics/cancertype/breast-racial-ethnic (accessed October 24, 2004); BlackWomens-

Health, *Breast Cancer* (BlackWomensHealth.com, 2004), www.blackwomenshealth.com/breast_cancer.htm (accessed October 24, 2004).

21. Lula A. Beatty, "Changing Their Minds: Drug Abuse and Addiction in Black Women," in *In and Out of Our Right Minds: The Mental Health of African American Women*, eds. Diane R. Brown and Verna M. Keith, 59–79 (New York: Columbia University Press, 2003), 59.

22. Ibid.

23. Tanya Telfair Sharpe, "Sex-for-Crack-Cocaine Exchange, Poor Black Women, and Pregnancy," *Qualitative Health Research* 11, no. 5 (2001): 612–30.

24. Wanda Thomas Bernard, "Including Black Women in Health and Social Policy Development: Winning over Addictions; Empowering Black Mothers with Addictions to Overcome Triple Jeopardy" (Halifax, Nova Scotia, Canada: Maritime Centre of Excellence for Women's Health, 2001); Carol A. Roberts, "Drug Use among Inner-City African American Women: The Process of Managing Loss," *Qualitative Health Research* 9, no. 5 (1999): 620–38.

25. June Moore et al., "Maryland Drug Scan" (College Park, MD: Center for Substance Abuse Research [CESAR], 2001).

26. Robert A. Johnson and Cindy Larison, "Prevalence of Substance Use among Racial and Ethnic Subgroups in the U.S." (Rockville, MD: SAMHSA, Office of Applied Studies, U.S. Department of Health and Human Services, 1998); Cora Lee Wetherington and Adele B. Roman, eds., "Drug Addiction Research and the Health of Women" (Rockville, MD: National Institute on Drug Abuse, 1998).

27. Sharpe, "Sex-for-Crack-Cocaine Exchange, Poor Black Women, and Pregnancy."

28. Kimberly Davis, "The Shocking Plight of Black Women Prisoners," *Ebony*, June 2000.

29. Irene C. Baird, "The Examined Life: A Study of Identity Formation, Agency, Self-Expression among Imprisoned Women" (paper presented at the Adult Education Research Conference [AERC], Northern Illinois University, DeKalb, Illinois, 1999).

30. Andrew Billingsley, *Climbing Jacob's Ladder: The Enduring Legacy of African-American Families* (New York: Simon & Schuster, 1992); Andrew J. Cherlin, "Marriage and Marital Dissolution among Black Americans," *Journal of Comparative Family Studies* 29, no. 1 (1998): 147–58; Robert Hill, "Indications of Recent Demographic Changes among Blacks: 1940 to 1970," *Journal of Social Biology* 18, no. 4 (1971): 341–58; Robert Staples, "Sociocultural Factors in Black Family Transformation: Toward Redefinition of Family Functions," in *The Black Family: Essays and Studies*, 6th ed., edited by Robert Staples (Belmont, CA: Wadsworth Publishing Company, 1998), 18–23; Ronald L. Taylor, ed., *Minority Families in the United States: A Comparative Perspective*, 3rd ed. (Upper Saddle River, NJ: Prentice Hall, 2002).

31. See chapter 1, note 73, for definition of "othermother."

32. Robert Hill, *Informal Adoption among Black Families* (Washington, DC: National Urban League, 1997), 9.

33. Charmaine Yoest, "Points of Light," *Children Today*, September–October 1990.

34. Hill, *Informal Adoption among Black Families*; Carol B. Stack, *All Our Kin: Strategies for Survival in the Black Community* (New York: Basic Books, 1974); Robert Joseph Taylor, Linda M. Chatters, and Aaron Celious, "Extended Family Households among Black Americans," *Perspectives* 9, no. 1 (2003): 133–51; Yoest, "Points of Light."

35. Staples and Johnson, *Black Families at the Crossroads: Challenges and Prospects*, 62.

36. See chapter 3, note 6.

37. Roberta Wilson, "Stolen Moments," *Essence*, June 1997. This same report also shows that blacks are more likely to acknowledge having an affair than whites, 24 percent and 15 percent, respectively.

38. *Ebony*, "Infidelity: Why Men Cheat," November 1998.

39. U.S. Census Bureau, "Sex by Age (Black or African American Alone)," ed. Census Summary File 1 (SF 1) 100-Percent Data (Washington, DC: U.S. Census Bureau, 2000); Raymond A. Winbush, "Beloved in Our Lives: Necessary Healing between African Men and Women" (paper presented at the Annual National Conference on the Black Family in America, Louisville, KY, 2002).

40. Scott J. South, "Racial and Ethnic Differences in the Desire to Marry," *Journal of Marriage and the Family* 55 (1993): 357–70. The gender-ethnic groups studied were white, African American, and Hispanic men and women.

41. Maxine S. Thompson and Verna M. Keith, "The Blacker the Berry: Gender, Skin Tone, Self-Esteem, and Self-Efficacy," *Gender and Society* 15, no. 3 (2001): 337.

42. Margaret L. Hunter, "Colorstruck: Skin Color Stratification in the Lives of African American Women," *Sociological Inquiry* 68, no. 4 (1998): 517–35.

43. Verna M. Keith and Cedric Herring, "Skin Tone and Stratification in the Black Community," *American Sociological Review* 49 (1991): 620–31; Cedric Herring, Verna M. Keith, and Hayward Derrick Horton, eds., *Skin Deep: How Race and Complexion Matter in the Color-Blind Era* (Chicago: University of Illinois Press, 2004).

44. Twinet Parmer et al., "Physical Attractiveness as a Process of Internalized Oppression and Multigenerational Transmission in African American Families," *The Family Journal: Counseling and Therapy for Couples and Families* 12, no. 3 (2004): 230–42.

45. Bill Lawson, ed., *The Underclass Question* (Philadelphia: Temple University Press, 1992), 94.

46. Rebecca Carroll, *I Know What the Red Clay Looks Like: The Voice and Vision of Black Women Writers* (New York: Carol Southern Books, 1994), 121. Carroll's chapter on Nikki Giovanni can be found on pages 114–21. In this passage, Giovanni is quoting from her book *Gemini: An Extended Autobiographical Statement on My First Twenty-Five Years of Being a Black Poet* (Indianapolis, IN: Bobbs-Merrill, 1971).

47. Study woman Dorraine was introduced in this chapter on page 98.

48. bell hooks, *Yearning: Race, Gender, and Cultural Politics* (Cambridge, MA: South End Press, 1990), 211.

49. Melissa Harris-Lacewell, "No Place to Rest: African American Political Attitudes and the Myth of Black Women's Strength," *Women & Politics* 23, no. 3 (2001): 3.

50. Also see Anita Jones Thomas, Karen McCurtis Witherspoon, and Suzette L. Speight, "Toward the Development of the Stereotypic Roles for Black Women Scale," *Journal of Black Psychology* 30, no. 3 (2004): 426–42.

51. Evelyn L. Barbee, "Violence and Mental Health," in *In and out of Our Right Minds: The Mental Health of African American Women*, eds. Diane R. Brown and Verna M. Keith (New York: Columbia University Press, 2003), 100.

52. Harris-Lacewell, "No Place to Rest: African American Political Attitudes and the Myth of Black Women's Strength," 24.

Chapter Five

Discord in the Sisterhood: Classed Patterns of Sentiment and Experience

One of the problems for us as Black women is the fact that although we are quite willing to engage in debates on sisterhood at local and global levels, we have failed to have constructive debates between ourselves about our differences and how we can unite through this diversity and the commonality of our experiences. The reality is that often Black sisterhood prevents us from speaking the truth about ourselves.

—Felly Nkweto Simmonds, sociologist and black feminist scholar[1]

Many of us learned how to bond with females who were like us, who shared similar values and experiences. Often these close-knit groups used the power of their intimacy to trash women outside the chosen circle.

—bell hooks, professor of English and black feminist scholar[2]

The large extended black family in which I was raised never referred to siblings as half or stepsisters or stepbrothers. I never heard anyone say that it was forbidden to use such terms explicitly, but I knew that if I did I would very likely receive a sharp "eyeballin'" from my mother, grandmother, or aunt. My grandfather, the Reverend William Offey "W. O." Bell, fathered at least twenty children, and my mother was the youngest (Gladys the "baby-waby"). Yet the blending together of the various branches of this huge family tree seemed to most of us virtually seamless; the offspring of these children simply operated in concert as "the Bell clan."

It was not until I had children of my own—one biological and two that were not—that I found myself using the term "stepchildren," against all of my othermothering instincts. The tension that surrounded the other two children's becoming part of my household was largely about their biological mother's need to make clear distinctions between the two of us in raising the children, and I wanted very much to honor her request. (I witnessed the same thing occurring with a number of my girlfriends who entered into blended families.) What is clearer now in retrospect, however, is that the quality of the relationships I had then with these children, and even now, was mainly due to conflicts of interest and perspective between their mother and me on this issue.

The gender-ethnic family composed of contemporary African-American women is likewise susceptible to relationship stress. Many believe that the gender-ethnic bonds that have historically sustained relationships among black women—the high currency of black sisterhood and the strong collective "struggle" identity among them—may be waning. It is fairly common to hear even the most outspoken of black womanist ideologues lament that this diversity is leading the sisterhood slowly into something more akin to black stepsisterhood and less akin to our cultural legacy.[3]

Evidence from this study confirms that such sentiments are reasonably founded. Conceptions and experiences of black womanhood are quite diverse, and there is discordant sentiment and experience around a number of important sistering issues, made all the more potent by the cultural-historical expectation that black women exhibit high levels of unity and cooperation. The most extreme cases of discord are experienced as the actual or perceived discrimination by one black woman against another, "an unfortunate phenomenon which violates the very foundation of female relationships" and "genuine sisterhood."[4] While sistering across lines of personal and social difference has been the cornerstone of black women's activism historically, the desire and ability to sustain that legacy and to relieve the strain of discord within the twenty-first-century black woman collective is—and always has been—a major concern. In reflecting on the formalized practice of black sisterhood in past decades, for example, historian Deborah Gray White reminds us,

> Had African-American women been perfectly united they would possibly have better fought their adversaries. However, black women were never a monolithic group. Race and gender united them as often as class, religion, sexuality, and ideology pitted them again each other.[5]

In the analysis that follows, I revisit the themes explored in chapters 3 and 4 to discuss specific instances of discord among the study women. In revisiting these themes, I determine where, as a whole, contemporary African-American women are largely unsettled (ambivalent) and where there are meaningful differences among subgroups of women in their tendency to support or reject certain ideas related to their gender-ethnic identity and consciousness.

Generational differences for any gender-ethnic group are generally anticipated and detected because, as research scientist Tom W. Smith points out, "[each new generation's] collective socialization creates a point of view distinctive from that of earlier generations."[6] Intergenerational phenomena are frequently cited among analysts of African America. Lois Benjamin concludes, as do many other scholars, that young blacks born about the time of the civil rights movement and brought up primarily among whites are less likely than those of earlier generations to have strong attachments to other African Americans and are more likely to lack a sociopolitical orientation toward black communalism and group survival.[7] Legal scholar Patricia J. Williams has said that, unlike older generations, her generation of black women (those currently in their thirties) has shunned their generally optimistic disposition toward pro–civil rights agendas for a more "radical individualism." And Professor Ella L. J. Edmondson Bell observes generational differences among black women in their workplace expectations. When asked about issues that black women encounter, especially on their road to middle management, Bell reports.

> We have a story in the book from a black woman executive who told us that her performance had to be sterling because she was in the spotlight. Her performance had to be beyond what anyone would ever expect, in order for it to even be accepted as O.K. We're seeing generational differences in this. Women in their forties and above, who've been in the corporate arena, they kind of know to expect this. The women who are younger believe that a lot of this has been dismantled. . . . When this reality hits them, they don't know what to do with it because they haven't encountered it.[8]

And in addressing the concerns of the "sistas of the post-Civil Rights, post-feminist, post soul, hip-hop generation," professors Astrid Henry (*Not My Mother's Sister*) and Gwendolyn D. Pough (*Check It While I Wreck It*) find both continuity and disjuncture between black women of the first two waves of feminism and the present wave.[9] Most notably, this new generation seeks to fashion a new set of womanist identities and practices steeped in racial complexity and in the contemporary language and rhythms of "wreck," rap, and hip-hop. It is also true, however, that despite these observations, many scholars find that "the youth of today are not necessarily more distinctive than in the past, nor are they especially distinctive among age groups."[10] Thus, recent reports on intergenerational attitudes and beliefs among blacks are a highly mixed bag.[11]

   In this study, it is unclear whether generational differences are mixed or uniform, given that such differences are virtually undetectable. They are evident only in two of the subject areas, but it should be no surprise that in the few areas where age does play a role, the youngest women stand out from the oldest.[12] One place in which generational differences among the study women arise is in regard to the oppressed-minority orientation.[13] Younger black women are more likely to believe that the struggle for black liberation in

America should be closely related to the struggle of other oppressed groups, whereas those aged fifty-five and older are less likely to believe that other people experience injustice and indignities similar to those of black women. Thus, older black women—particularly the eldest—appear more resistant to embracing other gender-ethnic groups in the struggle for freedom, whereas the "multicultural/multiethnic generation" of black women is much more open. The second observation of generational discord is that praise for the accomplishments of renowned black women is particularly heard from among older study women (aged fifty-five and older). Feelings of detachment from these accomplished women are more likely to be expressed by the youngest of the study women.

You may recall that the sites from which the study women were recruited were chosen in an effort to derive a socioeconomically diverse research sample. They were also chosen because of the differential patterns of social interaction that were likely to be exhibited among black women in those settings (see chapter 1, pp. 19–24). Though site-related discord was observed in several areas of gender-ethnic identity and consciousness, it is generally unclear what one is to interpret from these findings. Most of this discord is reduced to class-related differences; that is, the correlation between the women's social class status and research recruitment context site was generally quite high. I have speculated, nonetheless, about the four instances that do not appear to be simply reducible to class differences.

Relatively more tolerance for marital exogamy is exhibited among those women who were recruited from the staff of a predominantly white, elite university. This suggests that social environments within which black women interact interracially for a significant amount of time each day may be meaningful for shaping their ideas about black womanhood. In this particular case, black women who spend much of their time in white elite educational environments experience the severe black sex-ratio imbalance that exists, and this may play a role in how they feel about marrying interracially. They are also less admonishing of black women who are generally viewed as having not taken advantage of the opportunities paved for them by other black women. African-American women interacting in predominantly white, elite settings may more readily recognize the difficulties that all black women face, having witnessed firsthand the struggles they have had entering and remaining enrolled in college and in advancing occupationally as staff and faculty members, and they are therefore more empathetic toward those who are arrested in their social development.

It is interesting that though the study women recruited from black hair salons are significantly from the lower classes, they are more likely than women from other recruitment contexts to feel that black women should work within the system to improve their collective condition. I venture to guess that the black hair salon and the intimate, gender-ethnic-specific work that is performed there for and by African-American women every day may heighten and foster a sense of empowerment that encourages them to prove themselves through "legitimate" channels. This environment may also foster a strong sense of belonging among them that effectively distances them from women whom they feel cannot fully appreciate black sisterhood, which could explain why their feelings of detachment from white women is relatively stronger.

Pursuant to my agenda in this book, however, what is most important about the discord that is observed among these contemporary African-American women is that about half of it is driven by differences in their social class status. While some inconsistencies in the details exist, I am able to trace crudely coherent classed patterns of gender-ethnic identity and consciousnesses from this data. Class-based differences in conceptions and experiences of black womanhood are undoubtedly real to black women's lives, individually and collectively. This is particularly true between the most and the least privileged black women, those classes of women anchored at opposite ends of the deepening socioeconomic schism. This said, however, it is also true that the overall degree of separation between these classed patterns is *generally small*—moderate at best—and encourages a far more balanced outlook on contemporary sisterhood than the popular public debate on black "class warfare" would suggest. It is easy to lose sight of this once one ventures into the details of the class discord that is observed.

Two features of the survey and the interview are particularly relevant to the assessment of discord reported here. First, the questionnaire ends with asking the study women to review five vignettes and to choose the one that most reflects frequent thoughts they have about African-American women today (see table 4). These were five hypothetical quotes pieced together from popular literature and from research data collected for my previous studies. They were included as a means to help better differentiate the women on their primary concerns. As such, they also provide a means for helping to determine which issues tend to provoke ambivalence or division among the women. With the same purpose in mind, I incorporated a hypothetical scenario at the closing of the research interview:

> Suppose you had a day off where you could do anything you wanted and you could take along any black woman you would like. Let's begin by filling this room with one of every type of black woman you have ever known or heard of. To help you in choosing who you would like to take along, let's just get rid of all the black women you know you don't ever want to spend your time with. Describe who they would be.

The women's responses to both of these exercises are interwoven with other data revisited in this chapter.

Despite the integration of this new material, my report of intragroup discord is less rich with the study women's own voices than I would prefer. There are several reasons for this. First, some of the interview passages that are relevant here have already been presented in earlier parts of the book, and so their inclusion here would be somewhat redundant. Second, elementary quantitative analysis proved most useful in identifying where differences between subgroups exist on most subjects, and as a result a relatively greater portion of this discussion references details from the questionnaire. Finally, my assertion that black stepsisterhood is largely subverted by strong gender-ethnic identity and consciousness stems in large part from the fact that the study women generally gravitated more readily in the interviews to their shared experiences and sentiments than to those they believe divide them, even when they were intentionally pressed by the closing hypothetical scenario to focus exclusively on the issue of estrangement.

GENDER-ETHNIC CENTRALITY AND SISTERLY ATTACHMENTS

The single most conclusive fact to emerge from this research is that contemporary African-American women of all ages and social backgrounds are committed to embracing a strong and affirming gender-ethnic identity. This is particularly true, however, for black women from the middle classes; every one of the middle-class study women professes pride in being a black woman, and nearly as many say that their blackness and womanhood are important to their identities. It stands to reason that higher social class status in many ways affords middle-class black women more direct experience with and benefits from black women's accomplishments and, therefore, also the pride that accompanies them. Carol's professional status as a library materials specialist (age forty-nine) has assisted her in fulfilling her family role as the gatherer and preserver of the family genealogy. The process of researching documents of various kinds, in addition to interviewing family members individually and at family gatherings, has heightened Carol's appreciation for her womanist roots. It is a project that a female family member encouraged her to think about when she was just a teenager, a woman who Carol says shares her "Southern" taste for "goin' for the highest levels of achievement" and taking pride in that success.

While women of the lower classes also take great pride in black womanhood, their public image has been far more disparaged than that of the middle classes, and their success and contributions less celebrated. The weight of that disparagement can be experienced in any number of ways. For example, several of the women who as children did not ever realize that they were poor said that they "discovered" poverty when the world *told* them they were poor. Even worse, they learned that the world took the interchangeability of "poor" and "ignorant" quite seriously when referring to those materially lacking. Revelations such as these appear to undermine the strong gender-ethnic identity that some women of the lower classes might otherwise sustain, particularly among the most marginalized. Strong expressions of pride in black womanhood are most hindered among the incarcerated women. During one of my many visits to the women's detention center, Edith, a thirty-five-year-old recovering drug addict, became quite agitated while reflecting on suggestions that she believes are made regularly by the media (i.e., by television programming, the incarcerated women's primary source of information) about poor, addicted black women—suggestions of child abuse:

> I've never beat my kids. Never! I can't relate . . . relate to that. They're [those women] using their addiction as a excuse. For some people it might be, but I could never see myself doing that. They say they're weak. I'm not that weak. I know I'm hurtin' them by using [drugs], but I mean physically, I could never hurt my kids. Never.

Distorted representations of black womanhood among the marginalized make Edith terribly uneasy in her gender-ethnic skin. They not only alert her to the fact that these representations further malign her in society by extension, but they also encourage her to be condemning of black women toward whom she would normally be compassionate. This in some way helps to explain why, while Edith says that being African American is important to her identity, she is ambivalent about whether being a black *woman*—a more marginalized one, at that—is of any positive import in her life except among those closest to her. Thus, like most of the other women suffering her plight, Edith is much less convinced than her middle-class counterparts that society views black women as an asset.

Strong attachments to other African-American women are something also widely shared among the study women, and these attachments are fueled by a sense of belonging and "feeling close" to other "race" women with whom they share a common history and gender-ethnic experience, that is, by a feeling of black sisterhood. Yet, recall that I was a bit puzzled by why there was so much ambivalence conveyed when asked specifically about the idea of linked fate among them. Given the significance placed on sistering in many aspects of their lives, it was curious that so few women showed enthusiasm for defining these relations as shared "destinies." I have speculated that the notion of "destiny" in this context may have stumped at least some of the women. But it may also be that their lack of enthusiasm reflects their genuine hesitance to sound too deterministic about their collective outcome. If we assume the latter, this suggests that "linked fate" connotes a very different kind of social connectedness than sisterly "attachment" does. I found support for this suggestion by comparing responses to the "destiny" item on the questionnaire with those regarding strong attachment with other black women. Women who agree on both of these items amount to only about a third of the sample, again lower than what might be expected. Endorsement of the idea of shared destiny, and the association between the idea of a shared destiny and feelings of strong intragroup attachment, are somewhat stronger for women of the middle classes. Still, on the whole, these findings are consistent with Michael C. Dawson's observation: among African Americans, the notion of "linked fate varies very slightly with socioeconomic variables."[14]

As previously shown, the social relationships that are formed among African-American women are given special status and are viewed as distinct from those held with people from other gender-ethnic categories. A good proportion of the women say that their gender-ethnicity also plays a significant role in determining with whom *else* they will form social relationships. But differences by class status do exist on this issue: middle-class black women tend to claim that their gender-ethnicity factors—either positively or negatively—into the relationships they form with others, while women of the lower classes are less likely to claim that this is so, particularly those most socially marginalized among them. It could very well be that this latter group of women experiences fewer problems in forming social relationships with others because the range of gender-ethnic persons with whom they regularly interact is relatively narrow. Opportunities for meeting and bonding with nonblack men and women may be sorely limited. On the other hand, by virtue of the wider range of individuals with whom they regularly interact, middle-class black women may be highly cognizant of the fact that their gender-ethnic status can be a major attraction or repulsion for others. Some may view these other individuals as providing an opportunity for genuine multicultural engagement, while others may see them as a threat in some way.

On this issue of forming intergroup social relationships, race clearly trumps gender. Black women are most likely to form social relationships (i.e., friendships and romantic partnerships) with black men, the group with whom they most closely share a common history. Race also trumps class. While at least two of the study women are married to white men (Carol and Hannah), most shy away from intimacy or even friendship with white men. Tia (thirty years old) says that she once tried dating a white man, but,

> We had all the prejudice issues come up. He was an accountant. And he worked for a accounting firm that was prejudiced. So I was put in the background.

"History," Rochelle says, teaches you better than to put too much trust in white men who lead the world in spreading negative public regard for black women. Unfortunately, her most vivid personal encounter with this problem involved sexual harassment on the job:

> The myth is that African-American women are easy, they're always hot, and that they just want attention from Caucasian men. It's a myth. None of that applies to me. Because of history, I could never feel real comfortable having a close relationship with a Caucasian man.

Black women's feelings of closeness with white women are only slightly stronger than those with white men. The study women find that the two parties have racially divergent standpoints that are most readily revealed through differences in family and work dynamics. Many of the women argue that black women and white women are only superficially similar in their worldviews. Still, the vast majority claim to reject the notion that black women and white women can never be friends, with those from the middle classes generally showing more optimism than those from the lower classes.

Class discord around this issue is less potent than the survey data would suggest. There appears to be some political correctness at play with the questionnaire that is dismissed when the women are allowed more freedom of expression. In chapter 3, Natalie, Ashley, and Brittney—all middle-class women—had very strong, representative opinions about black-white woman estrangement. While the socioeconomic contexts from which they speak are certainly different, at least four study women from the lower classes carry equally strong opinions. At first glance, Nicole (age thirty-something) and Grace (age forty-three), both incarcerated, voice unusually strong optimism when discussing black-white female relationships. In fact, they go so far as to say that relationships with white women can be much more safe and reliable. But they also believe, it seems, that black-white female relationships are predicated largely on white women feeling "intimidated" by black women, and in saying so, they diminish significantly the cogency of their argument. I interviewed Nicole and Grace together at a women's correctional facility where they were being held:

> Nicole: I ain't gonna lie to you; sometimes I feel strongly that I can attach with a white woman better than I can with a black woman. Uh-huh. They lookin' out for my friendship in here. You know what I mean?
> *Now, I want to be clear, though, that when you say the women "in here," you're not making a special case out of the women [incarcerated with you here]. You ran into the same kind of stuff—*
> Grace: Out on the street too.
> Nicole: It's everywhere.
> Grace: It's everywhere.
> *I'd like to know a bit more. Tell me a bit more about the kind of things that have happened, to make you feel the way you do.*
> Grace: It's because you can't trust them. You just can't trust women these days. You know, my mother always told me, watch out for your friends, because they stab you in your back. They take your man, they steals from you. They . . . just little things . . . it's just little tiny things that you got to watch out for your black women. And the white woman, she basically trust you, and you can trust them more. Because of friendship. Because they, I think . . . we intimidate them a lot, too.
> Nicole: Yeah.

Just weeks later, I captured this exchange between Maisha and Glenda, also incarcerated (both age twenty):

Glenda: White women suspicious of black women's close friendships, especially when there are more than two black women. . . . I feel like, yesterday I made a announcement to the group, because I feel like this . . . we're incarcerated; it's thirty women in our dorm. When a Caucasian comes in there, she doesn't have to know anybody; she automatically goes to the other Caucasians, sit down, hi, how you doin', and then so-and-so, they give her a shirt, a pair of pants, toothbrush, whatever she may need, just coming in that dorm. But when a sister comes in the dorm, we usually look at her, and look at her shoes, her hair look a mess, her family must not be sending her no money. Us, we stick together. You know, Maisha, do you need some toothpaste? You want a extra tray? Would you like some of my potato chips? I think it's basically that they're expecting us, well, to be fucked up and so forth and so on.

Maisha: Yeah, to put each other down.

Glenda: To put each other down and to argue with each other, or to talk about each other behind each other's back. So that they can say, well, she not your friend for real. And I left a note yesterday [saying], I don't think it's fair that because we African Americans and we sticking together, that we have to be classified as a gang. When they stick together, what are they? We don't call them the Bloods or the Crips or the Pagans or none of that. We just stick together; we sisters.

Relationships across Class Lines

Positive sentiments about cross-class relationships are expressed by a large majority of the study women. Most say they experience close attachments to both professional and blue-collar women and are quite comfortable interacting personally and socially with either group. And because they believe that this is something most black women enjoy, they are quite certain that the two classes are fully capable of working well together in pursuing black women's interests:

Charlene (job coach, age twenty-seven): I think we all have our own ways of thinking, our own ways of doing things, but overall, I think we share a lot of the same ideas about community, about self-awareness, about love, about empowerment, about family. And the list goes on. Those are the things that mean the most to me; that's why I keep bringing them up. But I think . . . I think we do share a lot of the same views. I mean, it variates, though. It depends on the surroundings; it depends on if we're at work or if we're at school or if we're at church.

Tamara (secretary, age forty-two): There are a few [in my family] who didn't graduate high school, and their incomes may be lower, but their values seem to still be the same.

At age eighty-nine, Christina is the eldest of the study women, and she is a beloved member of the civil rights community of Baltimore. (We have a very special bond: I interviewed her the morning of September 11, 2001.) Though long since retired from teaching, Christina still keeps abreast of the goings-on in the black community. The sentiment she expresses about contemporary class relations among black women is shared by most:

Well, to my mind, I think [we're] beginning to mingle more. [We're] beginning to work together. I think they realize that women are women, and they all have the same ideas and ideals, even if they do not have the same chances. And we just have reach out and embrace the ones that don't have. That's the way I feel. Now, I don't know if that's fanciful thinking or not. But that's the way I feel about it.

From the women's elaborations on their personal experiences with class relations, important differences between the class groups are revealed. Women from the lower classes appear to experience greater attachment and comfort with a wide variety of black women. Amy (age thirty), who is employed as a hairstylist, says that she has no problem mingling in mixed circles or where either group is in the majority, though she admits that she makes a special effort to interact with middle-class women because she has learned that she can "get information" from them that may very well help her achieve their status someday:

If I'm at this level and somebody is [at a higher level], I want to get from you of how you became successful. . . . I'm always asking questions; I want to know. I just want to know, you know what I mean? How you got there, how you living, are you happy? You know, I just want to know. I just want to know. So I guess I have a connection with . . . with that class of people.

Middle-class women, on the other hand, are much more likely to say that they are strongly attached to women of their *own* class and spoke little about feeling comfortable with, admiring, and befriending the lower classes. In fact, while study women of both classes express a number of negative sentiments about class relations among black women, such sentiments are more abundant among the more privileged. Monique (age sixty) says that while she feels "a sense of [attachment] in terms of race and gender, there's definitely a social gap" between her and the women she serves at her job and the women who attend the church her husband pastors:

I mean, the women in the GED program are recovering drug addicts, and . . . and even some of the women in our church are—what do you say—their lives are unstable. They get evicted; they run out of money; most of them are single. It's just . . . the bridge is too . . . I mean, the gap is too wide.

Judy (age forty-nine) says she recognizes this wide "social gap" in speaking with groups of adolescent black girls as well:

If you're talking to a ghetto group, their whole perceptions of issues are very different than if you're talking to a roomful of—see, I'm getting ready to show some of my bias—a roomful of black folks who grew up out in Columbia [a suburb of Baltimore], [with their parents making] making fifty thousand a year each, or better. Very different issues, very different issues. Well, not different issues; different perceptions, okay? 'Cause I think a lot of the issues are the same. A lot of the issues are the same. But the way they perceive them are very different. And if you ask them if they have the same issues, they'd tell you.

Middle-class black women who offer negative sentiments about class relations say that the discomfort they feel in interacting with women from the lower classes has primarily to do with the crudeness, lack of good values, and general misbehaving they find typical of that class. They tend to characterize these women as "loud," "boisterous," "raunchy," and the like, and to say that feelings of estrangement between the two groups are fueled by sharp differences in such behavior exhibited in public and private. (It should be noted, however, that several of the lower-class women feel likewise about any woman who would act in such a way.) "Ghetto fabulous" is a popular term that middle-class black women—as well as other African Americans and, lately, folks in general—use to describe these and other estranging behaviors among the less privileged.[15] To be ghetto fabulous can mean any number of things. For Jessica, a thirty-eight-year-old special education teacher, the most dangerous form of ghetto-fabulous attitude is when black women "embrace the worst parts of themselves and tout them as being fabulous." For others, being ghetto fabulous means being frivolous and irrational in the way one spends what little money one has. It means her poor attempt at mimicking a life of luxury through the conspicuous consumption of cheap, tacky clothing and accessories. This topic sparked a brief though lively debate among seven of the study women. These women—Hattie, Rhonda, Nancy, Angie, Cynthia, Latrice, and Sarah—have organized a local book club, and I was invited as a special guest to one of their meetings. Because it was typical for the women to speak all at one time throughout the gathering, it is virtually impossible to determine whose voice is whose from the interview transcript; the important thing, though, is that they were all in agreement:

> I think [ghetto fabulous is] more the outward appearance—that's what I think—and some of the mannerisms, you know, like the real long fingernails [group laughter], the big high hair, the ghetto twist, and the, the—[group laughter]. All the girls on the block that don't have no job [group laughter], somehow you still are able to keep it [up]. I don't know if it's your man paying for it, but you still are able to dress to the nines.

Natalie (age eighteen) says that, unfortunately, she also sees such behavior among undergraduate women at her college who sometimes trade purchasing their textbooks for ghetto fabulousness. And Dolores (age thirty-five) worries that such behavior threatens the public regard of all black women, wherever it is exhibited: "I hope they don't mess it up for everybody."

Another concern shared among middle-class women is what they perceive as "disturbing" problems surrounding relationships between women of the lower classes and African-American men. While there are numerous remarks from the study women at large about the need to bolster certain black women's self-esteem in order to protect them from emotional overdependence on men, these women seem to say that the problem is much more prevalent among the lower classes:

Field notes on Leah (human resources administrator, age fifty-three):

> Interestingly, it was at the time when I asked her about women who were less privileged—I remember saying, for instance, women who may be on public assistance, or something like that; I was trying to get her to focus on women who were less fortunate—that Leah commented that she was very concerned that so many of these women tend to put so much emphasis on men, on men being the center of their lives. She said that these women can't see that to have a man is to complement her, not to have him be the center of her life. She believes that black men can be useful; they can be great sex partners, she said. It's okay if you have them around for sex, but you don't marry them on the basis of completing yourself. You don't have children by them as a way of keeping them in your life or completing yourself. And she seemed to think that that was a persistent problem. She wasn't quite sure how to get women out of that rut.

Thus, while some women from the lower classes hold these and other negative sentiments toward their own class, such sentiments are usually expressed by middle-class black women. Saundra (tax attorney and real estate agent, age thirty-one) is a notable middle-class exception. Saundra has become quite attuned, she says, to the black middle-class/lower-class divide, particularly among the elite set (e.g., members of the Links, Jack and Jill, and black sororities).[16] In childhood she was generally unaware that her family was itself part of this elite set, but she did notice some signs of socioeconomic difference between her family and those of the other kids around her. Today, she says that she experiences no discomfort moving around in blue-collar circles. In fact, she often seeks out opportunities to do so, like in making a conscious choice to take the bus to her job at the law firm because it gives her a chance to be among "everyday black women" and to converse with and share with them. Similarly, at times she has chosen to live in the city rather than in the suburbs, though today she lives in upscale Bethesda, Maryland, which is quite different from her hometown of Baltimore. Saundra says that her friends simply do not understand why she, given her capabilities and her resources, would choose to live among those who they feel are beneath her. Sometimes they even get upset with her. But Saundra says that she simply does not see herself that way: "I don't wear my education on my sleeve," making a point of not always letting others know what it is that she possesses. Saundra wants to be approached as an equal and makes a special effort to let others know that she is tangible. Saundra clearly still has very strong ties to the city of Baltimore, with her mother and father still living there, as well as to many of her friends from high school. And she says she finds that not having to always engage in "bourgeois conversation" is "liberating." She prefers talking meaningfully across class.

Many of the black women from the lower classes say that interaction across class has been made difficult by feelings of inferiority projected onto them by the middle classes. These experiences are particularly salient for those residing within the women's correctional facility. In general, women of the lower classes claim that the estrangement experience between the two groups is due to middle-class black women acting as though they "think they are better than other black women." Their sentiments are reminiscent of what Black Panther Assata Shakur wrote about her time spent at Riker's Island, about "the pseudo-motherly attitude of many of the guards":[17] they report that black female correctional officers frequently "walk up in here ready to tell me all that I done wrong, when fo' real they ain't no better than we are . . . probably worse" (Candice, age thirty-three). Elizabeth, a twenty-eight-year-old financial services specialist, was one of the most difficult study women to categorize by class. Though the final decision was to place her within the lower classes for this study, the fact that she possesses a college degree makes her subject to accusations generally lodged at the middle class:

> I've even had a black woman say, "you need to stop being so snobby." And I was like, how am I being snobby? I mean, I'm . . . we're in this together, we're . . . same position, same job. I have a degree; you don't. I'm not being snobby. We're on the same level. . . . She equates having a degree with being snobby or being on a level that she's not.

Tia says she feels that her cousin is an unnecessarily "snobby" black woman. What is more, her remarks about family conflict over social status issues also reveal the role of colorism in both family and class relations among African Americans:[18]

> I have family members like that. My cousin works for the [government], and she thinks, oh, she thinks she is up to sniffing God's butt with her nose, 'cause that's how far it be up in the air, uh-huh. And I'll be lookin' at her, and I told her one day, I was like, you know what? You ain't cute, I said, and I told her just like that, because her mother was a nurse, and my mother was on welfare.
> *Were they sisters?*
> Uh-huh, and her mother's light, and my mother's dark. . . . I think, honestly, she feels like she went to school; she feels like she did everything that she had to do to get where she's gotten. So she's not gonna let anything discredit it, and she's not gonna back down for anything. And I admire that in her. But when you're children, comin' up, don't try and make it seem like you better than me, 'cause you're not.

Phyllis (age twenty-five) and Shari (age fifty-four) say that one way "professional black women" make their sense of superiority known is by purposely using exclusionary language when in a mixed crowd. Shari in particular believes that this is their deliberate attempt to thwart the social mobility of lower-class women by limiting their access to information that could help improve their lives. Further, she believes that such actions violate the social contract among black women to sister one another.

The Special Case of Renowned Black Women

African-American women who are famous for having reached the top of their fields are a very small, special class of women. There have always been a few women among the black "talented tenth" or "black bourgeoisie," but contemporary African-American women have given new meaning to black female achievement. Oprah Winfrey undoubtedly leads this pack. Among her many accomplishments, Oprah is said to have "transformed popular culture," and "she epitomized what might have been another stereotype but was undeniably a positive one—the successful black woman." [19] Unlike her counterparts in white America, the renowned black woman is judged not only by her professional peers but by the standards that black America has set for her. In a recent study by sociologist Monica McDermott, it is shown that blacks in general "are continuing to achieve eminence through occupations that are different than those by which white ethnic groups achieve eminence; and eminence for blacks within the black community appears to derive from different occupational sources than does eminence on a national level." [20]

To my knowledge, none of the women of this study has the distinction of eminence. And, like most lower- and middle-class black women, the primary role they have played in thrusting other black women into the limelight is that of consumer or political voter. In spite of there being a huge experiential gulf between them and renowned black women, about sixty say that they generally embrace the renowned black woman and feel close to her in their feelings and ideas about things. But they also convey that with the limelight of eminence comes a rash of scrutiny. This scrutinizing has little to do with renowned women's professional performance and much to do with the policing of authentic black womanhood. Hannah, a thirty-three-year-old college training manager, explains:

> My concern is that *because* she is a black woman, folks who are viewing her or listening to her or reading her make the assumption that she's speaking as a black woman or *for* most black women. If there's someone who alarms me, that's why. Because, wait a minute, I know there's gonna be some white folks watchin' who are going to think she speaks for all black women, and I don't want her representing me [emphasis hers].

Clearly, a much larger proportion of study women feel that eminent black women are shining examples of authentic black womanhood than feel otherwise. There is an abundance of high praise for these women, their accomplishments, and their defiance of the public's general negative regard for black women. The words most often used to express their feelings of attachment are "inspiring" and "role models." Fifty-eight-year-old Myrna (clinical school counselor) says that she is impressed with how they have capitalized even on luck: "[They have] reached these peaks out of hard work and training, and luck and chance, and breaks, and all that stuff." Other women like Pamela (technical writer, age thirty-eight) are impressed with renowned women's determination (see pg. 69).

Such praise is particularly heard from elder study women (age fifty-five and older)[21] and, some may be surprised to learn, from women of the lower classes. Not only are women of the lower classes more likely than middle-class women to offer positive sentiments about members of this elite class, but they are also more likely to highlight particular women to whom they feel most attached, who they believe offer something special to the sisterhood, and who inspire them to realize their own ambitions. (These references are for the most part to entertainers, though there is also general discussion of women in politics and other arenas.) Further, virtually every reference to renowned women as having not "forgotten where they come from"—that is, as being appropriately "Afrocentric," committed to black women's issues, and even "true to their color"—comes from the lower classes. Lillian (college student and youth organizer, age nineteen) says she knows that there is plenty of negative sentiment among black women toward the eminent among them on such issues, but she does not concur:

> I love those women—Terry McMillan, Maya Angelou. I think they're very strong. And a lot of times people think that when black people make it, they kind of sort of forget about where they came from, or they want to turn away from their roots and their "hoods," quote, unquote. And I don't think they have.

Middle-class black women are certainly not absent from the voices of admiration for eminent African-American women, but it does appear that they are less enamored by them. It would seem that many of these women perceive the renowned as having failed the test of black social mobility—not in terms of their professional advancement, necessarily, but in terms of other aspects of their personal development and certainly the advancement of black women's causes. Where women of the lower classes are quick to highlight specific eminent women they admire, many from the middle classes name specific women who they believe have either failed or tainted the sisterhood in some way— names like Secretary of State Condoleeza Rice ("I question her always," and "I really commend just the fact that Bush thought highly of her enough to put her in that position, although . . . [sigh]"); writer Terry McMillan (for unnecessary "male bashing"); and rapper Lil' Kim (for enticing young black girls to aspire to something as useless as dancing in music videos).

Over lunch one afternoon, Saundra shared with me that "icons" of any sort are hard to wrap your mind around and that her taking the time to learn more about them than what the media portrays would be a step in the right direction. For now, anyway, she continues to feel strongly that renowned black women are disconnected from the "real" black experience, much more so than most middle-class black women are. She wonders why this is so and ventures to guess that it must be rooted in the materialism that surrounds their professions and strips them of their cultural authenticity. Trinity, a middle-class corrections worker thirty years Saundra's senior, has very similar sentiments about her estrangement from these women.

Perhaps middle-class black women are relatively more scrutinizing of this elite class because they hope to be held to the same standards of authenticity should they someday find themselves at that level of status. Nonetheless, it is ironic that these women say so frequently that they aspire to similar greatness and yet are also so condemning of the class they desire to enter. "I would prefer that they be there than not be there," says attorney Desiree (age fifty-seven) of the eminent, and she simply accepts that this is a quandary that black women must someday resolve.

BLACK WOMEN'S STRUGGLE AND ISSUES OF AUTHENTICITY

Real black women know what our struggle is about; they don't forget where they come from.

Astrid Henry, a women's studies professor at St. Mary's College, has recently proclaimed that "'to be real' has come to signify authenticity, something that can't be faked. Within the recent explosion of new writing by young black feminists, 'realness' or 'being real' has emerged as a central and recurring theme."[22] Many of my graduate students have tried to keep me even "fresher" by suggesting that "keeping it real" is the contemporary phrase of choice. However new these phrases may be, the practice of scrutinizing oneself and one another for signs of gender-ethnic authenticity has been common among black women for a good while.

It is for this reason that a vignette on the subject of keeping it real was very purposefully included in this research to represent one of several ideas that generally come to mind most about African-American women today. Among the five vignettes from which the study women had to choose, this vignette was the one most frequently chosen. The subject of gender-ethnic authenticity was also highly salient in the interview content, and the majority of that content was unsolicited. Contemporary black women are strongly committed to the notion of struggle and boldly embrace it as meaningful to their gender-ethnic identity—as a badge of honor and as a mark of their authentic black womanhood.

Feminist scholar bell hooks's experience with this subject gives us reason to anticipate that social class status might differentiate commitment to the notion of struggle and to embracing it as relevant to authentic gender-ethnic identity and consciousness. In her exchange with Cornel West, hooks bemoans what she sees as the rejection of struggle by many members of the middle classes:

> I was speaking on a panel at a conference with another black woman from a privileged background. She mocked the notion of struggle. When she expressed, "I'm just tired of hearing about the importance of struggle; it doesn't interest me," the audience clapped.[23]

Evidence from this study suggests instead that black women of all social backgrounds take ownership of struggle. Class distinctions can be drawn, however, among the various ways struggle is articulated among them.

To begin, for each of the four articulations of struggle that are identified, middle-class black women are far more likely to describe or explain the struggle they experience as indicative of that which all African-American women have had to endure for a very long time. They also have a greater tendency to articulate struggle as one's combat with negative public regard, which also largely involves evoking the history of black women's oppression. Thus, these two trends are closely associated. When Dorraine (social worker and real estate investor, age sixty-seven) conveys her frustration about a job recruitment experience that she believes was tainted by racism and sexism, she also explains that this was merely an extension of what "affected my ancestors and continues to affect me"; when Jessica tries to cope with combating negative public regard, she sees the "double dance" or "shifting" that she has to perform in order to please the dominant culture, and she recognizes that this is something that black women have had to learn to tolerate over their many years in this country; and similarly, when Shelley (database administrator, age twenty-three) feels pressured to conform to externally imposed standards of black womanhood on her job, she recognizes that these distorted "historical images" have haunted black women for centuries. It is not simply by chance that such references are clustered within the middle classes. As college-educated women, they are more likely to have formally studied black women's history and to have been expressive (that is, eloquent) about this history during our research interview. Nonetheless, this is their genuine contribution.

It should come as no surprise that the one articulation of struggle most often spoken by women from the lower classes is the struggle for economic and physical well-being. Though earlier I elaborated on a wide range of material and health-related concerns affecting African-American women across the board, those subsisting on the fewest economic resources bear a disproportionate share of that pain. Most of the middle-class women are highly conscious of this disparity, but they also are careful not to diminish the difficulties that they face in trying to maintain stability in their own lives. Stephanie (accountant, age twenty-four) raises an issue that few of her middle-class peers would dispute. She says that she is like so many other women of her class who walk a fine line between having and not having the money to make ends meet at any given time:

> I probably still have just as much debt as [the blue-collar black woman] does. After everything's all paid, I will only have twenty dollars left for me, you know? . . . What I've learned over time is that no matter how much money you make, you put your debt according to how much you make, so if you only make twenty thousand dollars, you probably have about fifteen thousand dollars in debt; if you make forty thousand dollars, you probably have thirty-five thousand dollars. It doesn't matter.

Black women of both the lower and middle classes are equally likely to articulate their struggle as a black family dilemma. Both groups say that they are preoccupied—and know plenty of other black women who also are preoccupied—with feeding, clothing, and nursing their children and other family members for whom they are responsible. They also have vivid memories of their own mothers scrambling to do the very same for them. Where economic struggles are highlighted here, women of the middle classes are most likely to reference work-related dilemmas as hindering them from stabilizing their family resources. Since black women know that workplaces rarely keep more than one black woman on staff at a time, particularly at the high administrative and managerial levels, they feel particularly vulnerable during times of corporate downsizing and job restructuring. In such times, household funds are often diverted from basic needs in order to pay for shoring up the woman's job-related skills or to help her gain new and necessary credentials. This can then lead the household to overextend its consumer credit in an effort to help restore some of those diverted funds. The woman is then pressured to devote more time to the labor market to help stave off bankruptcy.

Though both classes of women give equal weight to family dilemmas in articulating the "well-being" struggle, it is women from the middle classes who are more highly represented among those articulating black women's struggle as keeping and watching over black family members as they all navigate the complexities of life. The reason for this appears to be that the non-married members of their class group talk more about their desires to someday find a mate. (There is no indication that the *desire* for marriage is any greater among the middle classes, however.) It may also be due to the fact that much of this data focuses on middle-class women caring for extended family members, like in Terry's case (age thirty-nine), where she is caring for her drug-addicted sister's five children. Her case should remind us that even when public assistance is available (and accepted) to help in the support of other kinfolk, a solid middle-class income may still be required to sustain a family over time.

"Forgetting where you come from" is a theme of struggle that powerfully resonates throughout this study. Women across the social class spectrum express that the struggle to remain grounded and true to the culture is sometimes overwhelming. Eminent black women are frequently targeted for this scrutiny; they are required to have maintained a clear, authentic self throughout their careers, with which the masses of black women continue to identify. Women of the middle classes face similar scrutiny, and perhaps because they are more at arm's reach from the lower classes, the surveillance they experience may be even more taxing.

For these same reasons, middle-class women are more prevalent among those who speak of what I call the "social mobility" vein of struggle. What they express most often is how very difficult it is to please other women's sensibilities about their "forgetting" to give something back to their people. Terry says she often hears people say that women like her have "left the race." But what she says she truly believes is that "the black race has left me." Like so many other African-American women, Terry was socialized to believe that authentic black womanhood was about the struggle to achieve academically, professionally, and economically, and so she invested heavily in doing what she was told the black community expected her to do—make them proud by rapidly advancing. Yet now that she has met and surpassed that challenge, she finds little community support:

> I don't think people understand, when your day just consists solely of interacting with people that don't look like you and sometimes that may not want you there. [Here in the year] 2002, and you still have to be better [than whites] in all aspects. That's a lot to deal with, and you have to have some outlet.

At times, middle-class black women can be as scrutinizing about women "forgetting where they come from" as other women are, and even toward their own class group. Monique says that it was not until she observed on television a woman from the Masai people of eastern Africa that she realized just how differently black women of means in the United States toy with their wealth. She learned that this Masai woman was a queen among her people, yet her "dignity" kept her humble. Monique admits that she has seen similar qualities among some American black women, like, for example, her neighbor who she says most people would never know possesses an MBA and is married to a man who owns a successful business. More typically, however, she says that women of her class fail to "keep it real": "Once they hit the middle class, they got a bodacious car, and bodacious nails, bodacious rings, and a bodacious attitude."

Women from the lower classes certainly also get their share of criticism about having "forgotten where they come from." Many of their critics argue that the "ghetto fabulous" and the "boisterous and raunchy" among them have been duped into believing that *they* are more authentic representations of black womanhood. Similar accusations are made toward those who are perceived as having "given up their power" as black women by relying heavily on public assistance, or on other sources deemed "illegitimate," to support themselves and their families. But women from these classes, as well as those from the middle classes, understand that class status and its various trappings often have little to do with how they are evaluated. If her "hair is too long," her "friends are too white," her house is too big, or her skin is too "bright," the black woman, whatever her social background, can be dismissed as inauthentically black. As writer Sharon Brooks Hodge puts it, "Any black person who comes across as too white is eyed suspiciously from all sides."[24]

SOCIOPOLITICAL IDEOLOGY

Nowadays, I often find myself wondering whether black women will ever truly come together as a people. I mean, we all have different ways of expressing ourselves because of the things we've gone through. And frankly, it worries me.

Second only to the vignette on black women's struggle is the proportion of study women who believe that this sentiment best captures the kinds of thoughts they frequently have about contemporary African-American women. Nearly a third of the women are troubled that divergent gender-ethnic identity and consciousness among them hinders their collective ability to tend to the interests of black women and those of their families and communities. Yet their strong collective commitment to the ideological tenets of black feminism and humanism certainly gives reason for some optimism. Earlier evidence from this study shows that today's black women speak in virtual unison on the issue of black women's "double" and "multiple jeopardy" and on the need to combat the oppression that ails them on multiple fronts simultaneously. They strongly believe in equality for all gender-ethnic groups and that all groups are equally deserving of human rights protection. And they argue that any sociopolitical action taken on behalf of black women must be consistent with their humanity and that of others. But as is the case for other subjects addressed, there is sufficient discord around several important humanist concerns, as well as around assimilationist, nationalist, and oppressed-minority concerns.

Earlier, I reported that there is one ideologically humanist idea to which the study women hold particularly fast. Black women are highly supportive of the idea that people should be free to enter into marriage across gender-ethnic lines without fear of societal rejection. This closely parallels their anti–black nationalist position of rejecting the idea that black women should not marry interracially. While it is tempting to believe that black women's sentiment about this has changed over the last few decades, I know of no evidence to support this belief. What we do know is that over the years, studies on interracial relationships generally have found that African-American women are the least likely to hold favorable sentiments on this subject, and as a result they are frequently depicted as unconscionably "angry" or "bitchy" toward black men and their nonblack liaisons.[25] We also know that scholars and everyday folk have frequently argued that higher rates of interracial marriage among African-American men are attributed to men's belief that marrying into the dominant culture can significantly improve their social standing (i.e., attributed to their "false consciousness"); to the relatively greater access that black men have had to a pool of potential nonblack mates; and to black men having been hoodwinked by the myths surrounding black beauty. Black women, on the other hand, are said not only to have less opportunity to meet and form romantic relationships with nonblack men but to suffer greater repercussions from the black community when crossing racial lines.[26]

Results from this study suggest that, compared to those in the lower classes, contemporary middle-class black women are more open to interracial marriage. It may well be that as greater proportions of black women have entered high-paying jobs alongside nonblack men and as the pool of marriageable black men has remained shallow or even shrunk further in some places, middle-class black women may view marital options differently. Because these study women generally take the freedom to marry interracially for granted, few elaborated on their feelings. The only in-depth discussion was held with middle-class elementary school teacher Taylor (age fifty-four), and she admittedly takes a hard-line position against interracial marriage, aligning more with many of the correctional facility women than with her own class. Taylor also believes that she is just being more honest and less politically correct than her peers are. This excerpt is one of many like it from our interview:

> I'm telling you, that is such an issue for me. I have two boys [age twenty-one and twenty-five], and I have said to them, if I've said it once, don't bring one [white

woman] in here. I said, because your mother's black, your family's black. There are too many beautiful black women for you to choose that way. And you know how people say, but if you love someone [you'll let them make their own choices]. Well, find a black woman to love, 'cause Lord knows, there's plenty of them out there. And I guess what makes it such an issue for me . . . I mean, I'm married, so somebody might say, well, you have a husband, or whatever. But I guess because of church, school, sorority, I see so many beautiful black women who come in every shade, every length of hair, every hair texture; I mean, you just name it, there we are. Even those features that may look more European, what . . . I mean, you just name it, and you mean you can't find somebody in that [black] spectrum? . . . And as my sister, she's always said, well, don't push on it too much, 'cause that might make them go the opposite way. I said, well, I don't think I pressure them; I just let them know that's where I stand. And I can't determine who they marry, but I can determine who they bring in my home. And I think it's up to me as a black woman, as their mother, to remind them about black women.

The one humanist idea on which most black women generally agree is that "being an individual is more important than identifying as a black woman." Earlier I suggested that in taking this stand, black women assert their right to be ideologically humanist while also embracing a strong gender-ethnic identity. On this point, black women of the lower classes are significantly more comfortable than their middle-class counterparts. Not only may disparaging public images of black women undermine the strong gender-ethnic centrality that might otherwise sustain those of the lower classes, but they may pressure these women to assert their individualism in order to be viewed less stereotypically.

There are also signs of discord that speak to the potential benefits of embracing sociopolitical ideas that emphasize the uniqueness of black cultural content and black causes. These issues are mixed with humanist and black nationalist concerns. In general, African-American women are ambivalent about whether or not they should consider race when, for example, buying art or selecting a book to read, though the women with whom I spoke at the corrections facility were more inclined not to view racial content as important to their choices. They expressed that while they are always eager to keep abreast of what black authors and artists are producing "on the outside," they are happy to get there hands on any quality material. The women as a whole are equally irresolute about whether black social and political causes will be shortchanged if black women concern themselves more so with problems they share with other groups or if they move to establish themselves as a separate political force. What is clear, however, is that those from the lower classes are relatively less supportive of any of these issues.

Given the high premium they place on their individual and collective achievements (e.g., educational and occupational advancement) and on the virtues of their structural assimilation, one might expect contemporary black women to impugn the nonachievers among them for not fully participating in the sisterhood. The results on this subject appear quite mixed, however. On the one hand, the study women are ambivalent about whether nonachievers should be admonished for not taking advantage of the opportunities made for them by their foremothers. About half of the study women refuse to attack those who have not made the educational, occupational, and economic advancement expected of them in these times, where another third believe that such women must take personal responsibility for not seizing the opportunity to improve the quality of their lives. But when the study women are probed in regard to their feelings of estrangement from other black women, the women's tendency toward impugning nonachievers is much stronger. Those described as "not trying to better themselves" are their target:

> Lillian: It's harder for me to develop a relationship with women who I see have opportunities to do things for themselves but just kind of don't take advantage of them. I understand that the drive and the motivation hasn't been instilled. And a lot of times in those situations it's just generation after generation has been lulled into the process of just not being motivated to do so.

On the whole, my reading of these observations is that black women do tend to value holding each other accountable for their lack of social mobility, even as they also make delineating structural impediments to black women's advancement a cornerstone of their black womanist standpoint.

But class status does differentiate these findings somewhat. While black women from the lower classes are most likely to be the target of rebuke regarding nonachievement, they are also relatively more likely to agree that such rebuke is warranted. They are more likely to feel estranged from those whom they view as failing to do what is necessary to better themselves and to feel a strong sense of connection with those who they believe personify success:

> Candice (incarcerated, age thirty-three): Each and every time I see one of my sisters do something productive, and they are really getting their life together, I rejoice . . . just like . . . Mrs. McDonald, even though we've just met, I'm gonna tell you, when they told us that we were gonna have this survey lady come in, and she was gonna do this survey, and she was this doctor, the first thing I nearly thought—and I'm gonna be honest and blunt—is she was gonna be white. Honey, let me tell you, when you walked in that door, I said, oh no she's not! Thank you, Jesus. Because it makes me feel good to know that I am connected to a black woman of any standards that is bettering themselves—you know, getting things done, getting their lives in order, you understand? And that meant a lot to me.

This sentiment is particularly salient among the women recruited from the corrections community, virtually 90 percent of whom are from the lower classes. I attribute their relative intolerance of nonachieving women largely to the self-liberation content of the correctional facilities' social programs, where inmates, correctional officers, and corrections administrators focus almost exclusively on placing the blame for nonachievement squarely on the woman herself. Even as many administrators at various levels of the institution work to expose the gender-ethnic inequalities that are structured by the practices of the criminal justice system, they are resistant to empowering their inmates with education about these inequalities. Perhaps they are concerned that the women will use this education as an excuse to continue their criminal behavior, or that the women are ill equipped to process such information. Erin (age fifty), who served as my primary informant during the time I spent at the women's detention center, frequently lamented the struggle she has with balancing the women's personal rehabilitation with wanting to rehabilitate the correctional system. The best she could offer, she said, was educating inmate mothers—particularly the young ones—about the perils of the court system. (Because of Erin's position within the institution, I was especially careful protecting her identity, so she was never audiotaped):

> Field notes: Erin helps to maintain a very dense schedule of activities which includes Bible study meetings, exercise classes, meditation classes, meetings with detainees and their attorneys/public defenders or social workers, furnishing of dorms and other rooms, and coordinating meetings between researchers (there were a lot of us researchers in and out of there) and detainees, to name only a few. She is particularly concerned for the teens (charged as adults in a crime); they have to be kept separate from the adult women for they own safety. Erin believes that what innocence is left for these teens could be quickly destroyed unless they are given some hope that life would not be like this always. Hence, she tries very hard to make their surroundings bearable. . . . The one thing I clearly recall is Erin's numerous references to the drug courts. As I understand it, often the judges give drug-related offenders the option of serving a jail sentence or being released on probation. But what the women fail to understand is that if while on, say, a five- or even ten-year probation sentence, they commit a minor offense, this could land them back in jail to serve the full sentence or even a longer sentence. The problem here is that the women have to live their lives for five to ten years worried that they may get caught doing the slightest of things. Apparently, getting caught while on drug probation is far worse than serving out the original sentence. But of course most women take the probation so that they can get back to their children right away. This has had terrible consequences for many of the women.

Middle-class black women are generally much less likely to admonish nonachievers. Their awareness of the many obstacles that must be overcome in order to achieve such things as gainful, steady employment and a college degree is something they have gained through direct experience. Thus, Carol, like other women of her class, tends to be somewhat less condemning of non-achievers and more open to offering mentorship. She has this to say about another black woman whom she supervises:

When we had a training program where I could have been instrumental in helping her to move along, I did what I could, and she graduated from the program. But she chose to just stay there and not take advantage of the education here. She's just comfortable doing what she's doing, but the writing has been on the wall for our department a couple of times. . . . They could have easily removed her along with so many others. . . . She hasn't done anything to go beyond the position she's in, and I feel like if they were talking about downsizing again . . . scratch!

As a whole, African-American women feel strongly that as a group they should continue to strive for full membership in the American political system. Earlier, we learned that getting black women elected to public office and supporting the agendas these women put forward are seen as vital to the pursuit of black women's causes. It is not so surprising that women of the middle classes are much more likely to embrace this proassimilationist position and its potential implications for the redistribution of power across gender and racial lines. As such benefits are believed to eventually trickle downward, middle-class black women are among those who would reap them first.

Finally, the interviews I conducted for this research took place just as the nation was preparing to recognize the fifty years that have passed since *Brown v. Board of Education* (1964). The anniversary of this landmark decision reopened fierce debate over whether the promise of this legislation was "a sham at worst and an unfulfilled promise at best,"[27] whether the price of integration has been too great, and whether too many black cultural traditions have been lost in the process, such as the loss of "the black educator and their [*sic*] role in the shaping of the self-perception of the black student."[28] It was in this context that I learned that while there is strong consensus around black women's entitlement to political power, the study women are far less united on the issue of racial integration in these times.

Less than half of the women believe that working to integrate all of the nation's institutions that are still racially segregated is a priority or even worthwhile, and about a third clearly are against it. Further, class discord on this issue is fairly sharp: close to two-thirds of women from the lower classes believe that working to achieve full racial integration is still worthy of black women's attention, whereas this is true for only about one-third of middle-class women. What this appears to signal is not an all-out rejection of integrationist agendas by some in the middle classes but rather rejection of what they may view as strategies for achieving gender-ethnic equality that are too compromising of black women's sensibilities. These women seem to be advocating a more profitable route to equality that exploits the political power-brokering talents of black women who unapologetically advance the concerns in which black women are invested. Becoming full members of the American political system, then, may not be considered to be as much a reflection of black women's commitment to integration as a commitment to womanist agency. Thus, perhaps their shying away somewhat from integrationist causes reflects their desire to preserve certain race-based institutions; they may not want to draw too much attention to the few areas of social and political life that blacks still control. If in fact this is the case, there is some suggestion that they may have to put some serious work into building support for this among their counterparts in the lower classes.

SLOUCHING TOWARD BLACK STEPSISTERHOOD?

Sociologist Stanley Aronowitz argues that although "not powerful enough to replace the prevailing doctrine of classlessness," it is clear in all of America that "class has become an important component of our political and cultural unconscious. . . . In every crevice of everyday life we find signs of class difference; we are acutely aware that class plays a decisive role in social relations."[29] He contends that social relations are generally limited to those packed within what Annette Lareau refers to as "sharply defined categories" based on different "life-defining experiences."[30] A number of scholars are quick to point out that for African Americans, social relations are less stringently aligned by class position than they are among white Americans. As John L. Jackson explains,

> People have social interactions across class lines every day in contemporary black America. Sometimes they forget, downplay, and deny their existence, but folks are still theorizing and utilizing substantive and ephemeral exchanges across class lines.[31]

And this appears to hold true for the women of this study.

The results presented in this chapter confirm that the identities, consciousnesses, sentiments, and sociopolitical interests of contemporary black women are genuinely classed. They do not, however, run in opposition to each other at every turn. In fact, they rarely do. Class discord is primarily revealed in differences of small or moderate degree rather than by polar opposition. It is my conclusion that in areas where class differences are evident, they are much more subtle than we generally anticipate: the proportions of middle-class black women supporting or rejecting certain ideas are for the most part virtually the same as or only moderately different from those for the lower classes. Were it not for the expectation that the legacy of strong gender-ethnic identity and consciousness among black women would sufficiently suppress expressions of class-related discord, these reported instances of discord would simply be taken as a given. But inasmuch as we do fixate on class phenomena, it is necessary to recognize that class may exert a force stronger than collective identity and consciousness.

The crudeness with which I etch out the contours of class discord reflects both the evidence of subtle differences and the fairly simplistic way in which class categories are constructed for this study. Still, the distinctions are meaningful, as is the fact that these distinctions run deepest between the most and the least marginalized women. Those from the lower classes, who see their struggle as tied most to their economic and physical deprivation, express relatively less satisfaction with being black and female. This is something that may also stem from their knowing that women of their class group, more than any other, are cast as undeserving of the public's positive regard. Their greater tendency to render their gender-ethnicity less important than "being an individual" may be a means by which they cope with their social stigma.[32] This social stigma appears to be negatively internalized as the stiff intolerance they show for nonachievement among black women; by blaming these women themselves for their lack of social mobility, they demonstrate their ability to act more mainstream and less marginal. Developing interpersonal relations with white women is also difficult for these women, though not necessarily more so than for middle-class black women. Still, they show less resistance to the idea of working toward greater institutional integration, which would result in greater interaction with whites, and they do not appear to be as willing to employ racially separatist sociopolitical tactics to relieve black women's struggles.

In addition to diverging from their counterparts on these particular issues, women of the middle classes are more attuned to the sociohistorical forces that have given rise to struggle for black women of all social backgrounds. Because of this, they view struggle as largely about the public's negative regard for black women. Their substantial contribution to middle-class family income (biological and extended) serves also to make the struggle to hold black families together highly significant in their lives. Middle-class women generally believe that answers to many of their problems lie in gaining greater power through mainstream political channels, where they can exploit the political in-roads made by black women over the past few decades and can tend closely to black women's concerns. And perhaps their greater tendency to promote the conscious consumption of "things black," namely black art and literature, is in part an expression of their desire to preserve at least certain highly regarded elements of black culture.

These data also show that in crossing lines of class difference in everyday spaces, contemporary African-American women have developed perceptions about each other and "perform class-inflected social behaviors, actions that are said to differ depending on the class or status of the people involved."[33] So, not only do black women's opinions differ as to the nature of their condition and what would be best to do about it, but they hold certain negative sentiments about the other class group. Most scholars who have studied class relations among African Americans have found that those from the middle classes more likely feel a sense of distance from other blacks. According to a summary of this literature offered by Sandra S. Smith and Mignon R. Moore,

> Social distance is hypothesized to exist among those of higher SES because of their greater integration within mainstream America, their individual versus collective orientation toward success, and their reduced sense of collective fate resulting because their class status insulates them from many problems faced by more disadvantaged blacks.[34]

A very similar pattern is found in this study: there is a greater tendency for middle-class women to report distance from the lower classes. However, neither a more individualistic orientation toward success nor a reduced sense of collective fate seems to apply here. Based on my findings, both of these characteristics are more prevalent among the lower classes. In this study, women of the middle classes view poor class relations as the primary source of tension among contemporary black women, and they are more likely to point to the lower classes than to themselves as cultivating that tension. From their perspective, lower-class women tend to exhibit public and private behaviors that are disconcerting; middle-class women are more likely to identify the negative behaviors they find typical of this class as significantly driving the estrangement they feel. They also feel unfairly targeted by the lower classes for their supposedly having "forgotten where they come from," on the basis of having not adequately "given back," or for speaking, dressing, and otherwise acting in ways that are generally deemed "white."

Women of the lower classes express relatively less estrangement from middle-class women than middle-class women do from the lower classes. In fact, at times, lower-class women express that those of the middle classes serve as excellent models of socioeconomic and professional success. But they are also disappointed that women of the middle classes often effectively shut them out of potential opportunities to advance themselves, particularly by using language in mixed-class company that relegates other women to the margins of conversation. These women claim that what they are witnessing in such instances is the perpetration of a "superiority complex," another way of saying that women of the middle classes too often feel that they are better than other black women.

Elsewhere, I have argued that the consciousness of class differences and class tensions can be a particularly painful source of psychosocial stress throughout the social class spectrum.[35] Women from both class groups suffer the burden of having to adapt to their lives in various ways that are socially distant and detached from each other, particularly knowing that black women have traditionally shared many meaningful, sisterly connections. African-American women do develop and promote somewhat distinctive "behavorial repertoires"[36] in response to their knowing the vulnerabilities of their class status. That these repertoires at times transmit classism within the sisterhood is a highly sensitive issue (i.e., the "airing of dirty laundry"). Among all the discord shown among black women in their everyday lives, the internalization of classism may be the greatest threat to their gender-ethnic solidarity.

Those familiar with W. B. Yeats's poem *The Second Coming* (1921) and Joan Didion's collection of essays *Slouching Towards Bethlehem* (1968) know that both of these authors are apocalyptic in their visions of the future; they are exceedingly despondent about the splintering of society and about the loss of cultural values. I pose the question, "slouching toward black stepsisterhood?" not to signal a grave concern about the future of the black woman collective; on the contrary, I am relieved to discover that the discord we find is generally the discord we expect, and then not nearly of the magnitude we sense exists through such mundane things as "oil-and-lube-shop/ Oprah" encounters. But I do appreciate that many of us feel as though the sisterhood is slipping away from some of the best of its cultural principles. I also appreciate the need for an intrasisterhood dialogue through which real obstacles to addressing the problems that affect us all can be identified. As sister Audre Lorde has spoken,

> There is a pretense to a homogeneity of experience covered by the word *sisterhood* that does not in fact exist. Unacknowledged class differences rob women of each others' energy and creative insight [emphasis hers].[37]

NOTES

1. Felly Nkweto Simmonds, "Who Are the Sisters? Difference, Feminism, and Friendship," in *Desperately Seeking Sisterhood: Still Challenging and Building*, eds. Magdalene Ang-Lygate, Chris Corrin, and Millsom S. Henry (London: Taylor & Francis, 1997), 19–41.

2. bell hooks, *Yearning: Race, Gender, and Cultural Politics* (Cambridge, MA: South End Press, 1990).

3. This might be better stated as something more akin to poor stepsisterhood since by my own admission from childhood experience, the blending together of individuals with varying interests, values, and perspectives does not necessarily lead to poor bonding.

4. Clenora Hudson-Weems, "Africana Womanism: The Flip Side of a Coin," *The Western Journal of Black Studies* 25, no. 3 (2001): 137–45.

5. Deborah Gray White, *Too Heavy a Load: Black Women in Defense of Themselves, 1894–1994* (New York: W. W. Norton & Company, 1999), 16.

6. Tom W. Smith, "The Generation Gap Revisited," *Network on Transitions to Adulthood Policy Brief, MacArthur Foundation Research Network on Transitions to Adulthood and Public Policy* 6 (2004).

7. Lois Benjamin, *Three Black Generations at the Crossroads: Community, Culture, and Consciousness* (Chicago: Burnham, Inc., 2000).

8. Jennifer Gill, "Beyond Gender—Race," *BusinessWeek Online*, August 7, 2001, 2, www.businessweek.com/careers/content/aug2001/ca2001087_306.htm (accessed October

27, 2005). Ella L. J. Edmondson Bell and Stella M. Nkomo are the coauthors of *Our Sepa-rate Ways: Black and White Women and the Struggle for Professional Identity* (Boston: Harvard Business School Press, 2001).

9. Astrid Henry, *Not My Mother's Sister: Generational Conflict and Third-Wave Fem-inism* (Bloomington: Indiana University Press, 2004); Gwendolyn D. Pough, *Check It While I Wreck It: Black Womanhood, Hip-Hop Culture, and the Public Sphere* (Boston: Northeastern University Press, 2004). The quote, presented in Henry's chapter on third-wave black feminists, is by Joan Morgan, *When Chickenheads Come Home to Roost: My Life as a Hip-Hop Feminist* (New York: Simon & Schuster, 1999).

10. Smith, "The Generation Gap Revisited," 2.

11. See, for example, David A. Bositis, *Diverging Generations: The Transformation of African American Policy Views* (Washington, DC: Joint Center for Political and Economic Studies, 2001); and Lee A. Daniels, ed., *The State of Black America, 2001* (New York: National Urban League, 2001).

12. Such findings are common in social research. For example, a 1997 race relations poll conducted by the Joint Center for Political and Economic Studies showed younger-age cohorts of respondents to diverge most significantly from those of the oldest-age cohorts.

13. Recall that the oppressed-minority ideology emphasizes the similarities between the oppression that African-American women face and that of other gender-ethnic groups and is aware of the oppression that continues to confront black women (see table 2).

14. Michael C. Dawson, *Behind the Mule: Race and Class in African-American Poli-tics* (Princeton, NJ: Princeton University Press, 1994), 79.

15. Less familiar—among the study women and people in general—is the term "ghet-toisie," first introduced to me by my graduate student Mark King in 2000. It later surfaced in 2004 on Michael Bowen's Internet blog, *Cobb*, in a comic strip titled "Nation of Mil-lions," www.mdcbowen.org/cobb/archives/001889.html. "Ghettoisie" refers to those contemporary working- and middle-class black youth who, in an attempt to remain (or at least appear to remain) authentically black, don "ghetto" attire, walk in "ghetto" rhythm, and speak in "ghetto" language. Such youth are thought to be caught in what Mary Pattillo-McCoy calls the "ghetto trance." She reminds us that such behavior is not new: "Every generation of black youth has been influenced by some form (and usually many forms) of ghetto-based cultural production that was one part social commentary and resis-tance, one part deviance, and two parts fun." Mary Pattillo-McCoy, *Black Picket Fences* (Chicago: University of Chicago Press, 1999), 120.

16. Lawrence Otis Graham, in *Our Kind of People*, provides an insider's view of the Links Incorporated and Jack and Jill of America. The former is the largest and most influ-ential elite social club for black women who, among other things, give generously and strategically to political and charitable causes. The latter was founded as a nonprofit ser-vice organization to socialize elite black children to the educational, social, and cultural ways of their class.

17. Assata Shakur, "'Women in Prison: How We Are,' Assata Shakur, 1978," in *Let Nobody Turn Us Around: Voices of Resistance, Reform, and Renewal*, eds. Manning Mara-ble and Leith Mullings (Lanham, MD: Rowman & Littlefield, 2000), 31.

18. See chapter 4, pp. 113–14, for a discussion of colorism.

19. Darlene Clark Hine and Kathleen Thompson, *A Shining Thread of Hope: The His-tory of Black Women in America* (New York: Broadway Books, 1998), 304, 305.

20. Monica McDermott, "Trends in the Race and Ethnicity of Eminent Americans," *Sociological Forum* 17, no. 1 (2002): 137–60.

21. Feelings of *detachment* from renowned African-American women are expressed by the youngest of the study women, aged eighteen to twenty-four and twenty-five to thirty-four.

22. Astrid Henry, *Not My Mother's Sister: Generational Conflict and Third-Wave Feminism* (Bloomington: Indiana University Press, 2004), 148.

23. hooks, *Yearning: Race, Gender, and Cultural Politics*, 211.

24. Sharon Brooks Hodge, "Being Articulate Has Become a Measure of Authenticity," *Headway* 8, no. 7 (1996): 10.

25. See Patricia Hill Collins, *Black Sexual Politics: African Americans, Gender, and the New Racism* (New York: Routledge, 2004); and Erica Chito Childs, "Looking Behind the Stereotypes of the 'Angry Black Woman': An Exploration of Black Women's Responses to Interracial Relationships," *Gender and Society* 19, no. 4 (2005): 544–61.

26. Collins, *Black Sexual Politics: African Americans, Gender, and the New Racism.*

27. Charles Vert Willie and Sarah Susannah Willie, "Black, White, and Brown: The Transformation of Public Education in America," *Teachers College Record* 107 (2005): 475–95.

28. Edward Rhymes, "*Brown*balled? Desegregation without Real Integration Is an Invitation for Dysfunction," BlackCommentator.com, 2005, www.blackcommentator.com/108/108_guest_rhymes.html.

29. Stanley Aronowitz, *How Class Works: Power and Social Movement* (New Haven, CT: Yale University Press, 2003), 33, 25, 31.

30. Annette Lareau, *Unequal Childhoods: Class, Race, and Family Life* (Berkeley: University of California Press, 2003), 30.

31. John L. Jackson Jr., *Harlemworld: Doing Race and Class in Contemporary Black America* (Chicago: University of Chicago Press, 2001), 132.

32. Among the incarcerated women of this study, "being an American" is likewise viewed as more important than identifying specifically as a black woman.

33. Jackson, *Harlemworld: Doing Race and Class in Contemporary Black America.*

34. Sandra S. Smith and Mignon R. Moore, "Intraracial Diversity and Relations among African-Americans: Closeness and Black Students at a Predominantly White University," *American Journal of Sociology* 106, no. 1 (2000): 1–39, 5.

35. Katrina Bell McDonald, "The Psychosocial Dimension of Black Maternal Health: An Intersection of Race, Gender, and Class," in *African Americans and the Public Agenda: The Paradoxes of Public Policy*, edited by Cedric Herring, 68–84 (Thousand Oaks, CA: Sage Publications, 1997).

36. Nancy E. Adler et al., "Socioeconomic Status and Health: The Challenge of the Gradient," *American Psychologist* 49, no. 1 (1994): 15–24.

37. Audre Lorde, "Age, Race, Class, and Sex: Women Redefining Difference," in *Sister Outsider: Essays and Speeches*, The Crossing Press Feminist Series (Freedom, CA: Crossing Press, 1984).

Chapter Six

Embracing Oprah Winfrey

The fact that I was created a Black woman in this lifetime, everything in my life is built around honoring that. I feel a sense of reverence to that. I hold it sacred. And so I am always asking the question, "What do I owe in service having been created a Black woman?"

—Oprah Winfrey[1]

The further I ventured into conversations with the study women, the harder it was to resist sharing with them the Oprah encounter I had at the oil-and-lube shop a few years prior. It simply became one more instance of what we all agreed was customary "Oprah tampering" among contemporary black women. Sometimes my storytelling began by my explicitly asking the women whether they had ever had such an encounter, but many other times I was lured into it by their having voluntarily offered a similar scenario. Virtually every woman had an "Oprah moment" to report.

People who know me well know that I am a major fan of Oprah and that I would have been remiss in my duties as a fan not to have reserved a portion of this book for her, but I initially thought that engaging the concrete Oprah in this project would require compromising on my objective of merely using "embracing Oprah" as an analytical and metaphorical tool. Over time, however, I saw a chance to not only act as a good fan but, more importantly, to extend my analysis in a meaningful (some might even say obvious) way. "Oprah moments" are a significant portion of the contemporary fodder that *is* this project. Ms. Oprah Winfrey—talk-show host; philanthropist; business-woman extraordinaire; and, most recently, criminal justice crusader—is not only the most famous African-American woman the world has known, but she provokes debate that often leads to deep self-reflection by the black woman collective. Like other kinds of day-to-day encounters that black women have with one another, "Oprah tampering" relays much of the stuff of black sisterhood, what we like and dislike, and what we hope and fear about ourselves. Through assessing what and how Oprah does what *she* does, African-American women evaluate how well we do what *we* do.

The study women, like black women in general, have much to say about what they know and *think* they know about Oprah, and about what they believe she represents among the various representations of black woman-hood. Their fixation is driven as much by Oprah's unmatched fame as it is by the fact that Oprah in certain ways represents both segments of a sisterhood that some perceive as bifurcated along class lines. She embodies many of the experiences, beliefs, and sentiments observed among the lower *and* the mid-dle classes as they relate to gender-ethnic identity and consciousness. As such, she holds tremendous power to affect personal and collective self-eval-uations among black women, whether they admit it or not, whether they are avid consumers of her media products or not, and whether they like her or not. Devotion to that kind of power has resonated with black women from the time of precolonial Africa; through the Middle Passage, antebellum slavery, and Reconstruction; from within the Harlem Renaissance, the Black Wom-en's Club Movement, and the civil rights movement; and now today among African-American women (and quite clearly other women) from all walks of life.

In this brief chapter, I mine Oprah-related portions of the data for addi-tional insights on contemporary black sisterhood and the relative degree of unity and class discord that exists. Through this discussion is revealed what many of us already recognize, and that is that for black women to treasure Oprah is not to adore her, necessarily, but to respect her as a living legacy of black woman power. Now in her early fifties, black women marvel at Oprah's staying power—her ability to have survived some of most difficult struggles black women face and to have won the envy of a world that typically finds little regard for black women. But as is true for renowned women in general, there is ever a watchful eye scrutinizing whether Oprah is black enough to be black, woman enough to be woman, and sister enough to "keep it real." Posi-tive and negative sentiments regarding Oprah's life and legacy are about equally common among those from the lower and middle classes. Consensus is most obvious around the significance of her fame as a black woman, fol-lowed closely by concerns for the credibility of her spiritual life. There are other sentiments, however, that vary somewhat between the two groups, and the pattern of variation in these sentiments generally mirrors that observed in the previous chapter.

The study women often speculated that my data would support the notion that black women's sisterhood with Oprah is distinguished by favoring her "early years" or her "later years." Those from the lower classes, they assumed, would be more embracing of what Oprah exhibited before she "became Oprah," and middle-class women would be more embracing of that which came after "Oprah." I agreed that such a pattern seemed quite plausible given the metamorphosis of social class that Oprah has undergone over the course of her public life. But under closer examination, this dichotomy did not prove fruitful. Though the two classes of women respond somewhat differently to the significance and consequences of Oprah's struggle and to the choices she has made in fashioning her media and philanthropic empires, these classed sentiments straddle Oprah's professional timeline and thus make for less tidy interpretations.

Some readers may still be led on by the title of this book to anticipate disproportionate attention to this part of my analysis, but it simply is not the case that Oprah material predominates. Neither the survey questionnaire nor the research interview encouraged abundant exchange on the subject of Oprah, but as you will see, a sufficiently rich content did find its way in. In addition, this content does not extend into each of the dimensions of gender-ethnic identity and consciousness that together have formed the frame for my analysis thus far. Most notably, issues of sociopolitical ideology are scarce at best.

It is fair to assume that most readers know a good many important details about Oprah's personal and professional life and therefore have plenty of information from which to paint a backdrop for this discussion. Yet in spite of this assumption and the fact that numerous biographies (authorized and unauthorized) have been written and broadcast about Oprah, I begin this chapter with a summary of my own.

OPRAH, BRIEFLY

The name Oprah was assigned to Ms. Winfrey by mistake. Her given name is taken from the biblical character Orpah, but because the individual in charge of printing her birth certificate made a simple typographical error, Ms. Winfrey has never been known by that name. In 1954, Oprah was born in poverty to single mother Vernita Lee, who, fearing that life in the North (Milwaukee) would be too strenuous for her *and* Oprah, left her to be raised by her grandmother in Kosciusko, Mississippi. Oprah says that though she endured harsh disciplinary action from her grandmother, Hattie Mae Lee, and often resented her for it, she came to respect her grandmother as someone who truly loved and cared for her.

At age six, Oprah was rejoined with her mother in Milwaukee. But after about six years, her mother thought it best to have Oprah return to Nashville to live permanently with her biological father, Vernon Winfrey, and be closely supervised by him. People in Nashville (particularly those in her religious community) recognized and nurtured young Oprah's talent for speech and performance so that she continued pursuing spoken and dramatic art through high school. According to historian H. W. Brands, "[Oprah's] gift of tongue brought her into contact with an ever-widening circle,"[2] and before long Oprah landed her first job in the broadcasting field at a Nashville radio station. With anchorwoman Barbara Walters as her broadcasting role model, Oprah took her first television broadcast job in Nashville during college (Tennessee State University). This weekend anchor position gave her the distinction even then of being the "first" of many "firsts" to come: "She became both the first female co-anchor in Nashville and the first black co-anchor there."[3]

Soon Oprah moved on to another anchor job at a station with more exposure. Her performance in that post attracted the ABC affiliate station in Baltimore, Maryland, WJZ-TV, a station looking to expand its news format and add some flavor (i.e., racial diversity) to its team. At age twenty-two, Oprah found this new job and this new town ominous, but gradually she re-created herself as a more light-news, talk-show personality type. In this persona, she was allowed more subjectivity in addressing the news, and this fit far better with her personality. Oprah was extremely successful as the cohost of *People Are Talking*, and, having gotten a glimpse of what broadcasting to other metropolitan audiences would be like (*People Are Talking* was nationally syndicated for a time), she eventually accepted a job as host of *A.M. Chicago*. A short time later, this Oprah version of *A.M. Chicago* shot through the ratings roof. Then, two years later in 1986, the show was renamed *The Oprah Winfrey Show* and was distributed nationally in syndication. Her deal with King World Productions, the show's distributor, and subsequent deals have made Oprah the top-earning entertainer in America and have earned her the dubious title "Queen of Daytime TV."[4] Bolstering the show's enormous popularity is Oprah's Book Club, launched on her show in 1996. Many people attest that this club and Oprah's personal love for literature have gotten America reading again. Being placed on her book list means instant success for the author; her club boasts more than half a million members worldwide. Now in its twentieth season, *The Oprah Winfrey Show* is the highest-rated television talk show in history and is seen in virtually every television market in the United States and in 110 other countries. Her show is ranked highest among all talk shows and earned a Daytime Emmy virtually every year from 1987 to 1998. In 1998, Oprah won an additional Daytime Emmy for her lifetime achievement in the industry.

About two years after *The Oprah Winfrey Show* was launched, Oprah's own production company, Harpo ("Oprah" spelled backward), assumed ownership of and production responsibilities for her wildly received talk show. It also began looking to interesting film-project and other television venues in which to invest. (Oprah's appetite for movie production was whetted by her supporting role in Steven Spielberg's film adaptation of Alice Walker's novel *The Color Purple* [1985].) Since that time, Harpo Productions has produced numerous projects, including *The Women of Brewster Place*, a

miniseries based on a novel by Gloria Naylor (1989); a film based on Toni
Morrison's novel *Beloved* (1998); and the Emmy-winning made-for-televi-
sion movie *Oprah Winfrey Presents: Tuesdays with Morrie* (1999). In March
2005, Harpo aired its film version of Zora Neale Hurston's novel *Their Eyes
Were Watching God*, starring African-American Academy Award winner
Halle Berry. In addition, Oprah recently founded *O, The Oprah Magazine*
with Hearst Publishing and established herself as its editorial director. The
magazine is said to be "the latest vehicle to cement Oprah's power as a force
in American media."[5] At about the same time, she cofounded Oxygen Media,
which runs the Oxygen Network on cable television.

Finally, Oprah is also a dedicated philanthropist. She has summarized her
philanthropic objectives in the following way:

> What I really want to do is have an impact on major issues: putting child molesters
> away for life so that a person who's harmed a child will never have the chance to do
> it again, having free education available to every African child by 2010, using televi-
> sion as a channel for empowerment—telling stories from around the world about the
> plight of women and children who have no one to speak for them.[6]

Just a year after *The Oprah Winfrey Show* was first broadcast, Oprah backed
up these words by establishing a private foundation in her name "to encourage people around the world to make a difference in the lives of others . . . to
inspire individuals to create opportunities that help underserved people rise
to their own potential."[7] Developing schools internationally for young children is one of her favorite philanthropic ventures: she has helped to erect ten
schools in rural areas internationally. She also oversees the Oprah Winfrey
Scholars Program, which offers scholarships to students committed to using
their education to give something back to their communities. Perhaps the
most popular among Oprah's philanthropic projects is Oprah's Angel Network, announced on her show in 1997. Her website reports that this network
of charitable giving is Oprah's opportunity "to inspire people to use their
lives and reap the truest rewards that come from giving to others."

Although the world watched Oprah build a strong fortune from all of her
various media and charitable projects, most were stunned in 2003 to hear that
she had made the *Forbes* magazine list of American *billionaires*. That year,
Oprah became the first African-American woman to grace that list, with a net
worth of one billion dollars. This came just two years after Black Entertainment Television founder Robert Johnson made that list as the first black person ever to do so.[8]

There is little doubt, then, that Oprah Winfrey is one of the most (if not
the most) celebrated, accomplished, and powerful women of African descent
that has ever lived. But what some contemporary black women doubt is
whether her accomplishments and those of the people alongside whom she
has achieved her eminent status have desensitized her to the black sisterhood.

In a report of her recent interview with Oprah, journalist Audrey Edwards defends her by saying, "She has now come full circle, returning to the sisterhood, choosing to grant another interview, another cover, simply because she wants to."[9] But it is unclear here whether the sisterhood to which she refers is something broader than the staff of *Essence* magazine. Later, however, Edwards's remarks are less vague:

> Oprah, of course, has never left the sisterhood, despite the sniping of player haters who say things like "She's not really Black" or "She treats White people better than Black people." This has always been one of the burdens of Black success: Black resentment.[10]

The language of the Oprah debate is represented further in these comments made by writer Charlotte Allen, who contributes the comments to *Women's Quarterly* (and to my knowledge is not African American):

> Oprah preaches and practices exactly the right kind of "diversity." She's proud of being African-American, and both her show and magazine aggressively include and promote black celebrities (one of her biggest catches: National Security Advisor Condoleeza Rice), black fashion models, and ordinary black women trying on career clothes or being made over. Oprah's world, however, is a racially-integrated world, and her point is always to show that black women, indeed women of every ethnic group, are—or can be if they're not—every bit as smart, pretty, bright, and successful as their Anglo counterparts.[11]

In her book *Oprah Winfrey and the Glamour of Misery*, sociologist Eva Illouz argues that all of Oprah's intentions are guided by her unique "African American habitus," the components of which are

> her membership in the African American community; the rhetoric and moral outlook of the African American church, in which she was socialized; the experience of family as an arbitrary, secretive, and violent institution; and finally, the multiplicity of social worlds in which she has lived.[12]

But despite such attempts to demonstrate the significance of blackness to Oprah's womanhood and of the private and public attachments she has shown to black women all over the world, the question of whether Oprah is suitably authentic in her black womanhood still looms large among today's African-American women.

OPRAH'S RESONANCE AND DISSONANCE WITH CONTEMPORARY BLACK WOMEN

Through the study women's reflections on Oprah, it is quite clear that Oprah is by and large viewed by women of both the lower and middle classes as an

authentic product of black women's "struggle." There is virtual unanimity
on the subject of Oprah having thoughtfully constructed an "awesome" and
"amazing" life and career from humble and traumatic beginnings: she is
credited with "making much of something out of nothing." The women view
Oprah's childhood, for example, as highly illustrative of black women's
struggle for economic and physical well-being and of the struggle to hold
black families together. Not only was Oprah's childhood made difficult by
the meager resources her family was forced to live on in her rural farming
community, but it was also troubled by tragic events she today openly shares
with her audiences: teenage pregnancy and sexual abuse. Charlotte Allen,
again writing for *Women's Quarterly*, sums up well the study women's sentiments:

> Born out of wedlock in 1954 to teenaged parents, raised by her grandmother in Mis-
> sissippi until age six, when her mother moved her to Milwaukee and to a dysfunc-
> tional household in which she was sexually abused by men starting at age nine,
> slipping into early promiscuity and giving birth at age fourteen to a premature baby
> who didn't survive—such is not the stuff of which successful lives are made.[13]

As Oprah moved into adulthood, other struggles presented themselves.
Most notably, Oprah suffered the pain of obesity before a national audience,
winning and then losing one weight-loss battle after another. What is more,
Oprah publicly confessed on her show to having used illicit drugs: "The self-
degradation ran the gamut from the foolish but harmless (taking the seeds out
the watermelon for one man 'so he wouldn't have to spit') to the foolhardy
and dangerous (smoking cocaine with a boyfriend)."[14] Oprah has admitted
that her drug use was one of many manifestations of her having "allowed
herself to be used by men because she hadn't yet learned to love herself."[15]
She has confessed to having suffered a great deal of emotional abuse from
certain male colleagues who felt threatened by her early in her career; they
could see even then that Oprah would be fierce competition. Adrienne (age
fifty-two) is among several of the women I interviewed at the women's correctional facility who in hearing about Oprah's past indiscretion with drug
use began seeing Oprah as socially accessible. Her newfound sense of comfort was heightened in learning that a man had been the one to lure her. Adrienne says she has a clear memory of the Baltimore days when Oprah "was
going through something with that man in her life. . . . 'Cause she was really
going through something with that man. And now, look at all them men that
want her."

Terry (drug policy analyst, age thirty-nine) says that she learned a lot about
Oprah's early life and career struggles through her mother, who "knows her
personally" from a job she once had at a "food center" in Baltimore. What
she recalls most is her mother talking about how Oprah was frequently "in
need" of one thing or another stemming from her difficult history, and how

she often did not or could not seek the help she needed. But in time, Oprah began to trust many of the black women around her and "just gravitated" to the people willing to support her. Oprah's ability to survive such difficult circumstances makes many of the study women proud to call her "sister." Monica (nanny, age fifty-four) says that from her observations of Oprah in the days of Baltimore and from knowing some of the tragedy she had to endure, "I wished that I could have been somewhat like her, to climb, and have the ambition she had." Victoria (mental health social worker, age thirty-five) tells a somewhat amusing story about an event she believes serves as a metaphor for Oprah's difficult journey and for her sweet triumph:

> I remember Oprah when Oprah lived in Baltimore. Now, I was just telling my girl-friend about a show, when she [cohosted local news] with Richard, and they had this thing where they were looking at shoes, and to see if you have good self-esteem or something. And when he got to Oprah's shoes, Oprah must have worn the worst shoes she had, and he said, this person—I just remember him saying something like—this person has low self-esteem, and this person doesn't have [much], lives in poverty or lives close to it. And it was Oprah's shoes. And I can't remember if I had gone to the show for a taping or saw it on TV. And I just thought it was the most hysterical thing . . . now Oprah [is] the woman who has succeeded.

Oprah's status as a role model is something that greatly attracts black women of the lower classes. This attraction rests largely on the basis that Oprah, like them, has suffered significant personal struggle but has made it through in royal fashion. Tia, who now at the age of thirty is anxious to get out of prison and back on the right track, says she frequently reads material about Oprah's early struggles that help her to remember that she has the same "potential" to be a success story once she is released from detention:

> I see black women [like Oprah] who has had adversities in their lives, from whatever circumstances may be. But I see black women who has risen above those adversities.

And forty-two-year-old Michelle, also being held at a women's correctional facility, says that Oprah "seem[s] to try to push the word out to black women to not give up, because it's hard out there for us." These women also believe that what makes Oprah a strong role model is the leadership she has shown in her field; Oprah is hailed as the antithesis of the "sister slacker" who fails to take advantage of what life lays before her. They are proud to see that the best talk show on television is hosted by an African-American woman, and one who has made the conscious choice to emphasize content that helps black women viewers "think." Billie (administrative assistant, age thirty-four) says that she makes it a point to watch Oprah's show and ignores most other talk shows that do little more than contrive mindless "drama":

I'd rather look at Oprah than to sit and look at Ricki Lake or Jenny Jones. I don't have time for that drama, so give me something that's gonna help me grow and mature, to get to that point where I want to see myself, ten, fifteen, twenty years from now.

Megan says, "I'm just proud of the girl; I salute her" for having trusted herself enough to make such choices in an industry that can be exceptionally cruel. She, like Kitty, likes seeing Oprah "speak her own mind," a quality she would like to develop further within herself.

For middle-class women, it is primarily the boldness that Oprah has shown by crafting her life and career on her own terms that makes her their role model. They refer frequently to Oprah's "smart business decisions" in speaking of that boldness, particularly the decision to broaden her audience base. They even view Oprah's decision to "whiten" her audiences as necessary for her to survive in an industry where ratings mean everything. As Myrna (school counselor, age fifty-eight) says, Oprah has to go "where the economic structure is. All the people at the top are white, and all the people at the top got money." Not only, they say, is it important for her to remain financially solvent through the solicitation of white dollars, but it is also important that Oprah's show, magazine, website, and other venues evolve to meet the needs and tastes of an increasingly multicultural nation:

> Naomi (private school teacher, age twenty-six): Some of her choice[s], I think—her career, professional choices—were made because she was trying to make money, and because, as she evolved, she found, like, this common ground where all women can meet . . . and I think that's healthy for her individually, but I also think it's very lucrative for her.
>
> Tabitha (emergency room physician, age forty): We're changing colors. And if anybody doesn't see that, you know, ten, twenty, thirty years from now we're gonna be all mixed up. We're not gonna be just all black. There are gonna be more mixed couples and mixed children and Hispanic. They're taking over, and we're gonna be mixing up with them. . . . It's a big world out there where you really need to just embrace everyone.

Tabitha says that she also believes, however, that the strong-willed Oprah may not be making all these "racial" decisions on her own. She strongly suspects that there are others (i.e., whites) with a vested interest in her empire's success who may muscle her at times into changing her format: "But hey," Tabitha says, "whatever works." You may recall that middle-class women (and their counterparts in the lower classes) are irresolute about whether black women sabotage their collective goals by embracing a wider political partnership or constituency to combat oppression—that is, by concerning themselves with issues that they share with other gender-ethnic groups. By contrast, they are less ambivalent, it seems, about embracing other groups when the issues at stake are clearly economic. Oprah inviting a wider audience into her black womanist enterprises in order to ensure professional longevity and financial security is viewed as more legitimate than doing so for purely political reasons.

Oprah's decision to expand her audience base, particularly for her talk show, has not sat as well with women of the lower classes as it has with their middle-class counterparts. In fact, most of these women strongly object to the "sudden" sea of white faces that grace the seats of her television studio. Some claim to be offended by how this decision has led Oprah to venture into a new set of substantive areas—"white-related issues"—to which the lower-class study women find no connection. Wanda (temporary postal worker, early twenties) was particularly vocal about this:

> Field notes: Before I had a chance to go anywhere else on the subject of Oprah, Wanda jumped in and said, "I don't like Oprah. Oprah doesn't know where she's at right now, and I don't know where Oprah's at right now. I even couldn't begin to tell you what she's doing." Wanda said that she doesn't watch Oprah's show because to her it seems that she deals with issues that have no relationship to anybody but "white folks." She said, "I don't see black women fitting into any of her stuff, so I just don't bother."

Rosalee (administrative assistant, age thirty-one) had been similarly estranged from Oprah's "new" talk-show content:

> I look at her audience, and I think she reaches maybe a wider range of white people than she do black people. I don't watch her shows . . . maybe because of the topics. Black people topics, she really don't focus on.

I asked Rosalee what she might suggest to Oprah if she had the opportunity to address the issue of more appropriate content. She replied that more of her topics should include "getting back the family again" and the need for "fathers to play a bigger role" in work and family life. She also said that she would appreciate more discussion about how to help "young people turn their lives around." While certainly such issues are covered regularly on Oprah's show, especially when her friend and mentor Dr. Phil is a guest, many of these study women seem to feel strongly that these subjects need an infusing of authentic black experience.

Adrienne claims that Oprah's "love of white folks" is nothing new. Having spent some of her school years in Chicago, Adrienne had also encountered Oprah in that setting. There she recalls observing Oprah "work" the interracial crowds and witnessing what she describes as an overt need on Oprah's part to gain white people's approval:

> She was at this place, and we talked to her and stuff, and she really . . . she's a really nice person. But you noticed she tried to get most of the white people's attention.

She gave black people a little attention, but she put most of her surrounds around
the white people.

In addressing Oprah's love of white people and their love of her, writer
Tammy Johnson highlights what she and many other cultural critics have
argued is Oprah's disturbing role as "mammy" and "wise black matriarch"
to her white fans.[16] Her claim is that Oprah's relationship with whites helps
to ease their racial guilt by promoting "the mainstream spin" on racism and
privilege: both concepts are said to be cast simplistically on her show as interpersonal flaws rather than as deep-seated structural realities. From this perspective, the answers to such problems lie in personal transformation rather
than in revolutionary structural change, and Oprah is there to guide them
along the way. Cultural theorist Sherryl Wilson argues that Oprah's politiciz-
ing of racial issues is neither absent nor obscure, but rather her "'racial' identity is often foregrounded."[17] The presentation of Oprah's gender-ethnic
identity occurs most often, she says, "outside any political frame of reference"[18] and is generally embedded (some would say very deeply, too deeply)
within the broader topics she addresses on her show. Wilson provides two
examples of this embedded racial dynamic in her book, and while she
acknowledges their political hollowness, she also says,

Oprah's constant self-references as a black woman deny the possibility of effacing
her own racial identity and so is self-consciously an integral part of her persona.[19]

I do not recall having seen the particular Oprah segments Wilson highlights
here, but I have witnessed what I describe as Oprah's evolving to at least
a more public engagement with gender-ethnic phenomena. For example, in
February of 2005, Oprah's magazine and her talk show gave focused attention to news reporter Lisa Ling's travels to the eastern Congo in Africa,
where women shared their stories of having been brutally raped as part of the
civil war being waged there. It was only a brief statement, but Oprah made a
rare public pronouncement: the reason the world has not responded to these
atrocities and to atrocities like it elsewhere in Africa is because the people
being oppressed are *black*. That afternoon and evening, several of my sister-
friends called or e-mailed me to comment on what we all recognized as a
unique moment when Oprah "saw" black women.

As expected, the issue of Oprah having "forgotten where she comes from"
(or not having forgotten) permeates strongly throughout much of this discussion, particularly the "social mobility" vein, which scrutinizes the well-to-do
for not having adequately given back to their community. The women recognize that Oprah is wildly generous in her charity toward people around the
world, though some would like to see as much giving to African-American
causes as to those on the African continent. Further, the pattern of response
between the two class groups here is familiar: as is true for their sentiments

toward renowned black women generally, black women from the middle classes tend to be less forgiving of Oprah for having "forgotten." They frequently use language like "Oprah *used* to be black," and "I don't see her as down-to-earth as I used to see her." Taylor (elementary school teacher, age fifty-four) says that she hates to admit it but her devotion to Oprah as a fan dwindled as she became more famous:

> I used to be a big fan of hers. . . . I feel bad that I can easily say she kind of gets on my nerves. And I don't watch her show very often unless she's got someone on, you know? Because of her money, she's not as black as she used to be. Do you know what I mean?

Taylor goes on to grapple with what is really driving her to say such things and concludes that it must somehow be that "the money" has blinded Oprah's ability to "see" black people, particularly black experts who she feels deserve equal time on her show and in her magazine:

> I just think she should be promoting perhaps a few more black people. I think you shouldn't have to wait two weeks to see a black face.

Mariah (school counselor, age fifty-six) similarly struggles with why she is so "irritated" by Oprah these days. She says that her "blood pressure goes up" when she thinks about it all, and she believes that Oprah should somehow put her wealth to work in helping to make everyday black women look better in the public's eyes. On the contrary, she says that Oprah's "forgetting where she comes from" is sometimes revealed through her addressing social issues in such a way as to make African-American women "look bad." She is certain that the general public responds the way it does because it is incapable of understanding or lacks empathy for the black woman's standpoint:

> I think when she has different subjects on, especially that pertain to blacks per se, she doesn't try to identify or say this is what "we" do. You see what I'm saying? Now, I'm gonna give you a prime example. Both my coworkers are white females, and they are forever coming to me and saying, do you think we should report this to Protective Services? And I try to explain to them that black folks discipline their children a little differently. Now, I'm not saying put a mark on anybody, or break any bones or anything like that, but we have to do hands-on. For some reason, that's all our children will understand. They [white women] think a smack is abusive, and, well, maybe to them it is. [I tell them], you have to have been there to understand sometimes how the discipline in your house is [that] house.

Oprah has strongly advocated the protection of children from corporal punishment and sexual abuse; both have been a topic of major concern for Oprah personally. While Mariah says she certainly understands that this issue must be publicly debated and is anguished by Oprah's experience with violence, she feels that Oprah should make an effort to deliver this topic without appearing to demonize black people.

Black women across the class divide are about equally likely to argue that Oprah's immense wealth may have led her to being far more "uppity" than they can tolerate and less "down to earth" than they remember her "before." The "old Oprah," they say, was much more tangible and had not yet let the fame, money, and other luxuries "go to her head." But women of the lower classes are more prevalent among those *rejecting* the idea that Oprah's uppity ways have led to her no longer being "true to her race"; many feel that she is "just as black as she's always been":

> Brooke (single mother and homemaker, age fifty-two): I can't get it. I don't get it. Because to me, she's black. And I don't see her trying to act white. I just see her working in a white world. She got a whole bunch of money, and because she does have money, she gets the recognition she does. To me, Oprah has a heart of gold, and for *us*.

Thus, as is true generally, these women are less, rather than more, scrutinizing than middle-class black women about renowned women's gender-ethnic authenticity, despite their relatively greater social distance from them.

Finally, the particularly strong attachment the study women express toward religious, churchgoing black women is shown here through their concern for Oprah's religious affiliation and religious faith. There are many among the study women who—along with a great many other people, if you can trust what circulates on the World Wide Web—worry that Oprah has either been brainwashed into rejecting her good Baptist roots or that she has been dabbling in some newfangled, mysterious religious movement. It would seem that there are a good many people highly invested in whether Oprah's God is their God, or whether she worships any god at all. Speckled throughout our exchanges on this topic are study women claiming to have heard "that *one* time" when Oprah actually said something concrete about her religious beliefs, specifically about whether or not she is a Christian. It varies as to whether what was heard confirmed or denied her Christianity, but what is most important is that the need to know the truth about Oprah's spiritual life is as much about genuine concern for her salvation as it is about the authenticity of her black womanhood.

On this issue, there is no detectable class divide. Brooke says that she does not believe the rumors that Oprah "doesn't believe in God," as so many of the black women she knows believe. She argues that concerns about her straying from her faith appear unwarranted: "From what I know, that I heard from my ear, Oprah says she gets on her knees every day and pray to God." On the other side, Charlene and Saundra (both middle-class women) say they are well aware that Oprah is ambivalent about "to whom she belongs," meaning to which religious faith she adheres. Charlene says that the question of

Oprah's religious affiliation and religious faith comes up regularly in conversations she has with other black women: "What God does Oprah believe in?" She says that black women are concerned that Oprah is tiptoeing around the truth of her Christianity in not "calling the name of Christ" when she speaks of tapping into "one's spirit." Saundra says that Oprah's not openly professing her Christian faith (assuming this is in fact true) is "a spiritual issue," that somehow the process of becoming famous has disconnected her from the traditional African-American ethic of spirituality.

Ada (administrative aide, age forty-seven) says that attacks on Oprah for supposedly "forgetting where she comes from" may be primarily about people not wanting to think progressively and holistically about authentic black womanhood. She believes that the work Oprah does today should be the work of all black women—"more into educational things, improving our minds, improving our bodies." There is "a percentage of us," she concludes, "who just can't accept change," and as a result, the sisterhood remains mired in some of the same dilemmas that have troubled it for years.

*   *   *

The black woman collective is in a quandary about Oprah Winfrey, but what we learn from this analysis is that the quandary it is in does not organize itself strongly by camps of class-based sentiment. This conclusion is not likely to restrain the knee-jerk reactions we have when we find ourselves face to face with other black women at different places than we are on the continuum of Oprahness, but perhaps it will find its way into an intrasisterhood dialogue about how valuable personal and social capital like that which Oprah commands can best be exploited.

Oprah is simultaneously the most extreme and the most common kind of African-American woman there is, struggling to survive—yes, even in her immense wealth—and to live an authentically black womanist existence. This challenge to remain anchored within the black sisterhood can be both exhausting and invigorating, but seemingly always necessary. This is very likely why Oprah has taken such solace in the words once spoken to her by her beloved mentor, Maya Angelou. As Oprah tells it,

> [Coping with black resentment toward me] was the hardest thing for me in the beginning. I used to get criticism all the time, people saying you're not doing enough for other Blacks. I remember going to Sidney Poitier early on and saying, "God, I just can't handle this." It was Maya Angelou who told me, "You alone are enough."[20]

NOTES

1. Laura B. Randolph, "Oprah! The Most Powerful Woman in Entertainment Talks about Her Fame, Her Father, and Her Future in TV," *Ebony*, July 1995.

2. H. W. Brands, *Masters of Enterprise: Giants of American Business from John Jacob Astor and J. P. Morgan to Bill Gates and Oprah Winfrey* (New York: Free Press, 1999), 294.

3. Ibid.

4. Randolph, "Oprah! The Most Powerful Woman in Entertainment Talks About Her Fame, Her Father, and Her Future in TV."

5. Audrey Edwards, "The O Factor: Oprah Winfrey's First Interview with a Women's Magazine since Starting Her Own," *Essence*, October 1, 2003, 179.

6. Lisa Kogan, "The Oprah Show Turns 20 (Q & A)," *O: The Oprah Magazine*, October 2005.

7. Oprah's Angel Network, http://www2.oprah.com/uyl/angel/uyl_angel_about.jhtml.

8. Patricia Hill Collins, *Black Sexual Politics: African Americans, Gender, and the New Racism* (New York: Routledge, 1990), 142.

9. Edwards, "The O Factor: Oprah Winfrey's First Interview with a Women's Magazine since Starting Her Own," 179.

10. Ibid., 180.

11. Charlotte Allen, "O, How I Love You, Oprah: Oprah's Politics Are Sometimes O-Dious. Still, Charlotte Allen Finds Her a-O-Kay," *Women's Quarterly* 33 (2002): 22.

12. Eva Illouz, *Oprah Winfrey and the Glamour of Misery* (New York: Columbia University Press, 2003), 28.

13. Allen, "O, How I Love You, Oprah: Oprah's Politics Are Sometimes O-Dious. Still, Charlotte Allen Finds Her a-O-Kay."

14. Randolph, "Oprah! The Most Powerful Woman in Entertainment Talks about Her Fame, Her Father, and Her Future in TV."

15. Ibid.

16. Tammy Johnson, "It's Personal: Race and Oprah," Applied Research Center, November 29, 2001, www.arc.org/C_Lines/CLArchive/story4_4_04.html (accessed November 23, 2004). Also see Tammy Johnson, "Get Your Freak On: Sex, Babies, and Images of Black Femininity," in Collins, *Black Sexual Politics: African Americans, Gender, and the New Racism*.

17. Sherryl Wilson, *Oprah, Celebrity, and Formations of Self* (Basingstoke, Hampshire [England]: Palgrave Macmillan, 2003), 179.

18. Ibid.

19. Ibid.

20. Edwards, "The O Factor: Oprah Winfrey's First Interview with a Women's Magazine since Starting Her Own."

Chapter Seven

Conclusion: Restimulating the Black Sisterhood

At this point, whether African American women can fashion a singular "voice" about the black *woman's* position remains less an issue than how black women's voices collectively construct, affirm, and maintain a dynamic black *women's* standpoint. Given the increasingly troublesome political context affecting black women as a group, such solidarity is essential.

—Patricia Hill Collins, sociologist and feminist scholar[1]

A black women's movement for progressive social change needs leaders who understand black women's ambivalence, anger, apathy, and feelings of powerlessness as well as their strength, resilience, and commitment to their families and communities.

—Sheila Radford-Hill, author and black activist[2]

It is quite telling that an entire chapter of this book is devoted to the study women's articulation of struggle. It serves to remind us that the master narrative of black women's history, replete with victory of various kinds, is a story undeniably written from the struggle to overcome tremendous obstacles. The experience of struggle in black women's everyday lives is the primary mark of their authentic black womanhood. That this narrative must *re*document the history of black women speaks to one of the most ardent struggles of all: the struggle to combat the negative public regard historically shown for black women.

It is also telling that the theme of struggle is so highly salient among black women in this purported time of plenty. Billionaire Oprah Winfrey, Secretary of State Condoleezza Rice (next U.S. president?), Academy Award winner Halle Berry, two-time college president Johnnetta B. Cole—phenomenal as these women may be, they represent only the very tip of the eighteen million

175

black females in this country. Life for the vast majority of African-American women continues to be a material hardship. For those who manage to achieve some semblance of economic stability, the battle to maintain good mental and physical health, to keep black families together, and to live life with dignity remains.

It is given these and other harsh realities that we must keep in mind the significance of studying black women's gender-ethnic identity and consciousness. The black feminist/womanist standpoint has been forged in large part from the need to resist oppression in all its forms—from economic exploitation, distorted and controlling media images, and glass ceilings in the workplace to poor education in public schools. Because oppression is not uniformly realized across the population of black women, that standpoint and its vision are particularized. Black women are challenged, therefore, in their quest for collective empowerment: "Connections between Black women are not automatic by virtue of our similarities, and the possibilities of genuine communication between us are not easily achieved."[3]

The research that has produced *Embracing Sisterhood* can neither support nor deny claims of an increasing or waning identity and consciousness among African-American women over time. Such claims would require analyses that employ closely comparable data collected over the past thirty or forty years, and to my knowledge no such data exist. Even as there is much theorizing about the demise of black women's community and reports from a number of small-scale studies that reveal black women's angst about a gender-ethnic crisis, there is no strong evidence that what is observed today departs significantly from what black women experienced in earlier times.

What we know has changed over the past several decades is the proportion of African-American women who occupy high-status positions in this society, and of black women who have attained high levels of education. There have also been increases in the proportions of single black women heading family households, today about a third of which subsist below the poverty level. These changes signal in various ways a pulling away of women in these higher classes from the masses of women to whom they have historically been more akin in their socioeconomic condition. Granted, black women have never been a monolithic group, but the class structure among them was much more compact in times past. In these past times, it is argued, the concerns of black women were more immediate and universal, which provided for a more ready-made solidarity predicated on the notion that black women's fates were inextricably linked. But according to Sheila Radford-Hill, Patricia Hill Collins, and other black feminist scholars, concomitant with the changing socioeconomic dynamics among them are concerns that, over time, black women are becoming less committed to embracing the idea that black women constitute a meaningful cultural community.

The primary contribution that this research makes is to provide a snapshot of what is occurring at the intersection of race, gender, class, and group identity at a time in history when there is much speculation about the consequences of black women's unprecedented achievements. This snapshot is also situated at a moment when socioeconomic schism among black women is purported to be at its highest. Although the economic cleavage that is observed among African-American families and among black men is not duplicated for black women, their integral economic role in black families across the spectrum explains in part black women's inevitable experience of class schism.

Different schools of thought have made predictions about what the nature of intrarace dynamics would be under these kinds of conditions, but rarely are black women given specific attention. Thus, in addition, this research brings black women's concerns in from the margins of such study. These schools of thought—the race school, the class school, and the black feminist school—help form the theoretical framework that guides the process by which to answer very basic questions: What is the association between black class polarization and gender-ethnic identity and consciousness among contemporary black women? More specifically, what is the relative degree of gender-ethnic unity and class discord that exists? And, by extension, can there be political solidarity among black women in these times? A number of possible answers to these questions can be constructed from these various theoretical camps. I have conceded that most of these answers have not tended sufficiently to balance the precedent of a thriving, cross-class black woman collective with the potential for estrangement within the current polarized economic environment. So, despite my strong personal predisposition to assume that black *step*sisterhood would eclipse gender-ethnic unity, my scholarly approach was to take as firm a middle ground as I possibly could find.

I spent months wading through the voices of the eighty-eight contemporary African-American women I consulted for this study. I revisited the hair salons, the state corrections offices and facilities, the homes and offices of sorority members, and the meetings of black university faculty and staff in an effort to confirm what eventually jelled in this work. Discord is common among contemporary black women. Where in the everyday it may seem that black women are settled, both individually and personally, on most issues that concern them, there are several areas where ambivalence reigns. Class dynamics among today's black women are also very real, some of it troubling and some of it fairly benign. On the whole, the tendencies of black women who are more educated and more highly employed to embrace certain ideas about black womanhood can be distinguished from those of less educated, unemployed, and underemployed black women. This is true whether the issue at hand is their level of comfort with interracial marriage or their commitment to watching the next installment of the Oprah show, and it is particularly true when middle-class women are contrasted with those most socially marginalized. And, lest I be accused of overromanticizing about black sisterhood, I acknowledge that, for many black women, the view across class lines can be painfully unpleasant. But what is also real is that black women have typically imagined these tendencies to be miles apart, when in fact they are more like yards apart. What keeps the distance between them small (moderate at best) is that contemporary black women continue to view themselves firmly from the lens of collectivity. Their strong black womanist standpoint and the currency of sisterhood that is shown among them—particularly the currency of collective struggle—serve to temper the potential schismatic effects of class.

This study, like all social research, is limited in its scope. First, the sample I derived for this research is composed of African-American women who reside in a small geographic corner of the nation, and their number is quite small relative to even that population. What is more, the proportion of these women who are categorized as middle class is somewhat higher than is the case in the Greater Baltimore Area. Second, the range of issues (variables) and how they are addressed (measured) in this study constitute one of many possible options. Therefore, it is not possible to know with any certainty whether the sentiments expressed here closely align with those of black women in other parts of the country or whether the unity and discord that is observed here and potentially elsewhere is over- or underdrawn from the specific data-gathering tools I employed. Future research should work to replicate what was accomplished here in other geographic areas and to cover a wider scope of concerns with varied instrumentation. That said, I am confidant that at this juncture the strengths of this work far outweigh its limitations.

ENVISIONING A FUTURE

The desire for realness reveals a yearning for a political movement with real substance; more important, however, finding realness would mean building a genuinely new movement rather than merely imitating those of the past.

—Astrid Henry, womanist scholar[4]

Scholarly interest in determining the existence and nature of collective identity rests largely in being able to predict what social and political behavior might extend from that identity. The general hypothesis is that collective identities are reflective of collective interests and that collective behavior occurs as a means to advance and protect those interests. As we have learned, the historical praxis of black sisterhood has been manifest in a wide variety of ways, each involving the harnessing of woman power for the preservation and elevation of black women's lives. There are numerous examples of black women crafting all kinds of activism over the years through both formal and informal channels. As Patricia Hill Collins has stated, "Conditions in the wider political economy simultaneously shape Black women's subordination and foster activism":[5] activism has been the cornerstone of black women's gender-ethnic identity and consciousness.

What I believe is most valuable about this research is the realization it potentially brings to black women about the differences—and particularly the *lack* of differences—among them. If the nearly one-third of study women who expressed serious doubt about black women ever truly coming together have based their angst on inflated ideas about class discord, then this research helps to bring them hope. There is much evidence here of a sisterhood ripe for new activism and for new challenges, and there exists a unity that many black women may have thought had passed away. But as Astrid Henry warns us, today's black women, especially the youngest generations, are seeking a fresh approach to revitalizing the very ideals that gave birth to the sisterhood.

Talk of black women organizing a new social movement is always tantalizing, though people tend to evoke the term "social movement" without a full understanding of its character. The textbook definition of a social movement is "a collective, organized, and noninstitutional challenge to authorities, powerholders, or cultural beliefs and practices."[6] Social movement actors are in for the long haul. Furthermore, strong gender-ethnic identity and consciousness has proven to be sufficient for idea and resource mobilization in the short term and even for sustaining that activism in the long term. While social movements are not always initially constructed with clear, concrete goals in mind, it is helpful to have thought through what motivates the activism. In this instance, I would argue that the strong gender-ethnic identity and consciousness that is exhibited so vividly throughout this text strongly suggests that the motivation for contemporary activism by black women is this: black women *owe* each other, their communities, and the world at large to be engaged in progressive social change. And in that same spirit, black women owe each other the challenge of actualizing the vision of authentic cross-class activism.

Black feminist scholars today cry out for new birth and new leadership that will reempower black women to fully reclaim their legacy. Sheila Radford-Hill has had this to say about what will be necessary to move the sisterhood forward:

> The crisis in black women's identity and belief will end when every black woman has access to healing, solidarity, and political consciousness and when every black woman knows and accepts her share of responsibility to make all black communities places of nurture and transcendence for all black children. Although black women are more complex and heterogeneous than any current theorizing would suggest, black feminists can work with local community activists to achieve this goal.[7]

A potential project for the sisterhood is also suggested by this statement, and that is one focused on the nurturance of black children. This reminds me of the many interviews I conducted for this research that took place in and around public schools. In Baltimore and other major urban centers like it, public schools are generally considered a menace to black society. According to one report,

> 12 percent of African-American males dropped out of [Baltimore] city schools last year. But that's just one year. Over the course of their school careers, the numbers multiply enormously. According to a 2001 study at the Johns Hopkins University . . . 76 percent of the city's black males drop out before graduation.[8]

The figures for black girls are generally better but equally unacceptable. Very frequently, when my interviews with the study women were over and casual conversation would begin, it was these kinds of statistics that would be raised and lamented. Needless to say, the subject of reforming public education in the United States is one that many black women ponder, especially given the proportionately higher number of black children whose development is arrested by poor educational training.

For sure, the sisterhood could take on any project of significance to their lives as a starting point for encouraging systemic change. The idea is to organize around and fixate on something very tangible for black women across the socioeconomic spectrum that can illuminate the independency of social problems and solutions. Further, that project needs to unapologetically proclaim a cross-class leadership that is driven by black womanist ideals. The fresh new approach for which today's black women long may need to involve taking hold of an "intellectual and moral leadership" through which the hegemonic forces that oppress black women and their communities can be challenged.[9] To say that the ideals that would undergird the project would be black womanist in kind is not to mean that the project will be exclusive to black women or even to their communities, but rather it is to give black women the *authority to lead* whatever coalitions are built along the way. I do not claim that we have any specialized knowledge about social movements or about how they ought to be built. I am simply offering suggestions for what might be the necessary ingredients for igniting black women to progressive action. It is a start.

Oprah's Embrace?

My mother rang me up a few days ago. She called to say that she had just heard something on television that stopped her in her tracks: *Oprah had mentioned something about starting a social movement.* I had missed the show that day and could not imagine the context in which this was said, so I rushed to the Internet to find out. "Have You Let Yourself Go?" was the topic of that day's installment. Women had shared their confessions about having let everything take precedence over their taking good care of their physical health and appearance. Through all of that one hour of exchange, what registered most with my mother was not the substance of the material but that *Oprah* had spoken about leading a social movement. And she had to call me right then about it.

My mother was reacting in much the same way as I have seen the study women and other black women I know react over the course of this research. They get excited about the next big thing Ms. Winfrey will do; moreover, they are always hopeful that her next big project will be one that places everyday African-American women at the forefront. As was shown through my analysis of the women's sentiments toward Ms. Winfrey—my somewhat reluctant task of engaging the concrete Oprah in this book—reviews of Oprah's gender-ethnic authenticity are highly mixed, though there is the general feeling that black women are anxious to have Oprah "see" them as she has so obviously seen other groups. Some say that they are sure Oprah intends to do this by taking leadership in such things as film projects like *The Color Purple*, *The Women of Brewster Place*, and *Beloved*. Still, rarely are everyday black women the substance of discussion on the daily Oprah show or in the monthly Oprah magazine. Many of the study women, especially those from the middle classes, give Oprah license to do whatever she pleases to remain a powerful force in her field. That she chooses to construct her projects in ways that tend to render the masses of American black women invisible is something most black women have simply and respectfully accepted. Yet despite the quandary the sisterhood is in about her, it seems that any time the question arises as to who will lead the next social movement for black women, the *only* name that is taken seriously (if other names are even offered) is Ms. Oprah Winfrey. And so, in imagining a future project to restimulate the contemporary black sisterhood, we wonder what it would be like to have Oprah at the helm as both unparalleled charismatic leader and resource mobilizer.

NOTES

1. Patricia Hill Collins, "What's in a Name? Womanism, Black Feminism, and Beyond," *The Black Scholar* 26, no. 1 (1996): 9–17.
2. Sheila Radford-Hill, *Further to Fly: Black Women and the Politics of Empowerment* (Minneapolis: University of Minnesota Press, 2000).
3. Audre Lorde, "Eye to Eye: Black Women, Hatred, and Anger," in *Sister Outsider: Essays and Speeches*, The Crossing Press Feminist Series (Freedom, CA: Crossing Press, 1984), 145–75.

4. Astrid Henry, *Not My Mother's Sister: Generational Conflict and Third-Wave Feminism* (Bloomington: Indiana University Press, 2004), 152.

5. Patricia Hill Collins, *Black Feminist Thought: Knowledge, Consciousness, and the Politics of Empowerment* (New York: Routledge, 1990), 10.

6. Jeff Goodwin and James M. Jasper, eds., *The Social Movements Reader: Cases and Concepts* (Malden, MA: Blackwell Publishing, 2003), 3.

7. Radford-Hill, *Further to Fly: Black Women and the Politics of Empowerment*, 102.

8. Michael Olesker, "Dropout Rate in City Schools Needs Our Attention as Well," *The Baltimore Sun*, January 28, 2003.

9. Social theorist Antonio Grasmci as quoted in Giovanni Arrighi, Beverly J. Silver, and Iftikhar Ahmad, *Chaos and Governance in the Modern World System* (Minneapolis: University of Minnesota Press, 1999), 26.

Appendix

Table 1. Dimensions of black women's gender-ethnic identity

Centrality—the extent to which the woman normatively defines herself with regard to race and gender; her normative perceptions of self with respect to race and gender across a number of different situations.

Private Regard—the extent to which the woman feels positively or negatively toward African-American women, as well as how positively or negatively she feels about being an African-American woman (i.e., closeness and gender-ethnic pride).

Public Regard—the extent to which the woman feels that others view African-American women positively or negatively; her assessment of how African-American women are viewed (or valued) by the broader society.

Sociopolitical Ideology—the woman's beliefs, opinions, and attitudes with respect to the way she feels that African-American women should act; represents her philosophy about the ways in which African-American women should live and interact with society.

Ideology Subscales

Assimilationist[1]—characterized by an emphasis on the similarities between African-American women and the rest of American society.

Humanist—emphasizes the similarities among all humans across categories of race, ethnicity, gender, class, or other distinguishing characteristics.

Oppressed Minority—emphasizes the similarities between the oppression that African-American women face and that of other gender-ethnic groups, and is aware of the oppression that continues to confront African-American women.

Nationalist[2]—stresses the uniqueness of being a black woman; views the African-American woman's experience as being different from that of any other group; posits that African-American women should be in control of their own destiny with minimal input from other groups.

Notes:

1. I expanded the description of the assimilationist ideology from that offered by Sellers et al. (1997) after determining that theirs did not capture well enough the strong structural assimilationist content. Eight of the nine items speak to black women penetrating the social networks and institutions controlled by the dominant culture; only one speaks specifically to penetrating the dominant culture's value system (cultural assimilation).

2. Though some of the survey items related to the nationalist ideology make reference to black women specifically, they are intended as gender neutral.

Table 2. Share of aggregate total personal income by each fifth of black women, 1970–2000, aged twenty-five or older[1]

Census year								
	1970		1980		1990		2000	
Total	$58.0	99%	$104.4	100%	$154.7	100%	$219.6	100%
Lowest fifth	$1.8	3.2%	$3.9	3.8%	$5.3	3.4%	$7.7	3.5%
Second fifth	$4.3	7.5%	$9.0	8.7%	$12.8	8.2%	$19.1	8.7%
Middle fifth	$7.7	13.2%	$15.8	15.1%	$23.4	15.1%	$33.3	15.1%
Fourth fifth	$15.2	26.2%	$28.1	26.9%	$39.2	25.4%	$53.7	24.5%
Highest fifth	$28.7	49.5%	$47.2	45.2%	$73.9	47.8%	$105.9	48.2%
	1970		1980		1990		2000	
Bottom 5 percent	$0.1	0.2%	$0.3	0.3%	$0.3	0.2%	$0.5	0.2%
Top 5 percent	$10.0	17.2%	$17.0	16.3%	$27.0	17.5%	$46.0	20.7%

The top header reads: *Percent distribution of aggregate personal income (dollars in billions)*

Source: Steven Ruggles, Matthew Sobek, Trent Alexander, Catherine A. Fitch, Ronald Goeken, Patricia Kelly Hall, Miriam King, and Chad Ronnander, *Integrated Public Use Microdata Series: Version 3.0* [Machine-readable database] (Minneapolis, MN: Minnesota Population Center [producer and distributor], 2004), www.ipums.org.

Note:
1. Data based on weighted cases. Income reported in 1999 dollars for money acquired in 2003. Income data are reported for total incomes greater than $0 and where total personal income is equal to or greater than that for wage and salary income. The latter restriction corrects for coding that resulted in some women having less total income than wages.

Table 3. Survey questionnaire and basic results
McDonald survey of African-American women, 2001–2002[1]

PART A: Circle the number that best applies to you.	Disagree	Uncertain	Agree
1. For me, being a black woman supports a positive self-image.	1%	8%	90%
2. Black women are not respected by the broader society.	28%	24%	48%
3. It is important that black women go to white schools to gain experience in interacting with whites.	58%	16%	27%
4. Black women and white women have more commonalities than differences.	28%	22%	51%
5. The dominant society devalues anything not white-male oriented.	27%	24%	49%
6. Whenever possible, black women should buy from black businesses.	7%	11%	82%
7. White women can never be trusted where black women are concerned.	76%	16%	8%
8. My destiny is tied to the destiny of other black women.	43%	17%	40%
9. In today's society, if black women don't achieve, they have only themselves to blame.	47%	21%	33%

10. Black women should strive to be full members of the American political system.	12%	12%	76%
11. There are other people who experience racial injustice and indignities similar to black women.	5%	5%	90%
12. Black women should not consider race when buying art or selecting a book to read.	42%	12%	46%
13. Black women should try to involve themselves in causes that will help all oppressed people.	8%	10%	82%
14. A thorough knowledge of black history is very important for black women today.	5%	1%	94%
15. Being black is unimportant to my womanhood.	76%	10%	15%
16. In general, other groups view black women in a positive manner.	60%	28%	12%
17. Black women should try to work within the system to achieve their political and economic goals.	13%	16%	71%
18. Black women should strive to integrate all institutions which are segregated.	31%	21%	48%
19. Blacks would be better off if they were more concerned with problems facing all people than just focusing on black issues.	51%	18%	31%
20. Blacks will be more successful in achieving their goals if they form coalitions with other oppressed groups.	22%	33%	46%
21. It is important for Black women to surround themselves and their children with black art, music, and literature.	8%	7%	84%
22. Black women must organize themselves into a separate political force.	51%	27%	22%
23. I have a strong sense of belonging to black people.	4%	11%	86%
24. Overall, black women are considered good by others.	18%	48%	34%
25. In general, others respect black women.	29%	36%	35%
26. A sign of progress is that black women are in the mainstream of America more than ever before.	7%	12%	81%
27. Blacks should feel free to interact socially with white people.	1%	6%	93%
28. Being an individual is more important than identifying oneself as a black woman.	25%	15%	60%
29. The same forces that have led to the oppression of black women have also led to the oppression of other groups.	15%	19%	66%
30. Black women should not marry interracially.	80%	15%	6%
31. Black women would be better off if they adopted Afrocentric values.	42%	35%	23%

32. I have a strong attachment to other black women.	8%	4%	88%
33. Society views black women as an asset.	46%	34%	21%
34. Black women should view themselves as being Americans first and foremost.	35%	21%	45%
35. We are all children of a higher being; therefore we should love people of all races.	1%	2%	96%
36. Being a black woman is not a major factor in my social relationships.	46%	13%	41%
37. I feel that the black community has made valuable contributions to this society.	2%	7%	90%
38. Blacks should judge whites as individuals and not members of the white race.	6%	7%	87%
39. Black students are better off going to schools that are controlled and organized by blacks.	61%	30%	8%
40. I feel good about black women.	5%	4%	92%
41. Blacks who support separatism are as racist as whites who do so.	24%	17%	59%
42. It should be socially acceptable for black women to marry outside of the race.	2%	6%	92%
43. People, regardless of their race, have strengths and limitations.	4%	2%	94%
44. Black women and white women can never truly be friends.	90%	5%	5%
45. The struggle for black liberation in America should be closely related to the struggle of other oppressed groups.	31%	35%	34%
46. On a day-to-day basis, I find being a black woman difficult.	64%	5%	31%
47. I am proud to be a black woman.	2%	4%	94%
48. The plight of black women in America will improve only when they hold more of the important positions in society.	31%	29%	40%
49. Black women's values should not be inconsistent with human values.	6%	11%	83%
50. I feel that black women have made major accomplishments and advancements.	1%	1%	98%
51. Sometimes I wish I had been born of another race.	5%	5%	90%
52. Black women should learn about the oppression of other groups.	8%	16%	76%
53. The sexism black women have experienced is similar to that of other minority women.	35%	19%	46%

54. Black women should treat other oppressed people as allies.	37%	34%	29%
55. Being black is an important reflection of who I am.	4%	6%	90%

Note:
  1. See chapter 1, note 84.

PART B: Circle the number that best applies to you.

How close would you say you are to the following groups of women in your feelings and ideas about things?	*Very close*	*Fairly close*	*Uncertain*	*Not too close*	*Not close at all*
1. Black women in this country.	46%	45%	4%	5%	1%
2. White women in this country.	4%	33%	21%	39%	5%
3. Black women in Africa.	13%	17%	40%	12%	18%
4. Religious, churchgoing women.	34%	47%	10%	8%	1%
5. Young black women (younger than thirty years of age).	24%	42%	18%	15%	1%
6. Renowned black women, such as Oprah, Terry McMillan, Eryka Badu, Angela Bassett, and Maya Angelou.	22%	39%	21%	12%	7%
7. Black women in blue-collar jobs.	13%	46%	24%	15%	2%
8. Older black women (older than sixty years of age).	21%	40%	19%	18%	2%
9. Elected black women officials.	11%	39%	25%	15%	11%
10. Black women doctors, lawyers, and other professional women.	22%	53%	18%	6%	1%

PART C:
Now tell us a little about yourself.
(Write in or √ check your response.)

1. How old are you?	18–24	11%
	25–34	31%
	35–54	43%
	55 +	15%
	Median age	36

2. Are you currently . . .	Single (never married)	55%
	Divorced	10%
	Separated	2%
	Widowed	5%
	Married	28%

a. Are you currently living with a partner to whom you are not married?	Yes	16%
	No	84%
3. How many children do you have?	0	39%
	1	29%
	2	16%
	3 +	17%
a. Of these children, how many are *under the age of 18*	0	43%
	1	23%
	2	17%
	3 +	17%
b. Of *all* your children, how many are female?	0	34%
	1	42%
	2	16%
	3 +	8%
4. What is the *highest* grade of school you have completed?	Less than high school	6%
	HS/GED	15%
	Some college	23%
	BA/BS	21%
	Master's +	36%
5. Are you currently employed?	Yes	76%
	No	23%
a. What is your current occupation?	Exec./admin./mgr.	27%
	Prof	41%
	Tech/sales/admin. Supt.	15%
	Service	18%
7. What do you anticipate your total family income will be for the year 2001?	Less than $20,000	11%
	$20,000 to $34,999	21%
	$35,000 to $49,000	15%
	$50,000 to $74,999	19%
	$75,000 +	35%
	Median family income	$51,664.00

a. Will any of this income come in the form of public assistance, such as from social security, TANF (AFDC)?	Yes	8%
	No	92%
8. Do you belong to any local organizations, such as a church, lodge, sorority, civic league, women's group, or professional organization?	Yes	81%
	No	19%
a. If so, is this organization(s) *primarily* comprised of black women?	Yes	69%
	No	31%

PART V:
Finally, read through each of the following hypothetical quotes. CIRCLE the number of the one that most reflects frequent thoughts you have about African-American women today.

"Real black women know what our struggle is about; they don't forget where they come from."	38%
"Personally, all that matters to me is that black women don't straddle the fence; either you're black or you're not."	1%
"To me, it's sort of insulting as a black woman for someone to tell me that I am trying to be white. It's not so much that I'm trying to be white, but that I'm black and educated."	27%
"Are we still on the plantation? Why do some African-American women insist on looking and acting the way they do? These are not my sisters."	1%
"Nowadays, I often find myself wondering whether black women will every truly come together as a people. I mean, we all have different ways of expressing ourselves because of the things we've gone through. And frankly it worries me."	33%

Recruitment site/social context		
	Hair Salon	13%
	Referral	27%
	Sorority	24%
	Black Faculty/Staff Association	8%
	Corrections	28%

Table 4.   The study women

		Class status			
		L = lower class			
		M = middle class			

Pseudoname	Occupational title	Original designation	Final designation	Age	Educational attainment
Ada	Administrative aide, corrections	M	L	47	Some college
Adrienne	Unemployed, incarcerated	M	L	52	Some college
Alexis	Teacher	M	M	35	Bachelor's
Alice	Inventory control specialist, corrections	M	L	38	Master's +
Angie	Engineer, government	M	M	26	Master's +
Annette	RN, academic research	M	M	32	Master's +
Amy	Hair stylist and self-employed product salesperson	L	L	30	Some college
Arlene	Unemployed, incarcerated	L	L	36	HS
Ashley	Regulatory scientist (health), federal government	M	M	57	Master's +
Aurora	School administrator, public school	M	M	62	Master's +
Barbara	Customer account executive, communications company	L	L	24	Bachelor's
Beatrice	College administrator	M	L	25	Master's +
Billie	Administrative assistant, government	M	L	34	Some college
Brittney	Clinical social worker	M	M	35	Master's +
Brooke	Homemaker	L	L	52	Bachelor's
Candice	Unemployed, incarcerated	L	L	33	Less than HS
Carol	Materials specialist, research library	M	M	49	Some college
Charlene	Employment advocate/job coach, non-profit	M	L	27	Some college
Christina	Retired teacher; social activist and organizer	M	M	89	Bachelor's
Cynthia	Analyst/programmer, contractor	M	M	30	Bachelor's
Desiree	Attorney, corrections	M	M	57	Law degree
Dolores	Technical consultant, computing	L	L	35	Bachelor's
Donna Marie	College professor	M	M	54	Master's +
Dorraine	Social worker, residential treatment center, and real estate investor	M	M	67	Master's +
Edith	Unemployed, incarcerated	L	L	35	Less than HS
Elizabeth	Financial services specialist	L	L	28	Bachelor's

Emily	EEO Specialist, federal government, and academic advisor, higher education	M	M	58	Master's +
Erin	Administrative office, corrections	M	L	50	HS
Faith	Custodian, college campus	L	L	53	GED
Georgia	Unemployed, incarcerated	M	L	31	GED
Glenda	Unemployed, incarcerated	L	L	20	GED
Grace	Unemployed, incarcerated	L	L	43	GED
Gwynn	Social worker, methadone clinic	M	M	23	Master's +
Hannah	Manager, training program, community college	M	M	33	Master's +
Hattie	Computer systems analyst/ engineer, defense	M	M	30	Master's +
Jennifer	Community college administrator	M	M	60	Master's +
Jessica	Special education teacher	M	M	38	Bachelor's
Joanne	Probation agent, corrections	M	M	46	Bachelor's
Judy	Nurse	M	M	49	Some college
Julia	Unemployed, incarcerated	M	L	29	HS
Kathryn	Social security insurance agent	L	L	53	Some college
Kitty	Hair stylist	L	L	28	HS
Latrice	Mathematician, government	M	M	29	Master's +
Laura	Hair stylist and entrepreneur	L	M	38	HS
Leah	Human resources administrator	M	M	53	Some college
Leslie	Retiree, administrator, city government	M	M	69	Master's +
Lillian	College student and youth organizer, social services organization	M	L	19	Some college
Madison	Program analyst, government	L	M	46	Master's +
Maisha	Unemployed, incarcerated	L	L	20	Less than HS
Mariah	Guidance counselor, public school	M	M	56	Master's +
Maris	Unemployed, incarcerated	L	L	44	Some college
Margaret	Unemployed, incarcerated	L	L	37	HS
Megan	Administrative assistant, education	M	L	42	Some college
Melanie	Unemployed, incarcerated	L	L	36	HS
Michelle	Social security insurance specialist	L	L	42	Some college
Molly	Unemployed, incarcerated	L	L	18	Less than HS
Monica	Nanny	L	L	54	Some college
Monique	GED instructor, part-time	M	M	60	Bachelor's
Myrna	Clinical counselor, school	M	M	58	Master's +
Nancy	Software engineer, consultant	M	M	29	Master's +

Naomi	Teacher, private school	M	M	26	Master's +
Natalie	College student	L	M	18	Some college
Nicole	Unemployed, incarcerated	L	L	30-something	HS
Nina	Unemployed, incarcerated	M	M	36	Master's +
Pamela	Technical writer, research firm	M	M	30	Master's +
Paula	Teacher	M	M	27	Bachelor's
Phyllis	Unemployed, incarcerated	L	L	25	Some college
Rhonda	Software developer	M	M	27	Master's +
Rochelle	Physician	M	M	53	Master's +
Rosalee	Administrative assistant, corrections	M	L	31	Some college
Rose	Assistant high school principal	M	M	50-something	Master's +
Sabrina	Administrative support, community college	L	L	40-something	?
Sarah	Software engineer, information technology	L	M	32	Bachelor's
Saundra	Tax attorney and real estate agent	M	M	31	Master's +
Shari	Unemployed, incarcerated	L	L	54	GED
Shelley	Database administrator	L	M	23	Bachelor's
Stephanie	Accountant, accounting firm	L	M	24	Bachelor's
Tabitha	Physician, emergency room	M	M	40	Master's +
Tamara	Secretary, corrections	M	L	42	Less than HS
Tanya	Contract specialist, health care	L	L	35	Some college
Taylor	Teacher, elementary school	M	M	54	Bachelor's
Tia	Unemployed, incarcerated	L	L	30	GED
Terry	Drug policy analyst	M	M	39	Master's +
Trinity	Field supervisor, corrections	M	M	60	Bachelor's
Trisha	Program assistant, non-profit community development	M	M	22	Master's +
Victoria	Mental health social worker, corrections	L	M	35	Degree in mass communication
Wanda	Temp worker, postal	L	L	Early 20s	HS or GED
Wynona	Quality review technician	L	L	30	Some college

Bibliography

Adler, Nancy E., Thomas Boyce, Margaret A. Chesney, Sheldon Cohen, Susan Folkman, Robert L. Kahn, and S. Leonard Syme. "Socioeconomic Status and Health: The Challenge of the Gradient." *American Psychologist* 49, no. 1 (1994): 15–24.

Afonja, Simi. "Changing Patterns of Gender Stratification in West Africa." In *Persistent Inequalities: Women and World Development*, edited by Irene Tinker, 198–209. New York: Oxford University Press, 1990.

Aidoo, Ama Ata. "The African Woman Today." In *Sisterhood, Feminisms, and Power: From Africa to the Diaspora*, edited by Obioma Nnaemeka, 39–50. Trenton, NJ: Africa World Press, 1997.

Aina, Olabisi. "African Women at the Grassroots: The Silent Partners of the Women's Movement." In *Sisterhood, Feminisms, and Power: From Africa to the Diaspora*, edited by Obioma Nnaemeka, 65–88. Trenton, NJ: Africa World Press, 1998.

Allen, Charlotte. "O, How I Love You, Oprah: Oprah's Politics Are Sometimes O-Dious. Still, Charlotte Allen Finds Her a-O-Kay." *Women's Quarterly* 33 (2002): 22.

Anderson, Elijah. *Streetwise: Race, Class, and Change in an Urban Community*. Chicago: University of Chicago Press, 1990.

Anderson, Karen. *Changing Woman: A History of Racial Ethnic Women in Modern America*. New York: Oxford University Press, 1996.

Anderson, Margaret L., and Patricia Hill Collins. *Race, Class, and Gender: An Anthology*. Belmont, CA: Wadsworth Publishing, 1992.

Anthias, Floya, and Nira Yuval-Davis. *Racialized Boundaries: Race, Nation, Gender, Colour, and Class and the Anti-Racist Struggle*. London: Routledge, 1992.

Aronowitz, Stanley. *How Class Works: Power and Social Movement*. New Haven, CT: Yale University Press, 2003.

Arrighi, Giovanni, Beverly J. Silver, and Iftikhar Ahmad. *Chaos and Governance in the Modern World System*. Minneapolis: University of Minnesota Press, 1999.

Baird, Irene C. "The Examined Life: A Study of Identity Formation, Agency, Self-Expression among Imprisoned Women." Paper presented at the Adult Education Research Conference (AERC), Northern Illinois University, DeKalb, Illinois, 1999.

Bakare-Yusuf, Bibi. "Beyond Determinism: The Phenomenology of African Female Experience." *Feminist Africa* 2 (2003).

Banner-Haley, Charles T. *The Fruits of Integration: Black Middle-Class Ideology and Culture, 1960–1990*. Jackson: University Press of Mississippi, 1994.

Barbee, Evelyn L. "Violence and Mental Health." In *In and Out of Our Right Minds: The Mental Health of African American Women*, edited by Diane R. Brown and Verna M. Keith, 99–115. New York: Columbia University Press, 2003.

Beale, Frances. "Double Jeopardy: To Be Back and Female." In *The Black Woman: An Anthology*, edited by T. Cade, 90–100. New York: Signet, 1970.

Beatty, Lula A. "Changing Their Minds: Drug Abuse and Addiction in Black Women." In *In and Out of Our Right Minds: The Mental Health of African American Women*, edited by Diane R. Brown and Verna M. Keith, 59–79. New York: Columbia University Press, 2003.

Bell, Ella L. J. Edmondson, and Stella M. Nkomo. *Our Separate Ways: Black and White Women and the Struggle for Professional Identity*. Boston: Harvard Business School Press, 2001.

Benjamin, Lois. *Three Black Generations at the Crossroads: Community, Culture, and Consciousness*. Chicago: Burnham, Inc., 2000.

Bennett, Michael, and Vanessa D. Dickerson, eds. *Recovering the Black Female Body: Self-Representation by African American Women*. New Brunswick, NJ: Rutgers University Press, 2000.

Bernard, Wanda Thomas. "Including Black Women in Health and Social Policy Development: Winning over Addictions; Empowering Black Mothers with Addictions to Overcome Triple Jeopardy." Halifax, Nova Scotia, Canada: Maritime Centre of Excellence for Women's Health, 2001.

Billingsley, Andrew. *Climbing Jacob's Ladder: The Enduring Legacy of African-American Families*. New York: Simon & Schuster, 1992.

BlackWomensHealth. *Breast Cancer*. BlackWomenshealth.com, 2004. www.blackwomenshealth.com/breast_cancer.htm (accessed October 24, 2004).

Boris, Eileen. "The Power of Motherhood: Black and White Activist Women Redefine the 'Political.'" In *Mothers of a New World: Maternalist Politics and the Origins of Welfare States*, edited by Seth Koven and Sonya Michel, 213–45. New York: Routledge, 1993.

Bositis, David A. *Diverging Generations: The Transformation of African American Policy Views*. Washington, DC: Joint Center for Political and Economic Studies, 2001.

Boxill, Bernard R. "The Underclass and the Race/Class Issue." In *The Underclass Question*, edited by Bill Lawson, 2–32. Philadelphia: Temple University Press, 1992.

Brands, H. W. *Masters of Enterprise: Giants of American Business from John Jacob Astor and J. P. Morgan to Bill Gates and Oprah Winfrey*. New York: Free Press, 1999.

Brown, Diane R., and Verna M. Keith, eds. *In and Out of Our Right Minds: The Mental Health of African American Women*. New York: Columbia University Press, 2003.

Burlew, Ann Kathleen, ed. *African American Psychology: Theory, Research, and Practice*. Newbury Park, CA: Sage Publications, 1992.

Carroll, Rebecca. *I Know What the Red Clay Looks Like: The Voice and Vision of Black Women Writers*. New York: Carol Southern Books, 1994.

cbsnewyork.com. *Oprah Joins a Very Exclusive Club: Becomes First Black Woman on Forbes List of Billionaires*. CBS 2 New York News, 2003. http://cbsnewyork.com/top stories/topstories_story_058212927.html (accessed June 7, 2005).

Centers for Disease Control and Prevention, Office of Women's Health. "Leading Causes of Death by Age Group, Black Females—United States, 2001." Atlanta, GA: Centers for Disease Control and Prevention, 2001.

Chase-Lansdale, P. Lindsay, Jeanne Brooks-Gunn, and Elise S. Zamsky. "Young African-American Multigenerational Families in Poverty: Quality of Mothering and Grandmothering." *Child Development* 65 (1994): 373–93.

Cherlin, Andrew J. "Marriage and Marital Dissolution among Black Americans." *Journal of Comparative Family Studies* 29, no. 1 (1998): 147–58.

Cherry, Robert, and William M. Rodgers, eds. *Prosperity for All?: The Economic Boom and African Americans*. New York: Russell Sage Foundation, 2000.

Childs, Erica Chito. "Looking Behind the Stereotypes of the 'Angry Black Woman': An Exploration of Black Women's Responses to Interracial Relationships." *Gender and Society* 19, no. 4 (2005): 544–61.

Chukukere, Glo. "An Appraisal of Feminism in the Socio-Political Development of Nigeria." In *Sisterhood, Feminisms, and Power: From Africa to the Diaspora*, edited by Obioma Nnaemeka, 133–48. Trenton, NJ: Africa World Press, 1998.

Cole, Johnnetta B., and Beverly Guy-Sheftall. *Gender Talk: The Struggle for Women's Equality in African American Communities*. New York: One World/Ballantine Books, 2003.

Cole, Lorraine. "National Black Women's Health Project." *Ebony*, October 2002. www.findarticles.com/p/articles/mi_m1077/is_12_57/ai_97997705 (accessed October 10, 2004).

Collins, Patricia Hill. *Black Feminist Thought: Knowledge, Consciousness, and the Politics of Empowerment*. New York: Routledge, 1990.

———. *Black Sexual Politics: African Americans, Gender, and the New Racism*. New York: Routledge, 2004.

———. "What's in a Name? Womanism, Black Feminism, and Beyond." *The Black Scholar* 26, no. 1 (1996): 9–17.

Conley, Dalton. *Being Black, Living in the Red: Race, Wealth, and Social Policy in America*. Berkeley: University of California Press, 1999.

Cooper, Anna Julia. *Voices of the South*. Xenia, OH: Aldine Publishing House, 1892.

Coquery-Vidrovitch, Catherine. *African Women: A Modern History*. Boulder, CO: Westview Press, 1997.

Cornell, Stephen, and Douglas Hartmann. *Ethnicity and Race: Making Identities in a Changing World*. Thousand Oaks, CA: Pine Forge Press, 1997.

Cose, Ellis. "The Black Gender Gap." *Newsweek*, March 3, 2003, 46–51.

Cramer, James C., and Katrina Bell McDonald. "Kin Support and Family Stress: Two Sides of Early Childbearing and Support Networks." *Human Organization* 55, no. 2 (1996): 160–69.

Cruse, Harold. *Plural but Equal: A Critical Study of Blacks and Minorities and America's Plural Society*. New York: William Morrow, 1987.

Daniels, Lee A., ed. *The State of Black America, 2001*. New York: National Urban League, 2001.

Davis, Angela. "Reflections on the Black Woman's Role in the Community of Slaves." In *Words of Fire: An Anthology of African-American Feminist Thought*, edited by Beverly Guy-Sheftall, 200–18. New York: New Press, 1995.

Davis, Angela Y. *Women, Culture, & Politics*. New York: Vintage Books, 1989.

Davis, Elizabeth L. *Lifting as They Climb: The National Association of Colored Women*. Washington, DC: National Association of Colored Women, 1933.

Davis, Kimberly. "The Shocking Plight of Black Women Prisoners." *Ebony*, June 2000, 162–66.

Dawson, Michael C. *Behind the Mule: Race and Class in African-American Politics.* Princeton, NJ: Princeton University Press, 1994.

———. *Black Visions: The Roots of Contemporary African-American Political Ideologies.* Chicago: University of Chicago Press, 2001.

de Lauretis, Teresa, ed. *Feminism as a Model for Social Change.* Vol. 8, *Feminist Studies, Critical Essays.* Bloomington: Indiana University Press, 1986.

Dickerson, Bette J. "Ethnic Identity and Feminism: Views from Leaders of African American Women's Associations." In *Color, Class, and Country: Experiences of Gender*, edited by Gay Young and Bette J. Dickerson, 115–27. London: Zed Books, 1994.

Didion, Joan. *Slouching Towards Bethlehem.* New York: Farrar, Straus, and Giroux, 1968.

Donkoh, Wilhemina J. "Yaa Asantewaa: A Role Model for Womanhood in the New Millennium." *Jenda: A Journal of Culture and African Women Studies* 1, no. 1 (2000).

Duster, Alfreda M. *Crusade for Justice: The Autobiography of Ida B. Wells.* Chicago: University of Chicago Press, 1970.

Dyson, Michael Eric. *Is Bill Cosby Right?: Or Has the Black Middle Class Lost Its Mind?* New York: Basic Civitas Books, 2005.

———. *Race Rules: Navigating the Color Line.* Reading, MA: Addison-Wesley, 1996.

Ebony. "Infidelity: Why Men Cheat." November 1998.

Edwards, Audrey. "The O Factor: Oprah Winfrey's First Interview with a Women's Magazine since Starting Her Own." *Essence*, October 1, 2003, 176–80, 246.

Farley, Reynolds. "Indications of Recent Demographic Changes among Blacks: 1940 to 1970." *Journal of Social Biology* 18, no. 4 (1971): 341–58.

Feagin, Joe R., and Melvin P. Sikes. *Living with Racism: The Black Middle-Class Experience.* Boston: Beacon Press, 1994.

Feagin, Joe R., and Hernan Vera. *Liberation Sociology.* Boulder, CO: Westview Press, 2001.

Few, April L., Dionne P. Stephens, and Marlo Rouse-Arnett. "Sister-to-Sister Talk: Transcending Boundaries and Challenges in Qualitative Research with Black Women." *Family Relations* 52 (2003): 205–15.

Franklin, Raymond S. *Shadows of Race and Class.* Minneapolis: University of Minnesota Press, 1991.

Frazier, E. Franklin. *Black Bourgeoisie.* Glencoe, IL: Free Press, 1957.

Ganong, Lawrence H., and Marilyn Coleman. *Stepfamily Relationships: Development, Dynamics, and Interventions.* New York: Kluwer/AcademicPlenum Publishers, 2004.

Gatewood, Willard B. *Aristocrats of Color: The Black Elite, 1880–1920.* Bloomington: Indiana University Press, 1990.

Giddings, Paula A. *In Search of Sisterhood: Delta Sigma Theta and the Challenge of the Black Sorority Movement.* New York: William Morrow, 1988.

———. *When and Where I Enter: The Impact of Black Women on Race and Sex in America.* New York: William Morrow, 1984.

Gilkes, Cheryl Townsend. "Dual Heroisms and Double Burdens: Interpreting Afro-American Women's Experience and History." *Feminist Studies* 15 (1989): 573–90.

———. "Holding Back the Ocean with a Broom: Black Women and Community Work." In *The Black Woman*, edited by LaFrances Rodgers-Rose, 217–32. Beverly Hills: Sage Publications, 1980.

Gill, Jennifer. "Beyond Gender—Race." *BusinessWeek Online*, August 7, 2001. www
.businessweek.com/careers/content/aug2001/ca2001087_306.htm (accessed October
27, 2005).

Giovanni, Nikki. *Gemini: An Extended Autobiographical Statement on My First Twenty-
Five Years of Being a Black Poet*. Indianapolis, IN: Bobbs-Merrill, 1971.

Gomez, Michael A. *Exchanging Our Country Marks: The Transformation of African Identities in the Colonial and Antebellum South*. Chapel Hill: University of North Carolina
Press, 1998.

Goodwin, Jeff, and James M. Jasper, eds. *The Social Movements Reader: Cases and Concepts*. Malden, MA: Blackwell Publishing, 2003.

Gordon, Linda. *Pitied but Not Entitled: Single Mothers and the History of Welfare, 1890–
1935*. New York: Free Press, 1994.

Graham, Lawrence Otis. *Our Kind of People: Inside America's Black Upper Class*. New
York: HarperPerennial, 2000.

Greene, Sandra E. *Gender, Ethnicity, and Social Change on the Upper Slave Coast: History of the Anlo-Ewe*. Social History of Africa, edited by Allen Issacman and Jean Hay.
Portsmouth, NH: Heinemann, 1995.

Gurin, Patricia, Arthur H. Miller, and Gerald Gurin. "Stratum Identification and Consciousness." *Social Psychology Quarterly* 43 (1980): 30–47.

Guy-Sheftall, Beverly. "Introduction: The Evolution of Feminist Consciousness among
African American Women." In *Words of Fire: An Anthology of African-American Feminist Thought*, edited by Beverly Guy-Sheftall, 1–22. New York: New Press, 1995.

Gyekye, Kwame. *An Essay on African Philosophical Thought: The Akan Conceptual
Scheme*. Cambridge, MA: Cambridge University Press, 1987.

Hamilton, Tullia Kay Brown. "The National Association of Colored Women, 1896–
1920." Ph.D. dissertation, Emory University, 1978.

Harris, Robert L., Jr. "The Rise of the Black Middle Class." *The World and I* 14, no. 2
(1999): 40.

Harris-Lacewell, Melissa. "No Place to Rest: African American Political Attitudes and the
Myth of Black Women's Strength." *Women & Politics* 23, no. 3 (2001): 1–33.

Harley, Sharon, and Rosalyn Terborg-Penn, eds. *The Afro-American Woman: Struggles
and Images*. Port Washington, NY: Kennikat Press, 1978.

Harvey, Adia M. "Becoming Entrepreneurs: Intersections of Race, Class, and Gender in
the Black Beauty Salon." *Gender and Society* 19, no. 6 (2005): 789–808.

Helms, Janet E., and Thomas A. Parham. "The Racial Identity Attitude Scale." In *Handbook of Tests and Measurements for Black Populations*, edited by Reginald L. Jones,
167–74. Hampton, VA: Cobb & Henry Publishers, 1996.

Henry, Astrid. *Not My Mother's Sister: Generational Conflict and Third-Wave Feminism*.
Bloomington: Indiana University Press, 2004.

Herring, Cedric, Verna M. Keith, and Hayward Derrick Horton, eds. *Skin Deep: How Race
and Complexion Matter in the Color-Blind Era*. Chicago: University of Illinois Press,
2004.

Higginbotham, Elizabeth. "Black Professional Women: Job Ceilings and Employment
Sectors." In *Women of Color in U. S. Society*, edited by Maxine Baca Zinn and Bonnie
Thornton Dill, 113–31. Philadelphia: Temple University Press, 1994.

Higginbotham, Elizabeth, and Lynn Weber. "Moving up with Kin and Community:

Upward Social Mobility for Black and White Women." *Gender and Society* 6 (1992): 416–40.

Higginbotham, Evelyn Brooks. *Righteous Discontent: The Women's Movement in the Black Baptist Church, 1880–1920*. Cambridge, MA: Harvard University Press, 1993.

Hill, Robert. "Indications of Recent Demographic Changes among Blacks: 1940 to 1970." *Journal of Social Biology* 18, no. 4 (1971): 341–58.

———. *Informal Adoption among Black Families*. Washington, DC: National Urban League, 1997.

Hine, Darlene Clark, and Kathleen Thompson. *A Shining Thread of Hope: The History of Black Women in America*. New York: Broadway Books, 1998.

Hine, Darlene, and Kate Wittenstein. "Female Slave Resistance: The Economics of Sex." In *The Black Woman Cross-Culturally*, edited by Filomina Chioma Steady, 289–99. Cambridge, MA: Schenkman Publishing Company, 1981.

Hodge, Sharon Brooks. "Being Articulate Has Become a Measure of Authenticity." *Headway* 8, no. 7 (1996): 10.

Hogan, Dennis P., Ling-Xin Hao, and William L. Parish. "Race, Kin Networks, and Assistance to Mother-Headed Families." *Social Forces* 68, no. 3 (1990): 797–812.

hooks, bell. *Ain't I a Woman? Black Women and Feminism*. Boston: South End Press, 1981.

———. *Feminist Theory from Margin to Center*. Boston: South End Press, 1984.

———. *Yearning: Race, Gender, and Cultural Politics*. Cambridge, MA: South End Press, 1990.

Hudson-Weems, Clenora. "Africana Womanism: The Flip Side of a Coin." *Western Journal of Black Studies* 25, no. 3 (2001): 137–45.

Huggins, Nathan Irvin. *Harlem Renaissance*. London: Oxford University Press, 1973.

Hull, Gloria T., Patricia Bell-Scott, and Barbara Smith. *All the Women Are White, All the Blacks Are Men, But Some of Us Are Brave: Black Women's Studies*. Old Westbury, NY: Feminist Press, 1982.

Hunter, Margaret L. "Colorstruck: Skin Color Stratification in the Lives of African American Women." *Sociological Inquiry* 68, no. 4 (1998): 517–35.

Illouz, Eva. *Oprah Winfrey and the Glamour of Misery*. New York: Columbia University Press, 2003.

Jackman, Mary R., and Robert W. Jackman. *Class Awareness in the United States*. Berkeley: University of California Press, 1983.

Jackson, Jackson S., Wayne R. McCullough, Gerald Gurin, and Clifford L. Broman. "Race Identity." In *Life in Black America*, edited by James S. Jackson, 238–53. Newbury Park, CA: Sage Publications, 1991.

Jackson, John L., Jr. *Harlemworld: Doing Race and Class in Contemporary Black America*. Chicago: University of Chicago Press, 2001.

James, Joy. "Resting in Gardens, Battling in Deserts: Black Women's Activism." *The Black Scholar* 29, no. 4 (1999): 2–15.

James, Stanlie M. "Mothering: A Possible Black Feminist Link to Social Transformations?" In *Theorizing Black Feminisms: The Visionary Pragmatisms of Black Women*, edited by Stanlie M. James and Abena P. A. Busia, 44–54. London: Routledge, 1993.

Jaynes, Gerald D., and Robin M. Williams Jr., eds. *A Common Destiny: Blacks and American Society*. Washington, DC: National Academy Press, 1989.

Jell-Bahlsen, Sabine. "Female Power: Water Priestesses of the Oru-Igbo." In *Sisterhood, Feminisms, and Power: From Africa to the Diaspora*, edited by Obioma Nnaemeka. Trenton, NJ: Africa World Press, 1998.

Jenkins, Maude Thomas. "The History of the Black Woman's Movement in America." Ph.D. dissertation, Columbia University Teacher's College, 1984.

Johnson, Robert A., and Cindy Larison. "Prevalence of Substance Use among Racial and Ethnic Subgroups in the U.S." Rockville, MD: SAMHSA, Office of Applied Studies, U.S. Department of Health and Human Services, 1998.

Johnson, Tammy. *It's Personal: Race and Oprah*. Applied Research Center, November 29, 2001. www.arc.org/C_Lines/CLArchive/story4_4_04.html (accessed November 23, 2004).

Jones, Beverly Washington. *The Life and Writings of Mary Eliza Church Terrell, 1863–1954*. New York: Carlson, 1990.

Jones, Charisse, and Kumea Shorter-Gooden. *Shifting: The Double Lives of Black Women in America*. New York: HarperCollins, 2003.

Jones, Jacqueline. *Labor of Love, Labor of Sorrow: Black Women, Work, and the Family from Slavery to the Present*. New York: Basic Books, 1985.

Kaplan, Elaine Bell. *Not Our Kind of Girl: Unraveling the Myths of Black Teenage Motherhood*. Berkeley: University of California Press, 1997.

Keith, Verna M., and Cedric Herring. "Skin Tone and Stratification in the Black Community." *American Sociological Review* 49 (1991): 620–31.

Kimborough, Walter M. *Black Greek 101: The Culture, Customs, and Challenges of Black Fraternities and Sororities*. Madison, NJ: Fairleigh Dickinson University Press, 2003.

King, Deborah K. "Multiple Jeopardy, Multiple Consciousness: The Context of a Black Feminist Ideology." In *Black Women in America: Social Science Perspectives*, edited by Micheline R. Malson, Elisabeth Mudimbe-Boyi, and Mary Wyer, 265–95. Chicago: University of Chicago Press, 1988.

Kogan, Lisa. "The Oprah Show Turns 20 (Q & A)." *O: The Oprah Magazine*, October 2005, 278–79.

Ladner, Joyce. "Black Women Face the 21st Century: Major Issues and Problems." *The Black Scholar* 17 (1986): 12–19.

Ladner, Joyce A. *Tomorrow's Tomorrow: The Black Woman*. Garden City, NY: Doubleday, 1971.

Lamont, Michele. *The Dignity of Working Men: Morality and the Boundaries of Race, Class, and Immigration*. New York: Russell Sage Foundation, 2000.

Lareau, Annette. *Unequal Childhoods: Class, Race, and Family Life*. Berkeley: University of California Press, 2003.

LaVeist, Thomas A., Verna M. Keith, and Mary Lou Guiterrez. "Black/White Differences in Prenatal Care Utilization: An Assessment of Predisposing and Enabling Factors." *Health Services Research* 30, no. 1 (1995): 43–58.

Lawson, Bill. *Uplifting the Race: Middle-Class Blacks and the Truly Disadvantaged*. Philadelphia: Temple University Press, 1992.

——, ed. *The Underclass Question*. Philadelphia: Temple University Press, 1992.

Lerner, Gerda. "Early Community Work of Black Club Women." *Journal of Negro History* 56 (1974): 158–67.

Lewis, David L. *W. E. B. Dubois: Biography of a Race, 1868–1919*. New York: Henry Holt & Company, 1993.

Lincoln, Abbey. "Who Will Revere the Black Woman?" In *The Black Woman: An Anthology*, edited by Toni Cade, 80–84. New York: Mentor, 1970.

Lorde, Audre. "Age, Race, Class, and Sex: Women Redefining Difference." In *Sister Outsider: Essays and Speeches*. Freedom, CA: Crossing Press, 1984.

———. "Eye to Eye: Black Women, Hatred, and Anger." In *Sister Outsider: Essays and Speeches*, 145–75. Freedom, CA: Crossing Press, 1984.

———. *Sister Outsider: Essays and Speeches*. The Crossing Press Feminist Series. Freedom, CA: Crossing Press, 1984.

Mackenbach, Johan P., Karien Stronks, and Anton E. Kunst. "The Contribution of Medical Care to Inequalities in Health: Differences between Socio-Economic Groups in Decline of Mortality from Conditions Amenable to Medical Intervention." *Social Science and Medicine* 29, no. 3 (1989): 369–76.

Martin, Joanne M., and Elmer P. Martin. *The Helping Tradition in the Black Family and Community*. Silver Spring, MD: National Association of Social Workers, 1985.

Mathews, Holly F. "Killing the Medical Self-Help Tradition among African Americans." In *African Americans in the South: Issues of Race, Class, and Gender*, edited by Hans A. Baer and Yvonne Jones, 60–78. Athens: University of Georgia Press, 1992.

McClain, Leanita. "The Middle-Class Black's Burden." In *A Foot in Each World*, edited by Leanita McClain and Clarence Page. Evanston, IL: Northwestern University Press, 1986.

McDavis, Roderick J., and Deborah A. McDavis. "The Fruits of Integration: Black Middle-Class Ideology and Culture, 1960–1990 (Book Review)." *African American Review* 31 (1997): 314–16.

McDermott, Monica. "Trends in the Race and Ethnicity of Eminent Americans." *Sociological Forum* 17, no. 1 (2002): 137–60.

McDonald, Katrina Bell. "Black Activist Mothering: A Historical Intersection of Race, Gender, and Class." *Gender and Society* 11, no. 6 (1997): 773–95.

———. "The Psychosocial Dimension of Black Maternal Health: An Intersection of Race, Gender, and Class." In *African Americans and the Public Agenda: The Paradoxes of Public Policy*, edited by Cedric Herring, 68–84. Thousand Oaks, CA: Sage Publications, 1997.

McKinnon, Jesse. "The Black Population in the United States: March 2002." In *Current Population Reports, Series P20-541*. Washington, DC: U.S. Census Bureau, 2003.

Merriam-Webster's Collegiate Dictionary. 10th ed. Springfield, MA: Merriam-Webster, Inc., 1996.

Miniter, Richard. "Why Is America's Black Middle Class Strangely Fragile?" *American Enterprise*, November–December 1998.

Mintz, Sidney Wilfred, and Richard Price. *The Birth of African-American Culture: An Anthropological Perspective*. Boston: Beacon Press, 1992.

Mire, Amina. "In/through the Bodies of Women: Rethinking Gender in African Politics." Special issue, *Polis* 8 (2001).

Moore, June, Craig Winters, Kendra Smoak, Erin Artigiani, and Eric Wish. "Maryland Drug Scan." College Park, MD: Center for Substance Abuse Research (CESAR), 2001.

Morris, Aldon D. "What's Race Got to Do with It? Review of *The Declining Significance of Race: Blacks and Changing American Institutions*, by William Julius Wilson." *Contemporary Sociology* 25, no. 3 (1996): 309–13.

Morrison, Toni. "Cinderella's Stepsisters." In *Across Cultures: A Reader for Writers*, edited by Sheena Gillespie and Robert Singleton, 294–95. New York: Longman Publishers, 2001.

Mullings, Leith. "Images, Ideology, and Women of Color." In *Women of Color in U.S. Society*, edited by Maxine Baca Zinn and Bonnie Thornton Dill. Philadelphia: Temple University Press, 1994.

Nakao, Keiko, and Judith Treas. "Computing 1989 Occupational Prestige Scores." In *GSS Methodological Report*, 70. Chicago: National Opinion Research Center, 1990.

Naples, Nancy A. "Activist Mothering: Cross-Generational Continuity in the Community Work of Women from Low-Income Urban Neighborhoods." *Gender & Society* 6 (1992): 441–63.

National Cancer Institute. "Breast: U.S. Racial/Ethnic Cancer Patterns." Bethesda, MD: National Cancer Institute, 2004.

Nembhard, Jessica Gordon, Steven C. Pitts, and Patrick L. Mason. "African American Intragroup Inequality and Corporate Globalization." In *African Americans in the U.S. Economy*, edited by Ceclia A. Conrad, John Whitehead, Patrick Mason, and James Stewart, 208–22. Lanham, MD: Rowman & Littlefield, 2005.

Neverdon-Morton, Cynthia. *Afro-American Women of the South and the Advancement of the Race, 1895–1925*. Knoxville: University of Tennessee Press, 1989.

Nnaemeka, Obioma. "Introduction: Reading the Rainbow." In *Sisterhood, Feminisms, and Power: From Africa to the Diaspora*, edited by Obioma Nnaemeka, 1–35. Trenton, NJ: Africa World Press, 1997.

Nzegwu, Nkira. "Gender Equality in the Dual-Sex System: The Case of Onitsha." *Jenda: A Journal of Culture and African Women Studies* 1, no. 1 (2001).

Olesker, Michael. "Dropout Rate in City Schools Needs Our Attention as Well." *Baltimore Sun*, January 28, 2003.

Oliver, Melvin L., and Thomas M. Shapiro. *Black Wealth/White Wealth: A New Perspective on Racial Inequality*. New York: Routledge, 1995.

Oyewùmi, Oyèrónké. "Introduction: Feminism, Sisterhood, and *Other* Foreign Relations." In *African Women & Feminism: Reflecting on the Politics of Sisterhood*, edited by Oyèrónké Oyewùmi, 1–24. Trenton, NJ: Africa World Press, 2003.

Parmer, Twinet, Mary Smith Arnold, Tuoanyene Natt, and Christopher Janson. "Physical Attractiveness as a Process of Internalized Oppression and Multigenerational Transmission in African American Families." *The Family Journal: Counseling and Therapy for Couples and Families* 12, no. 3 (2004): 230–42.

Parpart, Jane L. "Women and the State in Africa." In *The Precarious Balance: State and Society in Africa*, edited by Donald Rothchild and Naomi Chazen, 208–30. Boulder, CO: Westview Press, 1988.

Pasley, Kay, and Marilyn Ihinger-Tallman, eds. *Remarriage and Stepparenting: Current Research & Theory*. New York: Guilford Press, 1987.

Pattillo-McCoy, Mary. *Black Picket Fences: Privilege and Peril among the Black Middle Class*. Chicago: University of Chicago Press, 1999.

Pegram, Amelia Blossom. "I Will Still Sing." In *The Heinemann Book of African Women's Poetry*, edited by Stella Chipasula and Frank Chipasula, 187–88. Portsmouth, NH: Heinemann, 1995.

Peterson, Charles. "Returning to the African Core: Cabral and the Erasure of the Colonized Elite." *West Africa Review* 2, no. 2 (2001).

Porter, Michael. *The Conspiracy to Destroy Black Women*. Chicago: African American Images, 2001.

Pough, Gwendolyn D. *Check It while I Wreck It: Black Womanhood, Hip-Hop Culture, and the Public Sphere*. Boston: Northeastern University Press, 2004.

Radford-Hill, Sheila. *Further to Fly: Black Women and the Politics of Empowerment*. Minneapolis: University of Minnesota Press, 2000.

Randolph, Laura B. "Oprah! The Most Powerful Woman in Entertainment Talks about Her Fame, Her Father, and Her Future in TV." *Ebony*, July 1995, 22–25.

Reid, Pamela Trotman. "Feminism versus Minority Group Identity: Not for Black Women Only." *Sex Roles* 10, nos. 3–4 (1984): 247–55.

Reid-Merritt, Patricia. *Sister Power: How Phenomenal Black Women Are Rising to the Top*. New York: J. Wiley, 1996.

Rhymes, Edward. "*Brown*balled? Desegregation without Real Integration Is an Invitation for Dysfunction." BlackCommentator.com, 2005. www.blackcommentator.com/108/108_guest_rhymes.html (accessed October 31, 2005).

Roberts, Carol A. "Drug Use among Inner-City African American Women: The Process of Managing Loss." *Qualitative Health Research* 9, no. 5 (1999): 620–38.

Rodgers-Rose, L. F. "The Black Woman: A Historical Overview." In *The Black Woman*, edited by L. F. Rodgers-Rose, 15–28. Beverly Hills, CA: Sage, 1980.

Roschelle, Anne R. *No More Kin: Exploring Race, Class, and Gender in Family Networks*. Thousand Oaks, CA: Sage Publications, 1997.

Rothstein, Richard. "Lessons: Linking Infant Mortality to Schooling and Stress." *New York Times*, February 6, 2002.

Rowley, Diane, and Heather Tosteson, eds. "Racial Differences in Preterm Delivery: Developing a New Research Paradigm." *American Journal of Preventive Medicine* 9, no. 6 (November–December 1993): supplement.

Ruggles, Steven, Matthew Sobek, Trent Alexander, Catherine A. Fitch, Ronald Goeken, Patricia Kelly Hall, Miriam King, and Chad Ronnander. *Integrated Public Use Microdata Series: Version 3.0* [Machine-Readable Database]. Minneapolis, MN: Minnesota Population Center (producer and distributor), 2004.

Sampson, William, and Vera Milam. "The Intraracial Attitudes of the Black Middle-Class: Have They Changed?" *Social Problems* 23, no. 2 (1975): 151–65.

Schmitt, John. "Recent Job Loss Hits the African-American Middle Class Hard." Washington, DC: Center for Economic and Policy Research, 2004.

Scott, Anne Firor. "Most Invisible of All: Black Women's Voluntary Associations." *Journal of Southern History* 56 (1990): 3–22.

Sellers, Robert M., Mia A. Smith, J. Nicole Shelton, Stephanie A. J. Rowley, and Tabbye M. Chavous. "Multidimensional Model of Racial Identity: A Preliminary Investigation of Reliability and Construct Validity." *Journal of Personality and Social Psychology* 73 (1997): 805–15.

Shakur, Assata. "'Women in Prison: How We Are,' Assata Shakur, 1978." In *Let Nobody Turn Us Around: Voices of Resistance, Reform, and Renewal*, edited by Manning Marable and Leith Mullings, 529–35. Lanham, MD: Rowman & Littlefield, 2000.

Sharpe, Tanya Telfair. "Sex-for-Crack-Cocaine Exchange, Poor Black Women, and Pregnancy." *Qualitative Health Research* 11, no. 5 (2001): 612–30.

Shaw, Stephanie. "Black Club Women and the Creation of the National Association of Colored Women." *Journal of Women's History* 3, no. 2 (1991): 10–25.

Simien, Evelyn M. "Race, Gender, and Linked Fate." *Journal of Black Studies* 35, no. 5 (2005): 529–50.

Simmonds, Felly Nkweto. "Who Are the Sisters? Difference, Feminism, and Friendship." In *Desperately Seeking Sisterhood: Still Challenging and Building*, edited by Magdalene Ang-Lygate, Chris Corrin, and Millsom S. Henry, 19–41. London: Taylor & Francis, 1997.

Skocpol, Theda, and Jennifer Lynn Oser. "Organization Despite Adversity: The Origins and Development of African American Fraternal Associations." *Social Science History* 28, no. 3 (2004): 367–437.

Smith, Robert C., and Richard Seltzer. *Race, Class, and Culture: A Study in Afro-American Mass Opinion*. Albany: State University of New York Press, 1992.

Smith, Sandra S., and Mignon R. Moore. "Intraracial Diversity and Relations among African-Americans: Closeness and Black Students at a Predominantly White University." *American Journal of Sociology* 106, no. 1 (2000): 1–39.

Smith, Tom W. "The Generation Gap Revisited." *Network on Transitions to Adulthood Policy Brief, MacArthur Foundation Research Network on Transitions to Adulthood and Public Policy* 6 (2004).

Sofola, 'Zulu. "Feminism and African Womanhood." In *Sisterhood, Feminisms, and Power: From Africa to Diaspora*, edited by Obioma Nnaemeka, 51–64. Trenton, NJ: Africa World Press, 1998.

South, Scott J. "Racial and Ethnic Differences in the Desire to Marry." *Journal of Marriage and the Family* 55 (1993): 357–70.

St. Jean, Yanick, and Joe R. Feagin. *Double Burden: Black Women and Everyday Racism*. Armonk, NY: M. E. Sharpe, 1998.

Stack, Carol B. *All Our Kin: Strategies for Survival in the Black Community*. New York: Basic Books, 1974.

Stanfield, John H., II. "African American Traditions of Civic Responsibility." *Nonprofit and Voluntary Sector Quarterly* 22, no. 2 (1993): 137–53.

Staples, Robert. "Sociocultural Factors in Black Family Transformation: Toward Redefinition of Family Functions." In *The Black Family: Essays and Studies*, 6th ed., edited by Robert Staples, 18–23. Belmont, CA: Wadsworth Publishing Company, 1998.

Staples, Robert, and Leanor Boulin Johnson. *Black Families at the Crossroads: Challenges and Prospects*. San Francisco: Jossey-Bass Publishers, 1993.

Steady, Filomina Chioma. "African Feminism: A Worldwide Perspective." In *Women in Africa and the African Diaspora*, edited by Rosalyn Terborg-Penn, Sharon Harley, and Andrea Benton Rushing, 3–24. Washington, DC: Howard University Press, 1987.

———. "The Black Woman Cross-Culturally: An Overview." In *The Black Woman Cross-Culturally*, edited by Filomina Chioma Steady, 7–42. Cambridge, MA: Schenkman, 1981.

———. "Women and Collective Action: Female Models in Transition." In *Theorizing Black Feminisms: The Visionary Pragmatism of Black Women*, edited by Stanlie M. James and Abena P. A. Busia, 90–101. London: Routledge, 1993.

Sudarkasa, Niara. "The 'Status of Women' in Indigenous Africa Societies." In *Readings in Gender in Africa*, edited by Andrea Cornwall, 25–31. Bloomington: Indiana University Press, 2005.

Taylor, Robert Joseph, Linda M. Chatters, and Aaron Celious. "Extended Family Households among Black Americans." *Perspectives* 9, no. 1 (2003): 133–51.

Taylor, Ronald L., ed. *Minority Families in the United States: A Comparative Perspective.* 3rd ed. Upper Saddle River, NJ: Prentice Hall, 2002.

Thomas, Anita Jones, Karen McCurtis Witherspoon, and Suzette L. Speight. "Toward the Development of the Stereotypic Roles for Black Women Scale." *Journal of Black Psychology* 30, no. 3 (2004): 426–42.

Thompson, Maxine S., and Verna M. Keith. "The Blacker the Berry: Gender, Skin Tone, Self-Esteem, and Self-Efficacy." *Gender and Society* 15, no. 3 (2001).

Townes, Emilie Maureen. *Womanist Justice, Womanist Hope.* Atlanta, GA: Scholars Press, 1993.

Troester, Rosalie Reigle. "Turbulence and Tenderness: Mothers, Daughters, and 'Othermothers.'" *A Scholarly Journal on Black Women* 1, no. 2 (1984): 13–16.

U.S. Census Bureau. "Sex by Age (Black or African American Alone)." Edited by Census Summary File 1 (SF 1) 100-Percent Data. Washington, DC: U.S. Census Bureau, 2000.

Wakschlag, Lauren S., P. Lindsay Chase-Lansdale, and Jeanne Brooks-Gunn. "Not Just 'Ghosts in the Nursery': Contemporaneous Intergenerational Relationships and Parenting in Young African American Families." *Child Development* 67 (1996): 2131–47.

Wallace-Sanders, Kimberly, ed. *Skin Deep, Spirit Strong: The Black Female Body in American Culture.* Ann Arbor: University of Michigan Press, 2002.

Washington, Mary Helen. "Zora Neale Hurston: A Woman Half in Shadow." In *I Love Myself When I Am Laughing . . . and Then Again When I Am Looking Mean and Impressive*, edited by Alice Walker, 7–25. New York: Feminist Press, 1979.

West, Cornel. *Keeping Faith: Philosophy and Race in America.* New York: Routledge, 1993.

Wetherington, Cora Lee, and Adele B. Roman, eds. "Drug Addiction Research and the Heath of Women." Rockville, MD: National Institute on Drug Abuse, 1998.

White, Deborah Gray. *Too Heavy a Load: Black Women in Defense of Themselves, 1894–1994.* New York: W. W. Norton & Company, 1999.

White, Marilyn M. "We Are Family!: Kinship and Solidarity in the Black Community." In *Expressively Black: The Cultural Basis of Ethnic Identity*, edited by Geneva Gay and Willie L. Baber, 17–34. New York: Praeger, 1987.

Willie, Charles Vert, and Sarah Susannah Willie. "Black, White, and Brown: The Transformation of Public Education in America." *Teachers College Record* 107 (2005): 475–95.

Willis, Deborah, and Carla Williams. *The Black Female Body: A Photographic History.* Philadelphia: Temple University Press, 2002.

Wilson, Roberta. "Stolen Moments." *Essence*, June 1997.

Wilson, Sherryl. *Oprah, Celebrity, and Formations of Self.* Basingstoke, Hampshire (England): Palgrave Macmillan, 2003.

Wilson, William Julius. *The Declining Significance of Race: Blacks and Changing American Institutions.* Chicago: University of Chicago Press, 1978.

Winbush, Raymond A. "Beloved in Our Lives: Necessary Healing between African Men and Women." Paper presented at the Annual National Conference on the Black Family in America, Louisville, KY, 2002.

Wright, Richard. "Blueprint for Negro Writing." In *A Turbulent Voyage: Readings in African American Studies*, edited by Floyd W. Hayes III, 322–29. San Diego, CA: Collegiate Press, 1992.

Yeats, W. B. *The Second Coming.* New York: Collier Books, 1962.

Yoest, Charmaine. "Points of Light." *Children Today*, September–October 1990.

Index

"acting white," 112, 114. *See also* struggle
Activism, black women, 26n8, 43–56, 99;
  concern for its waning, 11; and race
  consciousness, 14; restimulating, 178–
  81. *See also* the Birthing Project; black
  women's club movement; mothering
Afonja, Simi, 38
Africa: black women's power (woman
  power), 40–47; and civil war (Congo),
  170; meaningful connections to, 86;
  "secret" societies of women (and men),
  36, 42, 57–58n17
African-American culture, 93–94, 173;
  Black women's cultural history, 34–57.
  See also "deep collective roots";
  struggle
African American. *See* black. *African
  American Review*, 20
African Women & Feminism (Oyewùmi),
  35–36
"Afristocracy," 15
Aidoo, Ama Ata, 40
Aina, Olabisi, 37
AKA. *See* Alpha Kappa Alpha Sorority,
  Inc. Allen Charlotte, 165, 166
Alpha Kappa Alpha Sorority, Inc. (AKA),
  xii, 70, 72
Angelou, Maya, 69, 72, 173
Aronowitz, Stanley, 154
assimilationist ideology, 83–84, 90n39,
  150–54

authentic black womanhood. *See* black
  womanhood
Avery, Byllye, 70

Baird, Irene C., 102
Baker, Ella, 47
Baltimore, Maryland: and Oprah Winfrey,
  20; as research site, 20
Banner-Haley, Charles, 13
Barrett, Janie Porter, 54
Bassett, Angela, 69
Beale, Frances, 47
Beatty, Lula A., 101
Behind the Mule (Dawson), 12
Bell, Ella L. J. Edmondson, 130
Beloved (Morrison), 44, 164, 181
Benjamin, Lois, 9, 130
Berry, Halle, 164, 175
Berry, Sara, 40
Bethune, Mary McLeod, 54
The Birthing Project, 9, 17–18, 48, 70
black, 6
"black bourgeoisie," 13, 63n96, 142
the black church, 89n22; black women's
  club movement, 54–55. *See also* black
  women (religious, churchgoing
  women); sexism
black club women. *See* black women's club
  movement
black community: changing traditions, 6,
  130; giving back to, 117–19; maintaining ties to, 116–17

205

About the Author

Katrina Bell McDonald is an associate professor of sociology at The Johns Hopkins University in Baltimore, Maryland and is also a faculty affiliate of the Hopkins Center for Africana Studies and the Hopkins Populations Center. She received her Ph.D. in sociology from the University of California, Davis (1995) and also holds degrees from Stanford University and Mills College. She has served as an officer of the Racial and Ethnic Minorities section of the American Sociological Association; currently sits on the Board of Trustees for the Samuel Ready Scholarships, Inc. which provides funds to disadvantaged girls attending private K-12 schools in Baltimore; and is a regular speaker for My Sister's Circle, a Baltimore-based program to help transition fifth-grade girls to middle school.

Professor McDonald teaches courses on the African-American family, contemporary race relations, gender and work, social statistics, and qualitative research methodology. Her other published work include a book chapter ("The Psychosocial Dimension of Black Maternal Health: An Intersection of Race, Gender" in *African Americans and the Public Agenda: The Paradoxes of Public Policy* [1997]), and journal articles in *Social Science Quarterly, Review of Black Political Economy, Gender & Society*, and *Human Organization*. She is currently writing on the experiences of minority faculty at private K-12 schools and on egalitarianism in African-American marriages.